The
FUTURE
of AMERICAN
BUSINESS

The U.S. in World Competition

MARVIN CETRON

with ALICIA PAGANO
and OTIS PORT

McGRAW-HILL BOOK COMPANY
NEW YORK   ST. LOUIS   SAN FRANCISCO   HAMBURG
MEXICO   TORONTO   LONDON   SYDNEY

To my son, Adam, who in the third grade showed his business sense by selling half of his Lebanon bologna sandwiches to his classmates at lunch (until their mothers complained). MARVIN CETRON

To my family and the vision of the future we share.
ALICIA PAGANO

To Terry, whom I really do love more than my computer. OTIS PORT

1 2 3 4 5 6 7 8 9 DOC DOC 8 7 6 5

ISBN 0-07-010349-6

LIBRARY OF CONGRESS CATALOGING IN PUBLICATION DATA

Cetron, Marvin J.
   The future of American business.
   1. United States—Industries—Forecasting.
2. Economic forecasting—United States. 3. United States—
Economic conditions—1981-
I. Port, Otis.   II. Pagano, Alicia L.   III. Title.
Hc106.8.C45   1985   338.5'443'0973   85-6649
ISBN 0-07-010349-6

Book design by Mary A. Wirth

ACKNOWLEDGMENTS

This book wouldn't be in your hands had it not been for the help and collaboration of a small army of people who graciously contributed time and talent. Special thanks to Marcia Appel of Control Data, whose insight brought form to the theme and direction of this book.

Members of the Forecasting International staff were outstanding in lending technical and administrative support day in and day out: Cathryn Acton, Audrey Clayton, James J. Hendry, Susan H. McGuirk, Charles F. McFadden, Albert Small, Barbara R. S. Soriano, Sharon E. Sugarek, Donna VanPelt, and Barbara J. Weir.

Several experts in various fields reviewed chapters and provided valuable criticism, particularly Steve Gabbert of the Rice Miller Association; Robert Roland and Myron Foureaux of the Chemical Manufacturers Association; George B. Griffenhagen and Richard P. Penna with the American Pharmaceutical Association; and Dr. LeRoy Pagano, professor of management at St. John's University.

And then there is McGraw-Hill editor Leslie Meredith, who guided the work from beginning to end.

For the encouragement and contributions of these people, plus all the others whom I have failed to mention by name, my sincere gratitude. Any errors of fact or analysis are my sole responsibility.

CONTENTS

INTRODUCTION: WE AGAINST ALL OF THEM

There is no Mayo Clinic for corporate America, where a business or an industry can go for a checkup before competing in the fifteen-year international marathon that will take us into the twenty-first century. If there were, the results would not be terribly encouraging for the smokestack industries, on which the health of the U.S. economy was once based. Even America's strong new runners—electronics (principally computers, telecommunications, and semiconductors), biotechnology, and aerospace—will face stiff challenges in the coming years, sometimes from foreign nations that just a few years ago were dark-horse contenders. The U.S. steel and textile industries are in sorry shape, and they will have a tough struggle just to stay in the race with government-subsidized competitors from overseas. There will be more failures of auto and chemicals businesses. Agribusiness will continue to increase its production of food, but will use fewer and fewer workers.

The bright spot, at least in terms of domestic job growth, is the service industries. This sector of the economy spans an extremely diverse spectrum. On the "high-tech" end are services such as information processing, writing computer software, and hazardous-waste disposal. Among the more traditional service businesses are banking, insurance, real estate, airlines and travel, fast-food restaurants, nursing homes, and rental agencies. Lumped together, services already account for 70 percent of all U.S. jobs and 60 percent of the gross national product (GNP), and those figures will stand at 92 percent of jobs and 85 percent of GNP by the year 2000, maybe even higher. Close to half of all service jobs will be in some facet of information processing.

But, while a few service jobs pay very well indeed—a Ph.D. in computer science with a specialization in artificial intelligence software practically guarantees a starting salary of $70,000—these jobs are relatively scarce, and the number of qualified applicants still more scarce. Most people in the services sector take home less money than the average unionized factory worker—sometimes a lot less, as thousands of ex-factory hands in the Midwest's rust-bucket cities will attest.

What's happening to the industrial colossus that has been the envy of the world for most of this century, providing an unparalleled standard of living for blue-collar families? Answering that question—and its corollary: What does the future hold in store for American business and society?—is what this book is all about.

By almost any test, America is losing its edge in manufacturing. For the past three decades, the productivity of U.S. workers, though still the best in the world, has paled beside the gains made by workers in Japan and continental Europe; in fact, the United States ranks dead last among the industrialized nations. More recently, developing nations like South Korea, Singapore, and Taiwan have been coming on strong. Unless this country's productivity picks up, and quickly, by 1990 the per-person output of the U.S. work force will be matched and then surpassed in more than one overseas country.

Similarly, America has been trailing most industrial nations in the percent of GNP invested in capital goods. Our investment rate is only about half that of Japan's 29 percent and far below West Germany's 22 percent investment rate. As a result, the equipment used by American industry is woefully outmoded compared to the machine tools in almost every other developed nation. No wonder imports are soaring while U.S. export growth is flagging—except for the export of jobs to countries where labor is cheaper.

Back in the 1950s and '60s, when manufacturing, mining, and construction furnished a third of all U.S. jobs, no one would have dreamed that America's mighty industrial empire could be whittled down so quickly. But it's happening—and with a vengeance that too few Americans yet comprehend, despite the signs all around us, including the Japanese and European cars on the streets and the foreign-made stereos and videocassette recorders in our homes.

Think of the ramifications: In another fifteen years, industry will offer jobs to only 8 percent of America's work force. That is one-third of the present figure. And by 2015, that 8 percent figure will be cut in half, to almost the same level as today's agricultural jobs. Just thirty years hence, there won't be many more people in factories, proportionately, than there now are on farms. Until this nation's leaders in government and business come to grips with the unsettling changes gnawing away relentlessly at America's infrastructure, the old industrial centers will go on wallowing in a past that never will return.

Preoccupation with the past isn't just pathetic, it's downright destructive. If you spend too much time looking back, you can't spot the opportunities ahead. To the blind, goes an old saying, everything is a surprise.

There will be plenty of opportunities down the road to revive faltering sections of the nation. But it will require foresight, the liberal application of good old Yankee ingenuity, and a more enlightened posture by the government. Given half a chance, U.S. business will respond, because it has been cutting its teeth on challenge since colonial times—indeed, since Christopher Columbus persuaded Queen Isabella to put up venture capital and back a new idea to trade with the East Indies by sailing west. That spirit of adventure is alive and well. It's thriving among the business pioneers in places like California's Silicon Valley, Utah's Bionic Valley, North Carolina's Research Triangle, and along Route 128 in Massachusetts.

The crisis in U.S. industry today is largely a reflection of a past lack of confidence and perception at the top layers of management, as well as some ill-conceived federal policies. The will to succeed, the pride in workmanship, the dream of a better life—these basic characteristics of the American worker are as strong as ever. But they have been hobbled because the managements of some corporations couldn't see past their noses and were afraid to take risks and give their employees the tools they needed to compete effectively. Other American companies have been hampered by regulations that are unnecessarily antibusiness, which have put their workers at a competitive disadvantage in global markets. Neither of these structural defects will be remedied overnight, but they should be dealt with, before it's too late.

For executives and budding entrepreneurs who are ready to seize the initiative, and for investors undeterred by sensible risk, this book is a training manual for winning. It rediagnoses the condition of key U.S. industries—smokestack and high-tech—and prescribes exercises for shaping up. It probes major trends in technology and international affairs, and outlines what effects these currents will have. And it points to the best candidates for overseas investment by companies that take up the gauntlet of competing on a worldwide basis.

These glimpses of the future are neither magic nor Tarot-card sham. They draw on the expertise of a worldwide team of researchers and professional forecasters who regularly feed facts and careful analyses into a sophisticated computer model developed by Forecasting International. This model has proved uncannily accurate in recognizing seemingly obscure nuggets of information that signal critical turning points. For example, it spotted an impending crisis in oil thirty months before OPEC shocked the world in 1973. The model also enabled Forecasting International to warn its clients to pull out their investments in Iran three years before Western observers on the scene started to worry that the social unrest of 1977–78 might lead to the Shah's overthrow in 1979. The upheaval in Poland was also foreseen—three years in advance.

A Preview of Coming Changes

Even in comparison with recent years, the next two decades will be extraordinarily turbulent for business. To Ben Franklin's two certainties, death and taxes, you can add a third: change. Countries, companies, and individuals will endure wrenching transitions as the twentieth century gives way to the twenty-first. The juggernaut of technology gives no hint of slowing down; in fact, tomorrow the tempo of change will be absolutely blistering. This will put a premium on management's ability to make speedy decisions. At the same time, the stakes riding on those decisions will climb because more activities will become increasingly capital-intensive. Running tomorrow's companies won't be a task for the timid.

Some portents of the future are clear. Surely no one would quibble that the explosive spread of microelectronics technology, triggered by Intel Corporation's 1971 introduction of the microprocessor (a tiny computer on a sliver of silicon smaller than your little fingernail), will carry microchips into every cranny of people's lives, at work and at home. That's easy enough to say. But what will it *mean*?

For one thing, industry will be swept from an era of mechanization into one of automation. And business, having assimilated the personal computer, will next rush to embrace "thinking" computers. Just these two trends will have profound implications for executives, employees, and investors alike.

The difference between mechanization and automation isn't appreciated widely. The words are often used interchangeably—an understandable confusion, since automation initially was simply an advanced form of mechanization, using mechanical cams and timers and counters to automatically activate equipment. However, microchip-based automation is a new phenomenon, different not only in degree but also in kind.

As integrated circuits grow more and more powerful, or "smarter," some critics are raising doubts about the benefits of "micromation." One major concern is that the economic effects of mechanization and automation may be diverging. Mechanization substituted machines for human muscles; automation more and more substitutes machines for people's minds. The upshot, critics say, is that while mechanization expanded purchasing power by making it possible for almost anyone to secure factory work and turn out low-cost goods, automation is shrinking purchasing power—even though it lifts productivity—by eliminating workers, raising the skill levels needed to gain employment, and concentrating more profits in the hands of corporate and individual investors.

Some economists and sociologists contend that America is gradually eliminating the middle class, but failing to provide alternative work for the people displaced. Among the more outspoken critics is Lester C. Thurow, professor of management and economics at Massachusetts Institute of Technology's Sloan School of Management. He has charged that the new technologies are turning the United States into a two-tier economy, with a leisure class and a worker class and nothing in between.

Yet the microelectronics revolution has barely begun. In the 1990s, the semiconductor industry will be producing microchips crammed with so many transistors that one little chip will pack more data-processing power than today's mainframe computers. Two of them will be more than a match for a Cray supercomputer. These superchips will start out costing approximately $300 (in today's dollars), but if past experience is any guide, within four years the price will be down around $50—and it will keep on declining, to less than $10 within a decade. Ultimately, the price could end up as low as $3, or 1 percent of the original sticker.

The implications are truly awesome. The potentials of embedding a mainframe computer in virtually any appliance or machine are just starting to intrigue engineers, but clearly it will culminate in the merging of computer and communications technology that has already begun, with IBM and AT&T invading each other's turf. Before the turn of the century, for instance, today's cordless telephones will become powerful computerphones, able to do immediate translations of foreign-language conversations into English and vice versa.

In factories, this mainframe-on-a-chip technology will push automation to unprecedented levels. Today it is economical to equip individual machine tools with an adaptive controller, a rudimentary computer that can sense changes and automatically make compensations—say, by increasing the speed of a cutting tool that is getting dull. Tomorrow each machine will have its own computer-based expert system, programmed to "think" like the best human operators who have worked with that particular machine. Tireless, infinitely patient, and uncomplaining, computers implanted in robots and machine tools will monitor and control industrial processes faster and more accurately than people could. In other words, technology will give us the "brain" of the perfect industrial serf.

Many traditional job categories in factories will simply vanish, taken over by robots and computers. Over the next ten years, the number of robots in U.S. industry will mushroom tenfold to 200,000.

This "steel-collar" work force will displace 4.2 million people by the turn of the century, while creating roughly half as many new manufacturing jobs—no more than 2.5 million. Carnegie-Mellon University, a pioneer in robotics research, recently surveyed industry and concluded that even today's robots, which will seem antiquated a decade hence, could replace people in one-third of all factory jobs. And a study by the American Society of Mechanical Engineers predicts that, by 1990, robots will eliminate half of all the jobs of people who were working on automotive assembly lines in 1980.

The days of organized labor are clearly numbered. Pragmatic union leaders recognize the printouts on the wall and are treading water to buy time for older, less flexible members to retire gracefully. The contract signed by the United Auto Workers in late 1984 is a good illustration: The union actually took a *smaller* hike in wages than originally offered by General Motors, in return for a billion-dollar job security package.

With robots doing the heavy, hazardous, unpleasant work in factories in the near and far future, the last barriers to women in industry will fall, and male blue-collar workers will be faced with the toughest competition yet for manufacturing jobs. In 1996 or 1997, women will comprise just above 40 percent of the blue-collar work force.

Automation technology won't spare the office, either. Managers will turn to expert-systems software that will enable computers to give informed counsel in finance, legal affairs, library science, and various other disciplines. And when top managers finally feel comfortable with computers, the ranks of middle management will be decimated. That will certainly begin to happen in the 1990s, now that the premiere U.S. business schools—Harvard, Columbia, and MIT, among others—have launched programs to improve the high-tech savvy of their students.

Computer-based expert systems will be programmed to help engineers design better computers, to aid programmers in writing more efficient software, and to speed the search for cures for cancer and new drugs that improve memory and retard the ill effects of aging. With computerized assistance, biotechnicians will uncover new methods of genetically improving crops and farm animals, yielding such marvels as squarish watermelons (so they stack neatly in trucks and railcars), grains that thrive in saltwater environments, and cows that give more milk. Indeed, advances in bioengineering by the turn of the century will make it possible to farm both the oceans and the deserts, putting the end to hunger and famine within sight.

Computers are helping chemists and polymer scientists progress steadily toward breakthroughs that will yield new materials, such as plastics that are stronger and tougher than anything available today. These superplastics will replace steel in aircraft, oil rigs, and autos. Detroit's 1987 model-year cars will be the first to contain more plastics than steel. By 1991, the ratio of plastics to steel will be as high as 9 to 1 in some models. For the year 2000, cars will contain so much plastics that they will weigh in at only 1,000 pounds. By then, even engines will be nonmetal, molded and machined from advanced ceramics. Because they are immune to rust, the new breed of engineering plastics and ceramics will prolong the life of autos. By 1990 the average car can be expected to stay on the road for more than ten years, 50 percent longer than now, and twenty years will be the norm in the year 2000.

Although the coming generation of computers and expert systems will tend to constrict the number of traditional job openings for people, especially at the entry level, there will be a whole gamut of new jobs beckoning to those who have the foresight to prepare for tomorrow's world of work. The best-paying jobs will require creative insight and imagination—qualities that computers may never have—besides technical skills and the ability to work with computers and computerized machines. Despite automation, there will be no great shortage of jobs in the foreseeable future, only of people qualified to do increasingly technical work.[*] New technology has always created more jobs than it has destroyed.

The new jobs that automation and robotics create won't be anything like the ones that disappear. There won't be a simple exchange of workers from old jobs to new ones. The people replaced by industrial robots will not move directly to jobs in factories that produce robots because robots will build robots. Consequently, job dislocations, however temporary, will be extremely traumatic for the people laid off.

---

*Cetron, *Jobs of the Future*, McGraw-Hill, 1984.

The jobs of tomorrow will be so different—servicing and selling robots, writing the software that guides the steel-collar workers, et cetera—that a displaced blue-collar worker stands little chance of qualifying without going back to school for at least a year or two.

Even engineers and managers with good-paying positions in high-tech fields will find it necessary to recycle back through school after no more than ten years. In particularly fast-moving technologies, obsolescence will occur in five-year cycles.

The magnitude of the looming unemployment and retraining problems will galvanize a national program after the Democrats regain the White House in November 1988[*] by promising more jobs and better redistribution of wealth. The work week will be cut to thirty-two hours in 1990, and during the Democrats' second term, it will be slashed again—to facilitate job sharing, the work week will be limited to twenty-four hours. The reduced week will be mandatory almost immediately for hourly workers, and by 2000 most offices will be shared, too. Business leaders will support job sharing, now regarded as an unacceptable cost increase, because they will perceive that there's little point in having automated factories grinding out more low-cost goods if there is a shrinking number of consumers able to afford them.

The retraining effort will center on local schools. By the mid-1990s, school buildings will be in use sixteen or more hours a day, and their computer facilities—purchased with federal grants for the job partnership training program and the follow-on program that the next Democratic administration will launch—will be running twenty-four hours. Regular students will use the terminals during the day, adults in the evening for retraining courses, and at night the school will sell computer time to local companies and entrepreneurs.

Hand in hand with the retraining drive, a crash project to revamp the educational system will be launched. Starting in 1991, the academic establishment, bowing to the inevitable, will extend the school year

---

[*]This date and those following may get pushed four or eight years farther into the future if President Reagan resigns in 1986 to let Vice President Bush take over the Oval Office. In that case, Bush would win the presidency for the Republicans again in 1988 and probably in 1992. Forecasting International believes that the chances of a Reagan resignation are better than 50:50.

in stages to 210 days. The curriculum will be revised to require two years of computer literacy, four years of mathematics, and six years of science. Schools will no longer be grinding out graduates groomed mainly for industrial serfdom, where unquestioning obedience to authority and the ability to do rote memorization are valued traits. Education will instead stress critical thinking and the sharpening of students' creative faculties.

The payoff will be visible in the number of self-employed people, which will more than triple in the 1990s—a veritable bonanza of entrepreneurism. Many of these entrepreneurs will be doing the same type of work they used to do for a salary, only they will do it by "telecommuting" from home, using fiber optics communications links and personal computers to maintain contact via videoconferences and to receive data from and send information back to the company's computers. Large corporations will increasingly spin off costly staff functions, such as personnel and real estate administration, to former employees turned independent contractors.

From Model T to Moon Walks

If the scope of these predictions seems either overwhelming or overly fanciful, take a moment to reflect on the spectacular changes your parents or grandparents lived through. If you are between 30 and 50 your own father may have learned to drive a horse and buggy before he did a car, and he could have bought his first driver's license by mail order from Sears, Roebuck. He might recall the smell of kerosene lamps, before electricity, and the day when his parents first had a party-line telephone installed. He remembers the family's first refrigerator, and very likely he was among the kids who flocked to the home of the first family in the neighborhood to get a radio (yes, a radio; don't forget, commercial broadcasts started only in 1920, at station KDKA in Pittsburgh). No doubt he has a favorite yarn or two about the early, romantic exploits of barnstorming pilots in airplanes held together by baling wire. Yet he was still in his prime when Sputnik whirled past overhead in 1957, inaugurating the space age, and he hadn't retired when mankind first set foot on the moon. All that happened in just one lifetime!

Looking back, it seems to us that it must have been an exciting, glorious time to be alive. But imagine yourself transplanted back to 1920, hearing predictions of TV invading and reshaping home life, of freeway jams and jumbo jets, of spy satellites that can track a person strolling innocently through the park near a known KGB agent, of home computers and organ transplants and other marvels now commonplace. Surely you would feel apprehensive. Everyone tends to resist change—until after it happens. Only then, in retrospect, does new technology become idealized.

The spread of thinking robots and workerless factories may seem scary at first, but Sweden furnishes reassurance. The Swedes have thirteen times as many advanced robots per worker as does the United States. Yet Sweden is hardly a country that calls up images of labor unrest and rampant unemployment. In fact, Sweden enjoys the highest standard of living in the world.

The telephone provides another parallel. In the 1930s AT&T was rapidly expanding the foothold of the first "robot" of the communications age, the rotary dial telephone. Glenn E. Watts, now head of the Communications Workers of America (AFL-CIO), remembers how, as a young union firebrand, he fought against its use, fearing the loss of operator jobs. But soon the CWA realized that mechanizing the telephone meant more people could place more calls at lower costs, which spurred demand for more phones and created more jobs. Today, with Americans placing more than 750 million calls a day, AT&T would need every adult in the United States, and then some, to handle that traffic with manual switchboards. (Remember, with manual switchboards, long-distance calls required multiple operators: a local operator at both ends, and a long-distance operator at each switching center. So a cross-country call would need at least four operators—and making the connection could take several minutes. Also, the operators would be tied up whether or not the call was successfully completed.)

In 1934 a trade journal called *Tooling & Production* made its debut. In the first edition, one article proclaimed: "Model-T ideas should be junked. No business can escape change. . . . Manufacturers of the new machines and equipment have found ways in which to do things better and at less cost. Industry members will do well to reappraise their shops with an eye to the installation of new ideas and the latest models of machines and equipment [to] turn out only products of the highest quality.''

The article also noted that the new technology was having sweeping effects on employment patterns. "Between 1920 and 1930, the 19 principal growing occupations gained three times as many workers as the 19 vanishing occupations lost." Millwrights, draymen, and blacksmiths suffered the biggest losses, while new jobs were created by such growing industries as automobiles, motion pictures, and refrigeration. "A significant fact in connection with this change in occupation brought about by technological advancement is that the less arduous, more pleasant, and better compensated jobs displaced old, strenuous, hazardous occupations." The same sentiments, with slight adjustments, apply today.

Halfway Around the World and Back

The United States must continue automating because this nation is locked in an international struggle for productivity. The alternatives to automation are even more drastic: Either fence off the country and hide behind elaborate trade barriers that maintain artificially high prices on imports, or write off the sources of wealth that manufacturing represents and become dependent on other nations for almost all nondefense goods. Given these choices, and the fact that the United States cannot unilaterally turn back the world from the growing internationalization of business, automation is essential.

But the solution will never be more than transitory. When manufacturing equipment is automated, it makes little difference whether it draws power from an electrical outlet in India or Iowa. Undoubtedly, such newcomers as China, Brazil, and Malaysia will pull out all the stops to use such machinery to put growing pressure on manufacturers in the West—and on Japanese business, too. The new industrialists will flex their muscles by exploiting their countries' natural resources and low-cost labor forces to win bigger shares of world markets. To survive, American companies will be compelled to automate where feasible and shift most remaining manual-labor work to foreign lands.

"It's a nasty little choice," says Stephen S. Cohen, director of the University of California's Berkeley Roundtable on the International

Economy. He told the *New York Times* that "factory automation will result in a net loss of factory jobs. But if we don't automate, then there will be a massive hemorrhaging. If we lose the ability to be efficient manufacturers, then we've blown our economic future."

The "Buy American" slogan that some people glibly advocate as the answer to unemployment in the Midwest rust bowl simply won't work. It reflects an ostrichlike ignorance of the economic order of today's world. In fact, if Buy American should somehow actually become the law, it would wreak havoc with the U.S. economy. Very, very few products are made entirely by U.S. citizens employed at factories that are totally owned by American shareholders and use only American raw materials.

Nearly a third of all the clothing that Americans wear is imported. And much of the other two-thirds isn't made here—not entirely. Take your average button-down shirt, for example. Chances are good it was cut from domestic cloth, but the cutting and sewing may have been done in the Orient. Conversely, dresses and suits are often tailored in the United States with fabrics from Korea or Hong Kong or Scotland. Which is "American"?

Visit your local Ford dealer and you'll find cars on display that consist of parts made in the United States, Japan, and a handful of other countries. Some of the cars were put together at a plant in Mexico owned by Ford and Toyo Kogyo of Japan. On the other hand, if you test drive a Nissan, Honda, or Volkswagen, you'll be behind the wheel of a Japanese- or German-engineered car that may have been assembled by American workers at a plant in North Carolina, Ohio, or Tennessee, from a mix of imported and U.S.-made parts that provide work for other Americans. How do you decide which car is more American?

National borders are blurring everywhere. At a Sony plant in San Diego—the first Japanese factory in the United States, opened in 1972—American workers build TV sets that are shipped to stores throughout the United States and exported to other countries in this hemisphere as well. The plant turned out its 5 millionth TV set in May 1984.

Sony's plant presaged a wave of direct foreign investment in the United States. During the 1970s, foreign companies emulated the American multinational model and spent $20 billion on manufacturing investments in this country. (During the same decade, U.S. firms invested triple that figure in factories in Canada, Mexico, and overseas.) And the influx of foreign money is soaring. In the 1980s, Japan in particular has been pumping capital into the United States. Its cumulative total for manufacturing topped the $10 billion mark by the end of 1983—20 percent more than the total American investment in Japanese industry.

Last year alone, the Japanese opened or broke ground for fifty-odd new plants in the United States. For instance, a joint venture of Sony and CBS began making digital audio disks in Illinois. A few Japanese firms are even setting up research laboratories. Nippon Denso is building such a facility in Detroit to work on automotive electronics and new ceramics.

Even in those bastions of American high technology, semiconductors and computers, multinational pedigrees are the norm. There are few chips sold by U.S. companies that don't cross at least one border during their manufacture. Some of National Semiconductor's microchips are designed in California, fabricated in Scotland, tested and assembled in the Far East, then returned to America. So many high-tech plants have been built in Scotland—by Motorola, IBM, Hewlett-Packard, Ferranti, NCR, and NEC—that the tip of Britain has been dubbed Silicon Glen. Most semiconductor chips fabricated in America are assembled (put inside plastic or ceramic housings) in the Far East or Mexico. U.S. electronics companies have sixty manufacturing and forty-six technical plants in ten countries in southeast Asia. Advanced Micro Devices, for instance, does assembly in the Philippines and Malaysia and credits the low cost of these offshore operations for helping it to become one of America's fastest-growing chip makers.

The situation is even more complex in the computer industry. In addition to microchips shipped halfway around the world and back, the computer may have a video terminal from Korea, disk drives from Japan, and a keyboard from Taiwan. Tandon Corporation, the biggest producer of disk-memory drives for personal computers and a supplier to IBM, has factories in Singapore and Bombay, where the going wage is about $1 per hour.

Things get still more complicated when you realize that Japanese (or Italian) companies aren't necessarily Japanese (or Italian). Example: Merck, America's biggest drug company, owns a controlling interest in two Japanese pharmaceuticals firms—the largest foreign investment by any company in Japan. And AT&T has bought a 25 percent interest in Olivetti and is importing $250 million of Olivetti equipment to sell under the AT&T label in the United States.

Turning the tables, foreign companies find it increasingly attractive to buy into U.S. firms. Fujitsu has acquired 47 percent of Amdahl Corporation, which makes mainframe computers, for nearly $180 million. Sweden's Datatronic paid $25 million for a 90 percent stake in Victor Technologies, a troubled microcomputer company. Italy's Fiat and Allis-Chalmers have traded 10 percent holdings in each other. And Switzerland's Nestlé's signed a deal in late 1984 to take over Carnation for a hefty $3 billion.

Japanese steelmakers, reacting to tough new competition from South Korea, are concentrating on fewer, more modern sites. Nippon Kokan, Japan's second-largest steelmaker, last year bought 50 percent of National Steel for just under $300 million. Nisshin Steel, the number six producer, now owns 10 percent of Wheeling-Pittsburgh and is building a new production line in Ohio. Mitsui and Nippon Steel jointly own half of Alumax Mill Products, an aluminum producer. Canada's aluminum giant, Alcan, has acquired Atlantic Richfield's floundering aluminum operations in Indiana and Kentucky and Arco's 25 percent share of an Irish aluminum refinery.

The popularity of transnational joint ventures is spreading contagiously. General Foods recently launched four joint ventures in India, Brazil, Spain, and China. Boeing and three major Japanese companies—Mitsubishi, Kawasaki, and Fuji—will jointly develop a new jetliner, with Boeing retaining a majority interest. Himot is a blend of Hercules, Inc. and Italy's Montedison that is working on polypropylene resin. In aircraft engines, United Technologies and Rolls-Royce of Britain have pooled their expertise.

Another growth trend in international business is a form of barter called countertrade, and it also blurs national identities. Here, a company in an industrialized nation sells know-how to a developing country in return for part of the goods produced. Example: International Harvester provides Poland with the technology and equipment needed to manufacture tractors; in return, IH gets a royalty on each tractor sold and a portion of the plant's output. Levi Strauss has a comparable deal with Hungary in blue jeans. Countertrade now amounts to at least $100 billion a year, and we forecast more of it, because it aids developing nations in coping with hard currency and debt problems.

What is or isn't an American company becomes utterly bewildering when you examine how many private investors from overseas own shares of otherwise thoroughly red-white-and-blue-chip U.S. companies. Conversely, eighteen foreign firms, mostly from Europe, raised a record $1 billion in 1983 from shares offered to American investors. Roughly one-quarter of Sony's shares are owned by U.S. citizens. And mutual funds and closed-end funds specializing in foreign, particularly Japanese, stocks have been Wall Street hits in recent years. The latest is the Korea Fund.

The same patterns are evident in other countries, too. Take France, for example. Rhone-Poulenc, a chemicals and pharmaceuticals giant, is a partner in six joint ventures in Japan. Auto maker Renault has subassembly operations in Taiwan and Indonesia. Thomson, one of France's big electronics concerns, put up a factory in Singapore that exports its products globally. Inside France, meanwhile, Sony recently opened its second plant for final assembly of VCRs, and Canon produces copying machines.

This web of interlocking links among free-world companies will keep on multiplying, with no end in sight. Simon Ramo, cofounder of Ramo-Wooldridge Corporation (the "R" and "W" in today's TRW, Inc.) and former chairman of the President's Committee on Science and Technology, summed up the situation at a roundtable discussion sponsored by *Electronics* magazine to probe high-tech trends. By the year 2000, he believes, the us-against-them analogy will be next to meaningless. The answer to "How are we going to do against the Japanese?" begs another question, says Ramo: "What do you mean by 'the Japanese,' and what do you mean by 'we'?"

The internationalization of business defies simple definitions and tidy compartmentalization. In a sense, it's a kind of limbo land, lying somewhere between the sobriquet of "Buy American" and the idealists' dream of a world government.

International Winners and Losers

To compete in the global marketplace, American companies will be looking to disperse activities to more and more countries, chasing the lowest-cost labor, the cheapest capital, the best tax rates. Most of all, perhaps, executives will be seeking a high degree of political stability, since a manufacturing plant represents an investment of many millions of dollars that will take years to recover.

Divining political stability—the likelihood of revolution, social upheaval, or a radical reversal in either the political or business climate—is far more difficult than gauging the drift of technology. Part II of this book therefore offers valuable insights into the near- and long-term outlook for two dozen nations, with detailed analyses of those that seem destined to spring a major surprise or two on the business world. For example, two of the more spectacular and unexpected shifts will occur in Zimbabwe and Japan:

Zimbabwe, rich in natural resources, with a budding manufacturing industry rising on the country's mining base, is making dramatic progress under Robert Mugabe. The potential for tribal conflict still can't be dismissed, but if the country makes it through the 1980s without a disastrous outbreak of civil strife, it will blossom into a regional power by the turn of the century. The key will be attracting Western capital, technology, and managers with more favorable foreign-investment policies, which should be on the books before 1990. That will turn Zimbabwe into one of the prime investment candidates during the nineties.

Japan, on the other hand, is heading for a nose dive that will continue through the early 1990s, then will level out. Its aggressive trading groups will go on giving fits to competitors, but for the foreseeable future—well into the next century—it won't regain anywhere near the overpowering presence in international circles that it commands today. The causes will be a mix of internal and external factors, such as growing social service demands from an aging population, the strain of total reliance on imported energy and raw materials, and intensifying competition from Korea and other Pacific Rim nations—and then mainland China. Japan's chief hope of avoiding this slump is to become an innovator in technology, which appears dubious but is still an open issue.

Peering elsewhere into our crystal globe, Italy's stability will be sliding downhill steadily, with no signs of bottoming out for the next twenty years. Israel will keep on slipping over the near term, then bounce back once it resolves the Palestinian problem. In Libya, conditions will improve for a time, then deteriorate rapidly as its oil reserves start to peter out and Colonel Qaddafi no longer has the wherewithal to buy the allegiance of the people and the army. And Yugoslavia, after weathering some interim difficulties, will begin registering sharp gains in the late 1990s.

As for the United States, it'll take some licks as the twenty-first century draws near—even drop a notch in stability, from number 1 to number 2, with Australia replacing America at the head of the list. The reasons will be as much psychological as economical: alarm over the continuing erosion of industrial strength and domestic manufacturing jobs, uncertainty about the viability of becoming an almost-exclusive service economy, and the realization by the bulk of Americans that their own and their children's public schooling was based on obsolete assumptions about the workaday world. America's preeminent leadership in technological innovation, however, will carry the day—if we don't give away too much technology too fast, and if the politicians in Washington find the gumption to reduce this country's appalling deficit.

Without drastic action to balance the budget, the U.S. could slip even more in the 1990s. There are only two spending areas that offer any chance of making a significant impact: defense and social welfare. Economists can argue all day long over this cut or that one in smaller budget categories, but all of the possibilities put together probably won't come to much more than $50 billion over President Reagan's remaining three years. That just won't be enough. The Administration and Congress must think in terms of $200 billion over the next three years; otherwise, the government will keep on bidding for money—and bidding up the interest rate. And as long as interest rates here are substantially higher than in Europe, foreign investments will flow into the U.S. and American exports will find limited markets.

One example of the sort of hard decisions that must be made: The Navy has got to realize that there are two kinds of vessels—submarines and targets. The Navy needs to cut down building targets and instead build more submarines. And as for social security, the notion that people should retire at sixty-five is as out-of-date as the guy who first conceived it. More than one hundred years ago, when only about 2 percent of the population lived to be sixty-five, Prince Otto von Bismarck thought those few hardy souls deserved to live out the rest of their years at state expense. Today it's just too damn expensive to keep playing the game by mid-nineteenth-century rules; 65 percent of the population now lives to be sixty-five. So we need to lift the entitlement age to seventy-three.

None of this will be politically popular, obviously. Very likely supporting these measures will cost some legislators their chance of reelection. But it's high time that the elected officials in Washington put the future of the nation ahead of their own careers. Whether enough politicians have the guts to become statesmen is the question. But one way or the other, the day of reckoning is approaching fast.

PART ONE

1

THE GREAT TECHNOLOGY GIVEAWAY

America's industrial fortress may be cracking, but this country's technological leadership is unquestioned—so far. However, as a white knight that is supposed to rescue the U.S. economy from the perils of industrial decay, technology has one major fault: It's awfully easy to buy, or to copy or steal, especially given this country's open society and free-market economy. In fact, the federal government helps disseminate technical information to anyone who wants it, even Soviet spies. The National Technical Information Service, an arm of the U.S. Commerce Department, collects information on recent advances, then sells its reports for a pittance to all comers. Boxes of documents are regularly shipped to businesses and government agencies in developed and developing countries, including the Soviet Union.

The United States also transfers technology to foreign nations through multinational firms, through foreign students enrolled in the education system, and through technology and patent licenses. For example, multinational companies are frequently forced to transfer technology as the price of admission to an overseas country's markets. "Local content" laws are a common way of taxing technology: Some proportion of a product must be manufactured within the country where it is to be sold, which means the American multinational must either build a factory there or buy components from local manufacturers.

Either way, the U.S. company has to train foreign nationals to produce the components. Local content regulations are generally justified as insurance against the loss of jobs due to imports, but the net effect is more insidious.

Today, slightly more than half of the Ph.D. candidates enrolled in American universities are from other countries, and a third of the students working on a master's degree are "studying abroad" in the United States. They come because they realize this is the wellspring of basic science and technology. And American schools welcome them with open arms, if for no other reason than foreign students usually pay full tuition. Few universities are so financially secure that they can afford to turn away "profitable" students.

Most foreign nationals who earn a postgraduate degree here stay on to work at a U.S. company, because there may be few opportunities to utilize their skills in their native country, or because they can earn more money here. At high-tech centers such as California's famed Silicon Valley and Route 128 near Boston, it's quite common to find corporate R&D departments where one-third to one-half of the professional staff is foreign born. But if these people do return to their own countries, they take with them some of the know-how at the core of America's advanced technology.

As for technology and patent licenses sold to interested parties overseas, many such licenses have returned to haunt the U.S. companies that sold them. Because this nation is so huge, American companies, by and large, have tended to ignore the international marketplace. With the world's biggest market just outside the front door, why bother? Converting inches to centimeters and plowing through all the red tape to get a product out of the United States can be a real pain, not to mention the hassle of maneuvering through the exasperating bureaucratese encountered at ports of entry in foreign lands. So when offshore companies offered to buy technology, many U.S. executives jumped at the chance, figuring to pick up a few extra bucks and maybe some ongoing royalties as well. Or perhaps a basement inventor grabbed an offer from overseas after months or years of butting up against closed doors and closed minds at U.S. companies.

Whatever the reason for cutting the deal in the first place, technology licenses can easily backfire. Through one or more of the above means, U.S. companies have lost out on immense profits. Bell Laboratories, the venerable research arm of AT&T, invented the transistor in 1947 and launched the era of solid-state electronics. AT&T licensed its transistor technology to fledgling Sony in 1953 for a mere $25,000— and the rest is history. Today Sony is a $5 billion company that does an astonishing 70 percent of its business in foreign markets.

Sony has become a household name through a remarkable string of "firsts," most of which weren't—not in the strictest sense, anyway. The transistor radio that got Sony started was preceded by one produced in the United States, but it flopped because it was hand-made in small quantities and thus priced prohibitively. Sony, on the other hand, saw the promise of a cheap transistor radio and was willing to gamble on the manufacturing investment needed to minimize costs. Similarly, Sony's famous Trinitron color TV tube was invented in the United States, and so was the video-tape recorder, the precursor of the videocassette recorder (VCR) that Sony pioneered in 1975.

Today, VCRs are the hottest-selling and most profitable home entertainment product in the history of the consumer electronics industry. Worldwide sales have been growing 75 percent a year and last year topped the 25 billion–unit mark—double the number of color TV sets made by Japanese firms. The average factory selling price of a VCR, nearly $350, is 50 percent higher than that of a color TV. The VCR business last year accounted for nearly half of Japan's enormous consumer electronics industry. All VCRs, save a handful of European-made models sold only in Europe, come from Japan.

So if there's a choice between being first with an idea or invention, or being first with a successful innovation, an honest-to-goodness product, it's pretty clear which is the more lucrative.

American technology was the foundation for even more of Japan's consumer electronics industry. Around the same time that AT&T licensed the transistor to Sony, RCA sold its know-how for making color TV sets to several Japanese manufacturers. By the mid-1960s, Japanese TVs—plus hi-fi tuners and receivers, and related items— were rapidly wresting sales from U.S.-made equipment. During the 1970s, imports soared from one-third to two-thirds of the American market, and domestic employment in the consumer electronics sector plummeted from 160,000 in 1966 to 63,000 in 1982. Of the eighteen

U.S. firms that were making TV sets in 1968, only four are left, while the number of Japanese-owned—and more recently, Korean-owned—TV factories has jumped from zero to twelve. These foreign-owned plants supply 35 percent of the market, and imports of finished TVs represent another 15 percent, roughly. And virtually all radios and hi-fi gear are imported from Asian factories.

The Japanese robot industry also got started with U.S. technology, when Unimation, the pioneer of industrial robots, licensed Kawasaki Heavy Industries in 1968. Today, Japan builds and uses far more robots than the United States or any other country, which is one reason why Japanese companies can manufacture goods so cheaply. Moreover, GMFanuc, a joint venture between General Motors and Japan's Fujitsu Fanuc, is among the fastest-growing robot suppliers in America. Already the third-largest seller of robots, GMFanuc will be number one in the U.S. robot market by 1990, eclipsing Unimation, which ran into financial difficulties and was acquired by Westinghouse Electric, as well as Cincinnati Milacron, the current leader. GMFanuc's stated plan is to be the biggest robot company in the world by 1990.

Then there's Japan's computer industry, which also relied on licensed U.S. technology. Now the Japanese are increasing their share of world markets, largely at the expense of U.S. producers, and they have launched a national effort to develop a so-called fifth generation computer that will exhibit artificial intelligence and leapfrog everything available from IBM (more on this in a later chapter). Most of the Japanese giants participating in the "Fifth Generation Project" purchased U.S. technology in the 1960s: Hitachi got RCA expertise; Mitsubishi bought know-how from TRW and Xerox; NEC acquired Honeywell's help; Oki was licensed by Sperry Univac; and Toshiba took GE technology. (Several of these U.S. companies have since closed down their computer-making operations, but before the Japanese became serious competitors.)

The Leaking Bucket

The bottom line is this: Despite a twelvefold climb in dollar exports of U.S.-made products, American manufacturers have been steadily losing ground in international markets over the last twenty years. In 1962, American industry accounted for 22 percent of worldwide manufacturing exports; the current figure is more than five percentage points lower. Even America's two top manufacturing exporters, aerospace and chemicals, are feeling the crunch.

And the same trend is evident in the domestic market—where the rate at which market share is being lost is still more alarming. Manufactured imports have zoomed twentyfold in dollars in twenty years, and imports have more than quadrupled their 1962-vintage 3 percent share of the U.S. market. And as everyone must know, this home-market competition is spreading from labor-intensive areas, such as textiles, into capital-intensive industries—including steel, cars, and machine tools, the industrial equipment crucial to every manufacturing enterprise. Late in 1984 a Commerce Department study predicted that the decline in U.S. machine tools will continue into the next century, by which time the building of essentially all standard machine tools will have migrated to offshore plants, either U.S. or foreign owned.

No wonder American technology has been compared to a leaky bucket!

For the rest of this century, America faces two crucial challenges: first, keeping that bucket full; second, devising new sociopolitical mechanisms that give U.S. companies more incentives to cash in on their R&D investments by turning new technology into actual products, rather than farming out the technology to Japan or some other location.

To keep the bucket full, the United States can either plug the holes or it can pour in new technology at an ever-accelerating rate. The plug-the-holes scenario appears to be gathering support from hard-liners in and out of government. A few federal officials and corporate officers go so far as to suggest that the sort of export restrictions that now apply only to classified military information and products should be extended to all high-tech fields. They would bar foreign students from courses in semiconductor technology and computer science, and screen off non-American scientists from leading-edge research projects at universities.

But once embarked on such a course of action, where does one draw the line? Will newspapers and trade publications that write about high-tech subjects be censored? Will prominent scientists and technicians be told where they can and cannot travel and what they can and cannot say to fellow scientists in other countries?

The hard-liners are generally reacting to the Soviet Union's military exploitation of U.S. technology, sometimes obtained directly and legally from the United States, more often illicitly, via devious commercial channels and shell companies funded by the KGB or a sister spy agency in a Soviet satellite nation. The trucks that carried soviet troops into Afghanistan, for example, were built in a gigantic factory that the United States designed and helped construct only after the Kremlin gave assurance that the factory would never be used for military vehicles. Several pieces of some of the most sophisticated machines ever made—they are used in producing microchips—have mysteriously disappeared in Europe. The Central Intelligence Agency is certain that they ended up in Russia and are the heart of several chip-making lines that the Soviets would otherwise have had to spend years and many millions of dollars to develop.

Arresting that kind of technology transfer is worth a try, but let's be careful about stepping into the commercial arena. Apart from the dire impact secrecy controls would have on the fundamental makeup of the American way of life, there are very practical considerations, also. Who will replace the foreign scientists already making important contributions to new technology? If these scientists flee to Europe or Korea or some other place with high-tech aspirations, won't that eventually lead to even stiffer competition? If U.S. scientists can't exchange information freely with their counterparts around the world, how much will U.S. research be slowed? Inasmuch as U.S. R&D budgets aren't always keeping pace with inflation as it is, can America afford the bill to duplicate the research programs in other countries, to which we surely would no longer have access?

What's the competitive benefit that the United States realizes by "robbing" other countries of their brightest minds? Americans justifiably take great pride in the number of Nobel prizes that their scientists have won. But surely it is no mere coincidence that the number of Nobel prizes won by America has climbed dramatically since European scientists, fleeing Hitler and then Stalin, began arriving in droves on American shores. Before World War II, U.S. science ranked alongside such third-tier nations as Switzerland and Sweden, in terms of the number of Nobel laureates. From 1942 to 1960, Americans won forty-five of the eighty-nine Nobel prizes awarded in physics, chemistry, and medicine. Since 1960, U.S. scientists have collected more than half of these honors—triple the number awarded to the runner-up, Britain, and ten times as many as won by German scientists. No doubt some of America's Nobel laureates, as well as other scientists destined to win Nobels, are so devoted to their science that they might pack up and depart for a better environment if America imposed police-state controls on science—and the United States would suffer a brain drain.

Consequently, the plug-the-leaks tactic would end up being a classic case of cutting off your nose to spite your face. "If we lock up our basic research, we'll do far greater damage than if we allow the leakage," warns Michael Dertouzos, director of the Laboratory for Computer Science at Massachusetts Institute of Technology. This is not to say that some judicious patches shouldn't be applied to help companies realize better returns on their R&D investments. But hole plugging can never be more than a minor factor in protecting the U.S. edge in technology.

For one thing, the whole notion is based on a fallacious assumption: that the U.S. has a monopoly on high technology. Nothing could be farther from the truth. Between 75 percent and 80 percent of all high-tech products sold in free-world markets are manufactured elsewhere. Even in that most arcane high-tech area—processes and equipment for making microchips—European and Japanese companies have captured a healthy share of the business, not only in their home markets but in the United States as well.

Countries have been trying, vainly, to control technology transfer for centuries. *Newsweek* turned up a striking parallel: In 1565 King Sigismund of Poland wrote to Queen Elizabeth I, imploring her to curb Britain's trade with Russia. "The Tsar of Moscow, enemy of all liberty, increases his forces day by day through the advantages of trade and by his relations with the civilized nations of Europe. . . . Our only hope rests in our superiority in the arts and sciences, but soon he will know as much." So, only the names have changed.

Technology's Four I's

There is only one sure way of staying ahead: run faster than everyone else. Every year, each quarter, America has to pour new ideas and developments into that bucket of technology. And that applies to the military, too.

The rigid culture and structure of the military services has not been able to keep up with the private sector in exploiting technology, leading to such embarrassments as Assistant Secretary of Defense Richard N. Perle's recent attempt to embargo exports of Apple II computers. The Pentagon is worried that Apples could be used by the Soviet bloc as a portable battlefield-control computer. The nearest thing the U.S. Army has is so big and clunky it takes a jeep to haul it around.

Priming the pump of technology would be much easier if the lawmakers and government bureaucrats shed their antibusiness bias and tossed out some of the artificial disincentives that now hinder research and innovation, capital formation, and the competitive stance of U.S. firms abroad. There's no reason why American government and business can't work together, as in many other nations—except, perhaps, that Washington has too many lawyers in elected and appointed positions of leadership. Most of these lawyer-politicians have no business experience, little appreciation of how global competition works, and tend to project their adversarial bent into legislation and regulation.

Whether or not Washington comes to its senses, corporate America can't afford to forget for an instant what the "high" in high technology means: high rate of change. Technology is a dynamo that feeds off itself, constantly gathering momentum and speed. It's like the self-replicating machines in some science-fiction stories. Research leads to one invention, triggering other ideas and more innovation. The broader the base of accumulated science, the more wheels of technology that are set spinning. The more wheels that are whirling, the bigger the load of new concepts that can be supported, that become thinkable, and the faster each development can be nurtured through the stages of gestation.

These stages are the "Four I's" of science and technology: ideas, invention, innovation, and finally imitation. (Another "I"—internment—is always waiting for the unwary and, of course, the unsuccessful.)

Over the past decade or so, the diffusion of high-tech products, especially microchips, into general industry has sparked an incredible acceleration in the speed at which a development cycles through the Four I's. The lag between an invention and its manufacture, and particularly the time from a new product's introduction until the marketing of imitations, has shrunk significantly. "Every industry we look at seems to be undergoing shorter [product] cycles," says Joel Goldhar, dean of the business school at the Illinois Institute of Technology.

In the 1950s and '60s, the average time between invention and innovation was twenty-odd years, even longer in some industries. The life cycle of a home refrigerator, for instance, was thirty years. That was plenty of time to recover all development costs and then plow back profits into a new product for the next cycle. When microwave ovens came along, their average life cycle was ten years. Now most manufacturers can figure on only about eight years. IBM has always maintained a six-year life cycle for its business products, and in such fast-moving fields as personal computers, it's more like four years; in video games it may be as little as two. And copying another company's innovation can be done in a matter of months, sometimes, and rarely takes longer than a year or two. Consequently, a company has much less time to recover its costs before the competition gets hectic and price cutting sets in.

One of the primary forces behind this time squeeze is the ubiquitous microchip. Electronic engineers are designing chips that substitute for more and more electromechanical functions. That means product engineering doesn't have to bother with designing some complex mechanism; purchasing doesn't need to track down sources of special alloys and other raw materials; manufacturing doesn't get saddled with ordering special tools and machining those materials into cogs and cams and gears—all of which typically requires a lead time of a couple of years. Instead, the company orders a single chip that does the whole job. But, naturally, so can a rival manufacturer.

The furious pace of technology is nowhere better illustrated than in microprocessors, the "brains" in modern computers. The first practical designs were the 4-bit version introduced in 1971 by Intel and then Texas Instruments and others (4-bit designs are still widely used in industrial equipment), and the 8-bit "micro" that touched off the boom in home computers, video games, and powerful but inexpensive computer-aided design (CAD) systems. Those chips were superseded nine years later, when the semiconductor industry in 1980 unwrapped the 16-bit generation, which led to the IBM Personal Computer. Then, after only three more years, the 32-bit generation arrived, promising desk-top computers that rival the performance of big systems that used to require a special air-conditioned room. (The 8-, 16-, and 32-bit descriptions refer to the number of digits in the "words" that shuttle commands and data around the chip's tiny circuits; the longer the word, the faster the microprocessor can execute an instruction or retrieve information from its own memory or nearby memory chips. Most big mainframe computers process data in 32-bit words.)

A Contrast of Cultures

With all the technology that's floating around in the United States, one has to wonder why this country isn't doing a better job of capitalizing on it. Why can't American business be as adept, as fleet footed as the Japanese at turning its technology into products?

One reason, of course, is management's preoccupation with short-term results—the Harvard MBA syndrome that measures performance on the basis of profitability this quarter and next. But the problem runs much deeper.

Suppose Mr. Enlightened, president of Skytek Company, wants to make short-term sacrifices for a major long-term gain in five or six years. What happens? Well, he can count on bumping up against a jaundiced financial establishment. Wall Street analysts don't want to hear about potential returns even two years down the road, and to them a payoff that's five years in the future might as well be never. Don't forget, Wall Street firms make money from commissions on stock trades, both buying and selling. They like to see as much turnover as possible in their clients' portfolios. What incentive do they have to recommend that anyone buy Skytek's shares and sit on them for five years?

So the next analyst's report says that because Mr. Enlightened is diverting 15 percent of Skytek's quarterly dividends for at least the next two years, it's time to sell the stock—never mind that Skytek will triple in value in five years if the strategy succeeds. Hundreds of uncritical investors, who are just as shortsighted as the most callous businessman, immediately dump thousands of shares. What do they gain by hanging tough with Mr. Enlightened? So Skytek's shares take a nose dive, depressing the company's worth and thus limiting the capital that Mr. Enlightened can raise for up-front investments in his project.

Still, since Mr. Enlightened knew this would happen, he is determined to forge ahead. He lays out his plan to his bank and gets a loan at 12 percent interest, only one point above the prime rate (money being tight because Americans haven't increased their abysmal savings rate). Servicing the loan during the interim before the money starts generating revenues will eat up nearly half of the 15 percent being set aside from dividends.

The primary expense is for automating production of the skyhooks that the company recently introduced. Mr. E knows that the Japanese are working on a me-too imitation, but he's confident that if he buys advanced tools for his work force, at a cost of about $1,000 per person, Skytek can make skyhooks at least as cheaply as the Japanese can. More important, once Skytek's factory workers have a year or two of experience with the new equipment under their belts, the company will be ready to spring a surprise on the competition by unveiling a new blockbuster, the skypump. In addition, the factory will be able to trim production costs of the company's traditional skypole products. All together, Mr. E figures that Skytek will realize a gain of $2,000 per worker—a handsome 100 percent return on the initial investment.

And Mr. Enlightened pulls it all off, right on schedule. However, the workers aren't dummies; they know they are now worth a lot more to Skytek, so they demand a cut of their increased contributions— $900 per person in wages and fringes. Rather than lose their skills to competitors, a disillusioned Mr. E agrees to negotiate, and they compromise on $800, which the company can obviously afford.

And then Mr. (dis)Enlightened flies off to Japan to see if Nippon-Tek is interested in a joint venture to manufacture Skytek's latest invention, the skytop, which will require even more advanced production machinery that would have cost Skytek another $1,000 per person.

Nippon-Tek is delighted with the proposal. Mr. Hiteka, Nippon-Tek's president, sees all the same benefits accruing to his company— and privately figures he can eventually back into production of sky-poles, skyhooks, and skypumps for Skytek as well. He outlines the long-range strategy to Nitekki Bank, which already owns most of Nippon-Tek's outstanding stock, and the bank is enthusiastic. It was looking for new investment opportunities for its cash surplus (the Japanese savings rate is an outstanding 20 percent–plus of income, and workers not supported by the lifetime job policies of the top-tier companies often save one-third of their wages).

The bank's managers, concerned more with long-range return on equity than with quarterly dividends, eagerly put up 70 percent of the required investment, at the prime rate of 5 percent, with the first payment due in two years, or about when Nippon-Tek expects to begin shipping skytops. Also, the bank arranges for a low-cost government loan for the rest, repayable only from profits (if the scheme flops, the debt is simply canceled). There is no deflation of Nippon-Tek's price on the Tokyo stock market, and the favorable terms enable the company to get by with an investment of only $700 per person.

Two years later, Nippon-Tek is ramping up its output of skytops, and the workers who have been trained on the new production line hold a party to celebrate their new skills. Mr. Hiteka is the guest of honor, and the workers present him with a hand-lacquered box containing ten suggestions as to how they and their new equipment can be more efficiently utilized to the benefit of the company.

One suggestion proposes substituting nine robots for fourteen workers, who would then become missionaries and spread their new skills among people on the firm's other production lines. The workers who will be displaced know they have nothing to fear; the company will always provide work for as long as they choose to remain in the "family." Nor would they dream of gouging the company for a share of its enhanced profitability; if the company prospers, they know they will be rewarded at bonus time.

Another suggestion, from two graduate engineers serving their compulsory four-year factory apprenticeship before moving up to management, outlines how certain shifts in production scheduling and minor equipment changes would make it possible to use the new skytop line for turning out nutzinbolts. A nutzinbolt is the most complex part in a skypump, and the young engineers assert that Nippon-Tek can make it for about 20 percent less than what they estimate Skytek's cost to be. Mr. Hiteka awards elaborate certificates for both suggestions and six others as well, engendering considerable pride all around.

In due course, Mr. Hiteka relates the nutzinbolts idea to Mr. Enlightened, who, after much soul-searching, hands the job to Nippon-Tek—and pink slips to seventy of Skytek's workers. The day after the deal and the layoffs are announced, Skytek's stock gains 4.5 points on the Big Board.

A New Age for Entrepreneurs

What can be done about a system with the myopia to penalize innovation and reward the export of jobs? Plenty. But before launching into the changes that are needed, let's take note of the strengths inherent in American capitalism, the features we *don't* want to mess with.

Without question, one of the nation's great assets is the venture-capital system that funnels money to fledgling enterprises. It is unique, the envy of the world. America's venture capital phenomenon is directly or indirectly responsible for most of the 25 million new jobs generated in the United States since 1970—indirectly in the sense that legendary success stories in the computer, semiconductor, and biotech industries encourage people to strike out on their own, even if they don't ask for backing from venture capitalists. Small companies have always been the source of the lion's share of job growth in the United States, so society should do everything possible to nurture the formation and growth of small companies.

Venture capital may grease the wheels of start-up businesses, but it's obviously wasted without the drive and vision of entrepreneurs. America is blessed with more than its share of people who yearn to start their own company and make it big. In 1983 some 600,000 new businesses were born—three times as many as twenty years ago. In 1984 the number was almost 700,000. During the coming decade, the ranks of the self-employed will double.

"Clearly, there's been a radical rise of entrepreneurship," notes Karl H. Vesper, professor of entrepreneurship at the University of Washington. "There's a latent lust for it in all of us—it's the American way." Adds Donald C. Burr, the 43-year-old founder of People Express Airlines: "Entrepreneurship will be the major impetus for the decade immediately ahead of us, and what's ahead is terrifically exciting."

The new entrepreneurs are superconfident, willing to take risks, unscarred by the Depression mentality that caused people to seek job security above all else. Their reward can be handsome. Of the top 1 percent of Americans who earn the most money, three-fourths are their own bosses. But entrepreneurism demands persistence: Eight of every ten new businesses go under inside of five years. A study of well-known entrepreneurs in Minnesota a few years ago found that almost every one of them had had a string of failures before hitting it big. One went bankrupt seven times, but his personal fortune at the time of the study was estimated at $250 million.

Yet financial success is not the only motivating factor. Even people who are still struggling and not making very much money emphasize that they would never consider going back to work in a big company. They have an idealism that believes work should be self-fulfilling. They are ready to experiment with new values and new ways of organizing people. Doubtless this is why so many workers are willing to flee large institutions and rigidly structured management for smaller firms with more enlightened management policies.

Inc, a five-year-old magazine for small businesses, recently asked the definition of an entrepreneur: Someone who creates a company? Someone who takes risks? Someone with a bias toward action? Chief editor George Gendron concluded that "perhaps the phenomenon we are witnessing now has less to do with action or risk-taking than with the simple observation that people, not institutions, create economic wealth. In this respect, perhaps the entrepreneur is leading all of corporate America to a rediscovery of business as an enterprise, a rediscovery of business as a process limited only by the boundaries of each individual's intelligence, imagination, energy, and daring."

Still more such dreamers are needed, though. Despite all the publicity that the media has accorded start-up companies in the high-tech disciplines, the fact is that the number of new *technology* companies being created today is a fraction of the level in the 1960s, when as many as 400 to 500 new firms were founded each year. In the two decades after World War II, technological entrepreneurism flourished in the United States, not just in computers, solid-state electronics, and telecommunications, but also in chemicals, pharmaceuticals, copiers, instant photography, agricultural technology, jet transport, and other fields. Some of these are now verging on maturity, so America badly needs fresh infusions of technology.

Fortunately, the signs seem favorable. There is no reason to project any decline in the peculiarly American talent for invention. The country clearly stands on the threshold of two new technologies with vast potentials: biotechnology and telecomputing. In the 1990s and especially after the turn of the century, bioengineering will be no less catholic in its permutations than microchips are today, throwing off developments that will advance health care, agriculture, animal breeding, energy production, and industrial materials—and very likely yield a radically new type of computer: biocomputers.

Meanwhile, the merging of computers and telecommunications—telecomputing—will precipitate a synergistic deluge of new technologies in information processing, each of which will offer multiple new business opportunities. For example, two-way TV will foster electronic newspapers, shopping and banking at home, new forms of home entertainment, regional and national "town hall" meetings; those are just a few of the new possibilities. Telecomputing will enable a doctor to consult with top specialists anywhere in the country, as a patient's vital signs, X-rays, and diagnostic test results are being relayed as digital data over a videophone hookup. Already, business executives are beginning to hold simultaneous face-to-face conferences with offices in several different locations.

Such information processing and telecomputing capabilities will usher in a vibrant new era for entrepreneurs. The new technologies, says Alfred D. Chandler, Straus Professor of Business History at the Harvard Business School, are providing "entrepreneurial opportunities that simply weren't there prior to World War II."

In addition, the Defense Department is again trying to stimulate the private sector as it did in the 1950s and early '60s, when defense technology blazed the trail for industry. Since then, military technology has fallen further and further behind the private sector, and very little of the government's huge R&D budget has helped industry, except for aerospace companies and defense contractors. After a regrettable decline in federal R&D spending in the late 1960s, the Ford and Carter administrations reversed the downtrend, and the Reagan administration's budget for this fiscal year provides a whopping $35 billion for R&D in new technologies—double the figure existing when President Reagan took office. Apart from the so-called Star Wars thrust, the Defense Advanced Research Projects Agency is spearheading a multipronged push in artificial intelligence, supercomputers, and semiconductors that may surpass Japan's Fifth Generation Project, aimed at developing a computer that mimics the human brain.

The cumulative impact of all these thrusts will be as profound as the Industrial Revolution, when huge masses of people deserted farms and migrated to cities to take factory jobs. It clearly will overturn our concept of work, which now tends to be muddled by the notion that work should involve physical labor, even if it only is sorting and filing pieces of paper in an office. But why should a sentient human being be asked to do anything that a machine can do just as well? In tomorrow's telecomputing society, each individual will be able to develop his or her talents to the fullest, and the drudgery of so many of today's jobs will be turned over to machines that don't care if the chores are dull, monotonous, and boring. People will work with their hands or toil in factories only because they want to, because they enjoy that kind of labor—and there are plenty of machinists and lumberjacks and truckers who wouldn't dream of doing anything else.

Getting from here to there, however, won't be painless. The essential items on the agenda are these:

1. Since a primary root of America's manufacturing malaise is a relative lack of capital and a reluctance to make capital investments, modifying the tax laws is vital. To foster capital formation, interest that accumulates in savings accounts should be tax-free until it is withdrawn, and then it should be taxed on a sliding scale: 50 percent of earned interest would be taxed when withdrawn in the first year; 25 percent after one year through three years; and 10 percent after three years.

2. To make longer-term investments much more attractive, a similar slide scale should be applied to capital gains. For instance, 100 percent of the capital gains from sales of investments held for less

than one year would be taxed; 50 percent of gains on investments held for one to three years; 25 percent for three to five years; and 10 percent for more than five years.

3. Government must become more responsive to the needs of companies when they either are competing in global markets or are facing domestic competition from foreign rivals. For starters, if a manufacturer of a product that is 80 percent or more U.S.-made, by value, can show that imported products have captured in excess of 25 percent of the domestic market, the antitrust act should be suspended in that market. (An import would be defined as, say, anything with more than one-third foreign content, from a firm that is one-half or more foreign owned.) Antitrust provisions could be reimposed only on a company-by-company basis—for those whose market share exceeds double the total sales of all imports—or five years after imports have dropped below the trigger level.

4. To encourage companies, domestic or foreign, to do more manufacturing in the United States, the government should provide tax breaks and subsidies. For example, when a company shifts the capacity of an existing offshore factory into the United States, the government might underwrite part of the plant construction costs through a long-term loan at, say, one or two points above the going rate on government savings bonds. The interest would be repaid only from dividends.

5. The government must create a climate that stimulates innovation as well as invention, that helps put new technology into production in the United States at least as quickly as it happens in overseas nations. The first move would be to exclude from antitrust actions not only joint research partnerships but also cooperative engineering projects. In addition, Washington should empower the states to license regional and local joint-technology transfer institutes that would be sheltered from antitrust laws. These institutes would cater to small business, acquainting management with emerging opportunities and helping production workers to acquire new skills.

6. Because the small-business sector is so vital to creating new jobs, the government should devise incentives to encourage entrepreneurship, such as allowing 100 percent annual write-offs of investments

during a company's first five years. And to assist small companies in export markets, the Export-Import Bank should lower its minimum figure for loans.

7. Finally, a new accommodation with labor is imperative. The primary reason American companies have been losing so many battles is that U.S. labor costs are simply out of line. Today's distrust between labor and management must yield to a spirit of cooperation and joint responsibility, so that direct labor costs can be reduced while providing the means for workers to maintain their living standards. One way might be to give tax credits for bonuses paid from profits to factory workers—and make such bonuses tax-free to the workers. That should give the workers a strong motive to help the company thrive.

Give workers more responsibility and remarkable things can happen. Take the case of Hyatt Clark Industries, a unit of GM in New Jersey. It was losing $8 million a year because the primary market for its product, tapered roller bearings, was shrinking as the auto industry went from rear-wheel drives (which use tapered roller bearings) to front-wheel drives (which don't). The local union proposed that the employees buy the firm to save their jobs, and GM was agreeable because it would cut its losses and maintain a reliable source of tapered bearings. Employee ownership provided high motivation that led to almost unbelievable productivity improvements. Attitudes changed radically when the worker-owners realized in their guts that their futures were inextricably linked to the success of the plant. All is not perfect at Hyatt, but experiences like this prove that employees are an extremely valuable but often untapped resource—and more knowledgeable about business than many managers give them credit for.

Shifting into High-Speed Management

But until the above changes can be effected, all companies would do well to remember the catchwords of success. They've been around for twenty-five years or more, but they apply to the internationalist period no less than before:

Innovate and motivate
Automate or emigrate
or
Evaporate

Tomorrow's most successful organizations will use new management techniques modeled after practices perfected in the fast-paced high-tech industries. Andrew S. Grove, president of Intel, suggested one label for these techniques in the title of the book he wrote in 1983, *High Output Management*. They also have been dubbed high-speed and high-tech management. "High-speed management doesn't mean running faster on the same old treadmill," explains one executive. "It's a briefcase full of innovative techniques for coming up with new products, making sure that they're what the customers want, and getting products to the market in time to cash in big."

INNOVATE AND MOTIVATE. These two principles go hand in hand. Workers want and need to participate, to be recognized, to take pride in their work. When the employees' personal goals are in line with those of the company, the highest levels of innovation, product quality, and productivity result.

Many new, small companies—such as W. L. Gore & Associates, People Express Airlines, and Quad/Graphics—are rated as good places to work. Big companies with this reputation include Exxon, IBM, General Electric, and J. P. Morgan. These giants retain many little-company traits. They carve up operations into small units that stress teamwork, and they push responsibility for designing, manufacturing, and marketing new products down into the ranks.

The large-company masters of high-speed management take pains to emulate smallness for one overriding reason: Small firms produce more than twenty times the innovation, dollar for dollar, of big companies. Creeping bureaucracy, inflexible corporate cultures, and ponderous decision-making regimens obviously stifle innovation. And a constant stream of new products will be one key to survival in tomorrow's increasingly hectic business world.

In 1981 the management consulting firm of Booz Allen & Hamilton surveyed 700 U.S. companies about product development. The companies expected nearly one-third of their profits in the 1980s to come from new products, compared with slightly over one-fifth in the late 1970s. In really fast-moving markets, such as semiconductors, it's not unusual for products less than two years old to contribute between half and two-thirds of profits. More and more companies will have to learn to live with this pace of development, because the best and cheapest products will increasingly be those engineered around the very latest semiconductor chips.

Understanding is another prerequisite to successful innovation. Management must understand the dynamics of its customers' markets at least as well as its own market. A company must understand its competitors' strategies in order to counter them, to neutralize competitors' strengths and exploit weaknesses—and the company must be able to help its customers do the same. Only then can it respond to market forces both quickly and appropriately.

The optimum way of coping with rapid change is to anticipate it. The competition is always rougher on followers than on leaders. But sustaining a trailblazing posture for an extended period puts extraordinary strains on a company. The corporate culture must actively discourage conformity. That is no simple matter. In a sense, it means that management must cultivate an environment in which the status quo is chaos.

AUTOMATE. To open its new robot factory in Belgium, Asea, a Swedish company, programmed a 6-foot-tall, one-armed robot to cut the ribbon. "First the workers were automated, now the politicians [are]," quipped the Belgium minister of finance. Later, when the robot knocked over a vase of roses during the presentation, the minister added: "Thank God, the damn thing's human."

The survival kit for tomorrow's factories is automation. Traditional methods will not suffice to repel the combination of cheap labor and sophisticated manufacturing techniques heading this way not just from Japan, but from Korea, Brazil, Malaysia, Taiwan, and other emerging nations. To compete, the United States must move electronic "intelligence" in the form of robots and other computer-controlled machines onto every factory floor.

Computer-integrated manufacturing (CIM) is the cornerstone of the factory of the future. CIM technology will link up currently available systems—such as computer-aided design (CAD), computer-aided manufacturing (CAM), computer-aided process planning (CAPP), and flexible manufacturing systems (FMS)—so that all operations can share a common data base. That way, when a product engineer is finished working on the latest gizmo, he or she can shoot the specifications into CAM systems in the factory. (As it now stands, the two systems generally "talk" totally different languages, so design specifications have to be printed out on paper, physically carried to the factory, then laboriously "keyboarded" into the CAM computer's memory—a procedure that invariably results in mistakes and misinterpretations.) Then the CAM system will routinely issue commands to robots and automated manufacturing cells to turn out such-and-such a part from specified materials using particular tooling. Beyond trimming labor costs, totally automated factories will improve quality, generate less scrap, reduce the money tied up in inventories, and enhance a company's ability to respond to market trends with alacrity.

Athough it hasn't yet attained full CIM integration, Apple Computer's ultramodern plant puts out more than two Macintosh computers every minute; the labor content of a Macintosh is less than 1 percent of manufacturing costs. Xerox has a plant near Dallas that, in a three-shift day, can make as many as 2,000 electronic typewriters with fewer than one hundred workers per shift. Now that GE's Erie, Pennsylvania, locomotive plant has robots and computers, it can build a diesel engine block in sixteen hours with seven men; this task once took twenty-six days and ninety men. Even the apparel industry is getting into the automation act: Soon robots will be stitching men's suits.

EMIGRATE.   As competition in almost every high-tech business intensifies, "any company that limits its resources—money, people, ideas—to its home base will be restricted," says Yoshi Tsurumi, professor of international business at City University of New York. American companies are clearly taking this advice to heart. According to a Bureau of Economic Analysis survey, U.S. firms committed more than $42.4 billion to overseas capital spending in 1984. This was a sharp increase compared to recent capital spending.

And U.S. activity overseas is probably considerably higher than that figure indicates, because joint ventures are high fashion now and will be for at least the near future.

But there is a fine line to tread between exploiting overseas resources and giving away technology. The Japanese have been very adept at this (as have U.S. semiconductor makers). Japan's foreign plants are generally no more than assembly shops where workers in that foreign country bolt together key components that are made back in Japan and then put these into stamped-metal, low-tech cabinets that are purchased locally, along with knobs and nameplates and anything else that the Japanese owners can get from existing job shops. That way, the high-tech manufacturing skills crucial to any industrial society remain in the Japanese homeland, where they can be shifted from industry to industry when necessary. The Japanese set up full-blown manufacturing operations in foreign countries only when they must choose between that and losing business. By then, however, Japan's attention has likely already shifted to laying the foundations of some new technology.

To promote long-term growth and world peace, developing countries should be helped to start down the road to more high technology— but not at the expense of America's domestic industry. American firms should become more cautious in this regard.

2

THE "HARD" PARATECHNOLOGY: ELECTRONICS

COMPUTERS AND SEMICONDUCTORS

Two technologies cut across virtually all others, high- or low-tech, and will fundamentally affect progress in almost all types of business and industry for the foreseeable future. Over the next twenty years, at least, the effects of these supertechnologies will tend to cluster in different areas: organic and inorganic, or "soft" and "hard," applications. Biotechnology will chiefly influence medicine, pharmaceuticals, chemicals, and agribusiness. And the hard paratechnology—electronics—will continue to grind out breakthroughs in semiconductors, computers, telecommunications, robotics and automated manufacturing, and all manner of consumer durable products.

The provinces of biotechnology and electronics are far from mutually exclusive, though. One of the hottest markets for electronics, for example, is medical equipment, ranging from computer-aided tomographic (CAT) scanners to automated blood-analysis machines and all the sophisticated lifesaving equipment in intensive care wards. Agriculture is another area of overlap. Like progressive businesspeople everywhere, farmers use computers to help run their operations, and automated tractors that plow and seed and cultivate fields without anyone in the driver's seat are under development.

While biotechnology is just getting established as a business, electronics has come to play a central role in society. In fact, the electronics industry is the nation's biggest, employing more than 2.3 million American workers. The runner-up, according to the American Electronics Association, is the transportation equipment industry, with 1.9 million employees. Ranking all businesses—manufacturing and services—electronics comes in number six, after health care (6 million employees), restaurants, business services, wholesale trade in durable goods, and food stores.

The electronics industry has posted phenomenal growth in recent years, compounding at about 15 percent a year. Since 1978 the industry has created 850,000 new jobs. Yet that is only a partial measure of the importance of electronics. The industry's most important contributions are new tools and new technology that help boost the productivity and competitiveness of thousands of customer companies and service organizations.

Every facet of daily life is being enhanced by electronics. People learn at their own pace with the help of computers in the home, in schools, or at learning centers like those connected to Control Data Corporation's Plato network. At work, word processors and personal computers are replacing old-fashioned typewriters and calculators. (But the notion of a paperless office still seems a decade or more in the future; in fact, offices with computers are generating more paper than ever.) Factories are fast becoming computers with muscles. The computer is the manufacturing brain, and its peripherals include not just the customary hard disk drives and printers but also robots, numerically controlled machine tools, automated warehouses, and minions of programmable controllers.

Similarly, supermarkets and department stores are being automated with computer terminals disguised as checkout counters. The computer reads those odd bar-code patches on packages and automatically prints out the name and price of each item. Then it figures the total cost of all purchases, subtracts that sum from the money handed to the clerk, and displays the change due. But this is only a small fraction of the information that a store computer processes. It keeps tabs on each clerk's working hours and average time in handling shoppers. The computer also maintains an up-to-the-second accounting of inventory and notifies the store's purchasing department when to replace a given item (the computer may even automatically call up another computer at a regional warehouse and order the goods). This enables the store to maximize profits by keeping its inventory costs as low as possible without running out of stock. And the store's managers can watch buying patterns to see what effect various types of promotions have on sales.

Driving to work or the shopping center, electronic systems monitor engine performance to minimize fuel consumption and the emission of harmful pollutants out the tail pipe. Mobile telephones enable executives to keep in touch with far-flung enterprises even while stuck in a traffic jam. Tomorrow's car will have a computerized system that automatically pumps the brakes to prevent skidding on slippery roads and a video map that tracks the car's location on trips. And twenty-first-century cars will have robot drivers.

Video games are a popular form of entertainment. Similar techniques are used to provide exciting new computer-generated graphics and special effects for movies and TV, and one day soon computers will create entire films and maybe synthetic Hollywood "stars." Tiny computer circuits in cameras let vacationers "point and shoot" without worrying about f-stops and shutter speeds. Some travel agencies already have videodisk systems that provide video previews of popular destinations, and the next generation of these systems will enable you to "walk" through a distant city and, at each intersection, tell the computer which way you want to go. The computer will then search the videodisk and display successive scenes along the street you selected.

Isaac Asimov, a prolific author of science and science-fiction books who refuses to travel by plane, stretches the imagination and outlines the coming of multisensory proxy-travel: At a teletravel agency of the future, you get hooked up to a machine that emits signals which stimulate the brain's sensory areas. The agent dials up an office in Paris, say, and you request a stroll along the Left Bank. The Paris office dispatches an android that relays all sensory data into your brain. You see, hear, and smell through it. You feel the uneven pavement under your (its) feet, the gentle wash of air over your (its) swinging arms. Turn your head to the left, and the robot obligingly looks to the left. The result is so realistic that you can easily fool yourself into believing you are actually there.

Complex instruments in space relay voice conversations and computer data. In European hospitals, doctors routinely dial into the computer banks at the National Institutes of Health and, in a matter of minutes, have the results of computer scans of hundreds of thousands of medical records stored 3,000 miles away. Spy satellites monitor the military activities of potential aggressor nations. Future battles in the air, on land, and at sea will hinge on which side has the most advanced computers embedded in its weapons and at its command in space. America's military planners believe electronics is the leverage that can offset the numerical superiority of the Soviet bloc. So not only will the prosperity of the United States increasingly depend upon the strength of this country's electronics industry, but national security as well.

A Global Market Just Getting Going

Despite its amazing growth over the past three decades, electronics remains an emerging industry, promising a continuing stream of new technologies and innovations with enormous economic stakes. Electronics already ranks as the largest manufacturing industry in the United States, accounting for about 20 percent of all durable-goods manufacturing. The total output of the industry's core segments—semiconductors, computers, communications equipment, and consumer electronics—mushroomed from $5 billion in 1952 to $130 billion in 1982; the 1982 figure was half of the entire world's total output. In 1992, electronics production in the United States will more than double, reaching $340 million, while world production will climb to $700 billion. Still, there are some blemishes on that rosy outlook.

The electronics industry historically has made a small but welcome contribution to America's balance of trade—at least through 1980. That year, the trade balance in the four major electronics products was a $3.3 billion surplus. This contrasted starkly with the country's overall situation: a $27.7 billion deficit. The United States had maintained a surplus in all electronics areas except consumer electronics, where Japan is preeminent. Today, more than three-fourths of all radios and hi-fi systems sold in the United States are imported, primarily from Japan, although Taiwan is big in radios. Two-thirds of black-and-white TVs and nearly 15 percent of color sets are made offshore, split fairly evenly among Japan, Taiwan, and South Korea. And all videocassette recorders sold here are made in Japan, regardless of the brand name they carry (Korean VCRs will also begin showing up in mid-1985).

In 1981, though, the size of the U.S. electronics trade surplus dipped. This was largely due to the combination of a strong dollar, which depressed demand overseas, and a weak Japanese yen. The resulting price tilts helped the Japanese gain increased shares in foreign markets—including the United States, where Japan's blitz of semi-conductor random access memory chips (RAMs) kicked America's integrated circuit (IC) trade balance into the red for the first time. In 1984 exports of all electronic components—ICs plus capacitors, resistors, et cetera—grew an estimated 15 percent, to $6.7 billion, but imports rose even faster, nearing $8.4 billion, or an increase of 23 percent.

However, the statistics on U.S. trade in ICs should be taken with a large grain of salt. They exaggerate the value of imports because so many American companies have set up branches overseas to exploit low-cost labor to do assembly. When the finished products are reimported, they are worth more than when they left the country. Better than 50 percent of all IC imports, for example, come from U.S.-owned or -contracted offshore assembly facilities, located primarily in southeast Asia and Mexico. Malaysia accounts for more than $1 billion worth of ICs, making it the world's biggest exporter. Singapore and the Philippines are not far behind.

Still, without the policy changes outlined in Chapter 1, this situation is bound to become progressively worse. By 1992 domestic demand for chips will be so immense—close to $50 billion, up from $7.6 billion in 1982—that U.S.-based producers will be straining just to satisfy American customers. Japan, on the other hand, will be making more than twice as many ICs as its domestic market can use. As a result, Japanese chip makers could double their current 13 percent share of the total U.S. semiconductor market.

Moreover, the United States could be running a small but mounting trade deficit in finished electronics products as well, reaching perhaps $10 billion in 1992. BPA Technology & Management Ltd., a British consulting firm, projects that in the 1990s Japan will be the only industrialized country with a positive trade balance, let alone a growing surplus, in electronics equipment.

We believe an even bigger threat looms from elsewhere in Asia: Korea, Malaysia, Singapore, and Taiwan (see Part II for details). These nations are all eager to hop on the high-tech bandwagon, and many businessmen there harbor deep resentment or hatred of Japan for its merciless imperialism before and during World War II. They ache to cut back on purchases from Japanese suppliers, and they would like nothing better than to knock off a couple of Japanese competitors in international markets. U.S. manufacturers could get caught in the cross fire, just as European chip makers have slipped in the intensifying battle between the United States and Japan.

In 1980, two European firms—Philips and Siemens—were among the world's top ten semiconductor producers, along with five U.S. and three Japanese companies. But by 1983, Siemens had been displaced by a Japanese chip maker. In 1984, according to VLSI Research, the ranking was as follows: Texas Instruments on top, followed closely by Motorola and NEC, then Hitachi, IBM, Toshiba, National Semiconductor, Philips, Intel, and Fujitsu.

The erosion of America's position in electronics is due to several factors. The Office of Technology Assessment, a congressional watchdog agency, last year published a report called *International Competitiveness in Electronics*. It examines a number of technological issues and their interplay with the vitality of the U.S. economy. It found that the competitive status of the United States is undermined by the way America funds R&D and industrial innovation, the way the educational system operates, and the way Washington plans (or, more appropriately, doesn't plan) for the future.

In contrast to the haphazard U.S. approach, the government of Japan works closely with industry to mitigate the high cost of high-tech R&D and capital investment. The two camps collaborate on setting concrete goals in new technologies, and then jointly fund the effort needed to attain them. This practice of "targeting" specific technologies and markets has been telling, as the 64K RAM example makes evident. As explained in Part II, Japan's economy also boasts other unique elements that give Japanese manufacturers distinct advantages, not the least of which is being able to ignore short-term perturbations.

In the United States, though, high interest rates hang like a millstone around the necks of business leaders in high tech. The cost of money is one of the major factors pulling down management's attention to the short term. When business turns sour temporarily—and the semiconductor industry has more up-and-down thrills than a roller-coaster ride—companies have to rein in long-term projects because they can't afford to service loans that aren't generating revenues. During the recession of ten years ago, for instance, U.S. IC producers cut back on investments in plant and equipment. The upshot was that they were unable to meet demand when the economy picked up again. The Japanese didn't worry about curtailing their investment spending, and that was the main factor that enabled Japan to begin making big strides in the IC market.

And the competition in U.S. electronics markets is going to get more fierce. Other nations yearn to get in on the electronics bonanza, and for any company or nation, the only viable strategy in the electronics business is to peg output to global markets. Demand in almost any other country's domestic market just isn't adequate to achieve the economies of scale necessary to compete with the Japanese juggernaut and American giants such as IBM. And since the U.S. electronics market is the world's biggest and most wide open to all comers, the foreign firms naturally tend to gravitate here. Gold Star of Korea, Siemens of West Germany, Racal and Marconi of Britain, Olivetti and SGS Semiconductor of Italy—these are a small sampling of the foreign companies that have set up shop in the United States.

Surprisingly, China is the latest nation to make a move and is buying into a few American companies. Last November China's number one state-owned Beijing Machine Tool Plant and a mysterious operation called the Sausanto Group, jointly purchased Autonumerics, Inc., a Long Island producer of machine tools that had been in financial trouble. A year earlier, the Nanjing Telecommunications Works paid $2 million for a 19 percent interest in Santec, a small company in Amherst, New Hampshire, that makes computer printers.

Language Isn't the Only Barrier

U.S. manufacturers, attempting to penetrate foreign markets, rarely enjoy the freedom that this country extends to overseas competitors. Japan has been the most notorious at sheltering local markets from foreign competition. The strategy is simple and highly effective: When the "Japan Inc." consortium of industry and government has targeted a given technology or industry, all sorts of formal and informal barriers are thrown up while the Japanese cultivate a local market in the free world's second-biggest economy. Japanese companies essentially can charge whatever they wish during this period, so they are able to recover investments rapidly.

Unique product standards are a very effective means of blocking competition. For example, standards developed by Nippon Telegraph and Telephone (NTT) for electronics equipment are often based on design rather than performance, so a foreign firm has to modify its hardware to do the job. NTT's Japanese "family" suppliers, who are tipped in advance to what the standards will be (and likely have a hand in formulating them), are able to design their manufacturing lines to produce equipment that conforms. NTT in the past has further shielded its "family" by testing the patience of foreign companies and making it difficult for them to obtain a copy of the standards in the first place. It literally took years before Corning Glass Works, a premier pioneer in fiber optics technology, could get its hands on NTT's fiber optics "specs." And the final straw is that imports may be required to pass quality or performance tests in Japan before being delivered to the customer—a process that adds so much cost that the imported product generally cannot compete. So the government rarely worries about recovering industrial loans that are repayable only from profits.

Then, once Japan's companies have world-scale, large-volume factories in place and paid for, they launch an aggressive overseas drive. Undercutting prices in foreign markets until competitors are humbled is no problem because the Japanese products are being made on essentially free manufacturing lines. Only then does the Japanese government finally cave in to pressure from other nations and agree to negotiate ways to knock down trade barriers to Japan's own market. But by the time that's been done, it's too late. The Japanese have cornered so much market share that few companies can compete in terms of manufacturing costs.

There's a bit more to it than that, of course. Is there any American businessperson who hasn't been on the receiving end, as either a customer or a competitor, of Japan's fanatic devotion to engineering quality and reliability (and manufacturability) into products? Look at all the Americans—you might very well be one—who have been willing to pay premiums of up to one-third to get a Sony Trinitron TV. Most managers, *as consumers*, recognize and admit that the total cost of lifetime ownership is far more important than initial price. But as producers, many Americans somehow manage to draw the curtain on this concept, and concern themselves chiefly with minimizing cost.

The Japanese know that product quality is a double-edged sword. Not only does it help sell products, it's also cheaper in the long term. "You can pay me now, or pay me later." Too many American companies prefer later. The Japanese have shown the world that the extra up-front expense of engineering quality into a product is the best way to boost productivity, facilitate automation, and slash after-sale service and warranty costs. And lift the bottom line. In VCRs, Sony now offers some of the lowest prices in the industry, yet a Sony executive whispers confidentially that profits on VCRs last year bordered on the obscene.

The pattern has been repeated time and again, in 35mm cameras, cars and motorcycles, machine tools and robots, and in semiconductor RAMs. Japan's latest thrusts are in fiber optics, computers, ceramics and new materials, advanced ICs, and aerospace.

Europe's tactics are much less imaginative. Tariffs and local-content regulations constitute the main hurdles to free trade within the European Economic Community. "Rules of origin" agreements limit the amount of imported material that any item may contain and still receive duty-free treatment when shipped across national borders in the EEC. This discourages European producers of electronics systems from importing U.S. semiconductor devices, for example, because doing so could restrict the finished product's potential market. And because telecommunications in most European countries is a state-controlled enterprise (Britain is now the exception), about the only things that can be sold from a U.S. factory are essentials unavailable anywhere else.

Brazil is one nation so determined to foster local high-tech industries that it practices unusually tough protectionism. Once the government has arbitrarily decided that Brazil should have its own computer industry, say, it becomes extremely difficult to import computers. The Brazilians may be the best red-tape generators in the world. Few U.S. businesspeople have the patience to persevere and comply with Brazil's extensive import licensing process. And if a shipment is allowed in, the duty will probably be 100 percent of the computer's price and maybe even a higher multiple of its value.

Semiconductors: The Crude Oil of the Twenty-First Century

Electronics is concerned with regulating the flow of subatomic electrons through wires or circuits so that the stream of electrons can transmit information. The jargon of electronics is already seeping into everyday vocabulary—"bit" and "byte," for example. *Bit* is simply shorthand for "binary digit," the basic unit of information in the digital realm. A bit must correspond to one and only one of two (hence binary) states: the presence or absence of an electrical charge. It is comparable to a light switch, which is either on or off. The on/off states are written as 0 (off) or 1 (on).

So how does a computer deal with bigger numbers? In clumps of eight bits, called *bytes*. There are enough combinations of 8-bit bytes to represent the digits 0 to 9, plus the ninety-odd letters and symbols on a keyboard, plus more than thirty control functions, such as "carriage return" and "delete." Under the byte code known as ASCII (American Standard Code for Information Interchange):

"1" is 00110001	"A" is 01000001
"2" is 00110010	"B" is 01000010
"3" is 00110011	"a" is 01100001
"4" is 00110100	"b" is 01100010

In other words, a byte is an alphanumeric character. If a computer's memory capacity is 256K bytes, it can hold 256 kilobytes or about

256,000 characters. That is more than 200 double-spaced typewritten pages.

The progress in computer technology has been astounding. The first automatic digital computer was the ENIAC (Electronic Numerical Integrator and Computer), developed at the University of Pennsylvania in the mid-1940s. It was a monster, weighing 30 tons, occupying a 30-by-50-foot room, and needing nearly 200 kilowatts of electricity to power almost 19,000 vacuum tubes. Those tubes gave off enough heat to boil an egg on the machine's surfaces, and they blew out so often that one-third of the time ENIAC was turned on was spent tracking down and replacing tubes.

By 1959, vacuum tubes were being replaced by transistors—invented at Bell Labs in 1947—and the second generation of machines was born. These were a lot smaller, used less energy, cost less, but were still quite large by today's standards. They were superseded in the mid-sixties to early seventies by the third generation, built with the integrated circuit technology pioneered from 1958 onward by Texas Instruments, Fairchild Camera & Instrument, and a growing flock of firms in the area around San Jose, California, that would come to be world famous as Silicon Valley.

Integrated circuits, or ICs, are the marvel of the electronics age. This technology is so crucial to any industrial nation that W. J. Sanders III, president of Advanced Micro Devices, has dubbed ICs "the crude oil of the twenty-first century."

On a thin slice of a semiconductor base material, typically silicon (but a special grade of silicon that is the purest substance ever made by humans—99.999999 percent pure), the wizards of Silicon Valley first crammed hundreds, then thousands, then tens of thousands of tiny on/off switches, or transistors. These stages of evolution are known as small-, medium-, and large-scale integration (SSI, MSI, LSI). Each switch is a solid-state replacement for a vacuum tube. By the late 1970s, a hand-held calculator powered by little hearing-aid batteries packed as much raw processing power as ENIAC.

To connect these tiny transistors into a functional whole, the surface of the silicon "chip"—which usually is smaller than your little fingernail—is blanketed by minuscule circuit lines in a pattern so complex that it might be some geometrically precise spider web woven by an arachnid from another world. If all the circuit lines on a modern chip were straightened out and laid end to end, they would literally stretch for miles! All this is squeezed into an area smaller than your little fingernail. To protect this microelectronic wonder, the chip is inserted in a protective package with multiple connector legs; the finished product has the deceptively sinister look of a centipede.

The number of transistors and circuits that can be shoe-horned onto each chip is important because semiconductor transistors switch on and off with blinding speed. Consequently, the major limit on the speed of an IC, and thus a computer or any other piece of equipment designed around ICs, is the time it takes to get data to and from the proper group of transistors. Even though the electrical signals travel through ICs at almost half the speed of light, this is slow in the microelectronics realm. And if signals have to travel from one chip to another, across a printed circuit board, the wait seems interminable. To avoid that, the goal is to pack each chip with as many transistors as close together as possible.

In the past couple years, the transistor count on ICs pushed past 100,000, ushering in the era of VLSI, or very large-scale integration—and the fourth generation of computers. For the first time, a microprocessor, or computer-on-a-chip, could execute more than 1 million instructions per second (mips).

Before 1990, the semiconductor industry will begin turning out integrated circuits with more than 1 million transistors, and early in the 1990s the transistor count will be more than 10 million, with operating speeds of up to 100 mips, maybe more. Passing the 1 million–transistor level will mark the onset of a new IC generation, which may be called ULSI (ultra-large-scale integration) or 2VLSI (very-very LSI). The industry hasn't made up its mind what moniker to give these superchips. But all chip makers are busy designing them.

The 10 million–device chip may be called 3VLSI (very-very-very LSI). It will pave the way for the fifth generation of computers—systems that mimic certain functions of the human brain and exhibit rudimentary intelligence. But building a silicon-chip equivalent of the brain will still be a long way off even at the turn of the century, when 4VLSI chips with 100 million or more transistors and speeds of 1,000 mips and up will become available. The brain has an estimated 100 trillion "transistors" (synapses) that process information at the incredible rate of 100 quadrillion operations a second.

Still, an assemblage of 3VLSI chips the size of a person's head, roughly, should come very close to those astronomical figures. Will someone try to patch together such a silicon "brain"? You can bet on it.

But what if it's so good a copy that the silicon brain starts to learn on its own? That cannot be dismissed as unadulterated science fiction; indeed, it's probable.

Isn't that kind of scary? Not really. The human race seems to yearn for contact with another intelligent species, the progressively expanding search for extraterrestrial intelligence has not yet been successful and, as search distances increase, the feasibility of a dialog with any life forms found diminishes. It might therefore be fitting—and psychologically beneficial—if we ended up being the creators of another entity carrying the seeds of a separate line of evolution. As Isaac Asimov remarked in a private conversation, "There's no cosmic reason why the evolution of intelligence should be restricted to biological organisms."

But computers that learn—won't they be so smart they'll make humans feel inferior? To a certain extent, perhaps. But we all know people who are smarter than we are, and our psyche manages to accommodate that fact. Besides, psychologists say that people only use about 10 percent of their mental capacities. Maybe the challenge of competing with silicon minds will be just the trigger we need to make the next jump in evolution.

"Brainy" Chips, Memory Chips

Microprocessors are the "brains" of computers and other chip-based systems because they supervise all operations. They read the instructions in a system's program, fetch data from memory (stored in a nearby memory chip, on a rotating disk that resembles a phonograph record, or on a magnetic tape), perform the processing steps stipulated in the program—add, subtract, insert, delete, et cetera—then put the results back into memory.

The first microprocessors appeared in 1971, almost simultaneously from Intel Corporation and Texas Instruments (TI). They handle data in 4-bit "words" and are still widely used in undemanding applications, such as simple calculators and digital watches. But retrieving and processing information only 4 bits at a time limits their use. It took the next generation of 8-bit microprocessors to launch the personal computer revolution. Early 8-bit designs cost $400 in 1972. By 1976 volume had expanded enough that the price sank to $32, then to $6 two years later, and less than $3 by 1982. That's 1 percent of the original price a decade earlier, and the price is still falling.

The IBM Personal Computer and work-alike PCs, such as the Compaq computer, use 16-bit microprocessors. Last year, 32-bit microprocessors appeared, the first to employ the 32-bit word length used by most big computers. Combined with VLSI densities of 150,000 to 600,000 transistors, these chips can process a million or more instructions every second—equal to the raw processing power of a minicomputer. When systems designed around these chips begin appearing in a year or two, their performance will make today's 16-bit equipment seem as old hat as that built with those first 4-bit microprocessors.

The 2VLSI microprocessors coming within the next several years will match the power of present mainframe computers. To cram a million or more transistors on a chip, the transistors and connecting circuit lines will have to be so tiny that they will be invisible; only very high-power microscopes will be able to discern them. Carver Mead, a computer scientist at the California Institute of Technology, has likened the circuits on today's chips to a detailed street map of Los Angeles. The upcoming versions will approximate a map of California, with such mind-boggling accuracy that every city alley and suburban cul-de-sac is included on that fingernail-size slice of silicon. And 3VLSI circuits will be totally invisible to any optical microscope— the size of a transistor will be smaller than a virus—and each chip will hold the equivalent of a street map of the entire United States.

The same geometric progression in capabilities is evident in computer memories, where the amount of digital data that could be stored on a random access memory (RAM) chip has notched successive fourfold jumps from 256 bits in the late 1960s to 1K, 4K, and 16K capacities in the 1970s. In 1980, the semiconductor industry raised the ante to 64K. In 1983, 256K memory chips began entering the market.

And now a couple of semiconductor producers are selling prototypes of so-called Meg memories or megabit RAMs—chips that can hold 1 million bits. Three years hence, 4 megabit chips will be available. One of these fingernail-size slices of silicon will hold 450 typewritten pages.

Chip makers strive constantly to pack more and more transistors onto their little slices of silicon, because each new level of density means that the per-bit price of computing power declines substantially. That enlarges the market by making the technology affordable to an ever-expanding base of increasingly price-sensitive applications. The rule of thumb known as Moore's Law (after Gordon Moore, one of the founders of Intel) holds that every two to three years IC density doubles and per-bit costs halve.

The implications of Moore's Law are truly astounding. Here's what has happened to the cost of building a RAM that can hold 1 million characters: From $50,000 in 1973, it went to $5,000 in 1978, then to $500 in 1983. Come 1988, it will be a mere $50. If the auto industry behaved this way, a Rolls-Royce that cost $50,000 in 1961, the year TI and Fairchild introduced the first integrated circuits, could be had today for under $2, and it would get 1,500 miles to a gallon of gasoline.

Japan's Onslaught

"Memory is where the money is." That sentiment used to be expressed often by Motorola, the world's second-biggest chip maker, with 1983 sales of $1.63 billion (closely trailing TI's sales of $1.67 billion). As a motto, it made good sense. RAMs are the workhorse of the computer industry and pop up in a dazzling array of other products as well—virtually anything controlled by a microprocessor. Each successive generation of memory chips has become far and away the biggest-selling product in semiconductor history. The 64K RAM will probably crest in 1986 at roughly 1.2 billion chips. And the 256K RAM should easily top 2 billion units, perhaps 2.5 billion, at the end of this decade—a market worth a conservative $4 billion.

In the early 1970s, Japan's emerging semiconductor industry took one look at the juicy RAM market and decided it was too ripe a plum not to pick. In 1976, with substantial government funding, Japan launched a three-year, joint government-industry program with the avowed goal of surpassing the United States in memory-chip production. The so-called VLSI Project was coordinated by the Ministry of International Trade and Industry (MITI) and involved Japan's four largest chip makers* plus Mitsubishi and Nippon Telegraph & Telephone's central R&D laboratory (NTT is Japan's counterpart of AT&T). Estimates of the amount of government subsidies, grants, and loans repayable only from profits range as high as $2 billion.

The upshot was amazing. Fujitsu became the first semiconductor maker in the world to market a 64K RAM, in 1979. By early 1981 all five chip makers in the VLSI Project were producing 64Ks in volume—versus only three U.S. firms—and Japanese 16K and 64K RAMs were pouring into America. Early in 1981, when the prevailing U.S. market price for 64K RAMs was $25 to $30, Fujitsu was offering them for $15. Throughout 1981 Japanese prices were consistently below those of American chip makers, despite the cost of shipping the chips across the Pacific. Japan's aggressive marketing practices hammered down prices at a precipitous rate, unprecedented even in the semiconductor industry. By year-end 1981, the sticker on a 64K RAM was less than $8—and Japan's low-ball pricing policies had captured 70 percent of the worldwide market for 64K RAMs. American firms have since staged a comeback, but the Japanese still command more than half of the computer-memory market in the country that invented RAMs.

Seven of the twelve U.S. companies that had been making 16K RAMs either backed out of the market without a fight or threw in the towel for lack of profits. That, of course, is precisely what the Japanese had hoped for. Industry experts contend there was no way that any company could have turned a profit in 1981–82. So the Japanese companies were soaking up their losses to buy market share and eliminate some competition. They could afford to do that because of the government subsidies and because until recently Japan's domestic IC market has been sheltered from American imports, so Japanese chip

---

*NEC (1983 semiconductor sales of $1.6 billion), Hitachi ($1.5 billion), Toshiba ($1.1 billion), and Fujitsu ($700 million). Mitsubishi's sales were $580 million. Worldwide, these companies now rank as numbers three, four, six, ten, and twelve, respectively.

makers could charge more at home to help offset losses abroad. Integrated circuits from U.S.-owned companies account for less than 20 percent of Japanese consumption, and many Japanese users practice an unwritten "buy Japanese" policy.

America's chip makers believe that they can hold onto a bigger share of the emerging 256K RAM market—at least 50 percent of the U.S. market—but the preliminary indications aren't encouraging. At the end of 1984 several Japanese companies had been in volume production for six months or more, while the first American 256K plants were just starting to move into full output. That six-month lag may not seem important, but the market for each new generation of memories blossoms quickly, then gives way after about three years to the next fourfold jump in capacity. So six months can mean the difference between profit and loss in this dynamic market.

Because of Japan's lead in 256K memories and the strong demand for 64Ks, Japanese chip imports in 1984 vaulted past the $1 billion level for the first time, all the way up to $1.4 billion. That is an increase of nearly 60 percent over the prior year and triple the 1982 import figure from Japan.

Japan's takeover in RAMs is all the more ominous because these ICs have traditionally been the proving ground for new technology. It would be next to impossible for a company making 16K RAMs to avoid the bloodbath in 64Ks by leapfrogging directly to 256K chips. The tricks and shortcuts essential to profitability have to be picked up in little steps—what the chip makers term "going down the learning curve." So the U.S. semiconductor firms that have dropped out of the RAM business for more profitable types of chips are unlikely ever to return to the memory market.

But backing away from the confrontation in memories offers only a temporary respite. With the memory-chip business as a base, the Japanese will be able to diversify into other markets. And they are now ready to do just that. The biggest Japanese semiconductor firms are developing their own microprocessors, an area in which the United States is the unquestioned pioneer and reigning champion. The bulk of all microprocessor fabrication in Japan and Europe is done under a license from Intel, Motorola, National Semiconductor, Texas Instruments, or Zilog. "We want to be a major semiconductor supplier," says Keiske Yawata, president of NEC Electronics USA, the American offshoot of Japan's largest chip maker. "And there's more to the semiconductor industry than memory."

NEC announced in mid-1984 that it was working on its own 32-bit design, and late last year Hitachi boasted that its proprietary 32-bit microprocessor is the world's fastest—at 4 to 5 mips, double the speed of American designs by National Semiconductor and Motorola. But the Hitachi chip won't be in volume production until 1986. By then National will be producing an improved version that should match and possibly surpass the performance of the Hitachi design. Still, Japan's new challenge in microprocessors must not be treated lightly.

Microprocessors account for less than 10 percent of semiconductor industry sales, but that figure belies their crucial role. Because these ICs function as the brain in any electronics system, the microprocessor sets the ground rules for other chips, which must be able to communicate with it. Should Japan's chip makers succeed in winning customers for their microprocessors, then U.S. companies that want to supply those same customers with so-called peripheral chips—microcontrollers for the keyboard, the video display, and the disk drives in a personal computer, for example—could end up licensing technology from the Japanese.

If Japan puts the same brutal pricing pressure on microprocessors and other chips as it has on memories, some semiconductor executives candidly worry about the U.S. industry's ability to fund growth. Even Texas Instruments, the biggest U.S. chip maker, may not have sufficient capital resources to last in the face of Japanese determination to win more and more market share, says Harold L. Ergott, Jr., who left the Dallas company to become president of Mostek Corporation, a subsidiary of United Technology.

Market Share Above All Else

As transistors get tinier and tinier, the cost of the equipment for making ICs is escalating faster than revenues. In the mid-1970s, a wafer fabrication line for MSI chips ran about $5 to $10 million. By the end of that decade, an LSI wafer "fab" meant an investment of about $20 million. Today's VLSI lines cost $60 million. To manufacture tomorrow's 2VLSI chips will require $150 million, maybe more. And a 3VLSI facility may cost upwards of $500 million.

"This is a tremendously cost-intensive business—and it's getting worse," says Douglas L. Powell, a vice president of Motorola. That's because the equipment is growing increasingly esoteric. Andrew Grove, president of Intel, emerged from a capital budget planning session last year and quipped: "I just spent several hours approving science fiction for capital equipment." At the same time, there's no letup in the rate of technological change, the need to buy new equipment every two or three years in order to be able to produce the latest chips. "Put those two unarguable facts together," declares Roy H. Pollack, the executive vice president who oversees RCA's chip-making operations, "and it becomes an extremely difficult capital-financing proposition—for everybody."

Furthermore, designing million-transistor chips will be very expensive. Even with computer-aided engineering systems, putting a map of California, let alone the United States, on the head of a thumbtack takes several work-years of meticulous labor by a team of one or two dozen engineers. Development costs of the latest VLSI chips can mount up to many millions of dollars, and a 2VLSI design may take $50 to $100 million.

These skyrocketing costs pose a threat to America's chip-making industry. Traditionally, Silicon Valley has thrived on spin-offs and venture capital. An engineer working at one company has a bright idea, finds a venture-capital backer willing to bet a few million bucks on his (or her) idea, and forms his own company. Fairchild Camera & Instrument spawned a dozen start-ups, including Intel, which has in turn served as the training ground for entrepreneurs who have founded several new firms. But when the cost of designing a single new integrated circuit zooms to several tens of millions of dollars, the venture-capital pool could recede dramatically. The risk-reward ratio would tilt too steeply toward risk. Consequently, opportunities for budding entrepreneurs could shrink to applications of existing technology, not new breakthroughs. If such a structural change should occur in Silicon Valley, the momentum in semiconductor innovation could shift to Japan.

While even America's established chip makers may have difficulty raising the capital it will take to stay at the cutting edge of IC technology, Japan's semiconductor producers are almost immune to any financial pinch. They are all part of diversified, multibillion-dollar conglomerates, and semiconductors typically account for only 5 to 10 percent of their total business. Moreover, except for Sony, the major IC firms belong to one of the thirteen multicompany trading groups, called *zaibatsu*, that control about 80 percent of Japan's trade. The unifying force within each zaibatsu is a special type of bank—Mitsubishi Bank, Fuji Bank, et cetera—whose raison d'être is to make money available to the group's firms, typically at less than half the interest rate charged by U.S. banks.

The trading-group banks, which for some strange reason are called city banks, are also willing to lend far more money than would any American institution. The debt-to-equity ratio among Japan's four largest chip makers in 1980 ranged from 150 to 230 percent, according to a study by Chase Manhattan Bank for the Semiconductor Industry Association. Despite the fact that Japanese firms have short- and long-term debts that add up to some multiple of their assets, they still manage to get by on profitability levels that are even lower than the low interest rates they pay. Such a situation is unheard of in the United States, where lenders demand that the returns on capital exceed the "price" paid to obtain the money.

Under Japan's business strategy, however, profitability is subordinate to market share—for a bank as well as for the manufacturers it supports. So long as a company is expanding its market share, it will always have access to low-cost capital. "The Japanese perspective is that, when you are still making inroads into a market, you can't afford the luxury of making money." That revealing insight, reported by *Business Week*, comes from Keiske Yawata, president of NEC Electronics USA. The Japanese figure that eventually a commanding market share has to translate into profits. It's just a matter of waiting until enough competition has been squeezed out.

The United States must not allow this to happen. The simile between ICs and crude oil is no exaggeration. If this country loses its edge in the basic building blocks of the electronics industry, it will be just a matter of time until the slippage spills over into the products and systems engineered around integrated circuits. One reason is that, as ICs grow more powerful, they will take on more functions and represent an increasing proportion of the total worth of finished systems and products. In 1982, the "chip content" averaged out at roughly 5 percent for all electronics industry products (7 percent for personal computers). By 1992, the average semiconductor content will triple to 15 percent of the value of finished products. By 2002, it will be 20 to 25 percent. That means chips more and more are going to become computers and telecommunications and stereo components.

In 1983, IC sales in the United States climbed 24 percent over the preceding year, and the industry closed the books on 1984 with sales up a spectacular 45 percent, to about $14 billion. The producers have temporarily outgrown their markets, so most forecasters predict a relatively flat year in 1985, with conventional growth rates of 15 to 25 percent annually resuming in 1986. By the year 2000, assuming the industry finds the funds to underwrite growth, semiconductors will be one of the top three industries in America.

A Computer in Every Pot

Without integrated circuits, modern computers, especially personal and home computers, would not be possible. Thanks to microchips, computers have gained footholds in every walk of life. They are affecting society in ways at least as profound as did the telephone, the automobile, and television—but far more rapidly. By 1987, only a decade after the first personal computers began appearing, there will be 35 to 40 million electronic keyboards in U.S. homes. That's four of every ten households—40 percent—up from 15 percent in 1984. Before twenty years go by, the penetration of home computers will reach 80 percent, according to InfoCorp, a market research firm in Cupertino, California. It took seventy-five years for the telephone to diffuse through society to that extent, seventy years for cars, and thirty years for TV sets.

Today, many people jokingly wonder why on earth they need a home computer. Tomorrow, they will marvel how they ever got along without one. Telecomputing will be just as essential to home life as electricity.

Most market researchers predict that home computer sales will rocket from $1.75 billion in 1983 to about $9 billion in 1990. And that's just computers that cost $1,000 or less. Add on software and the 1990 home-computer market will be more than $14 billion.

But while home computers will grow the fastest in terms of unit sales, personal computers—machines with price stickers of $1,000 to $10,000, used primarily in offices—will greatly outstrip home computers in dollar sales, jumping from $6.5 billion to $30 or $35 billion over the same period ($40 to $45 billion including software). In fact, late 1985 or early in 1986, personal computers will surpass big mainframes as the computer industry's number one source of revenues. Even for IBM, the unquestioned king of mainframes, PCs represented one-quarter of 1984 sales—and gaining.

A fair percentage of PC units end up in homes where more computing power is needed for such sophisticated chores as doing taxes and tracking investments. Inexpensive home computers, by comparison, are most often used for playing games, running educational programs, keeping household budgets, and doing limited word processing. At the end of 1983, about 20 percent of all home computers (excluding those normally used in conjunction with work brought home from the office) cost more than $1,000, according to a survey by New York's Link Resources. In addition, one-third of the entrepreneurs who run a business from home already do so with the help of a PC.

As might be expected, the explosion in home and personal computers has attracted a gaggle of competitors. The prominent names are Atari, Commodore, IBM, Radio Shack/Tandy, and Texas Instruments; the second tier's A-to-Z list would include AT&T, Compaq, Hewlett-Packard, Kaypro, and Zenith. But for every one of these there are twenty other lesser lights. At a recent industry trade show, there were almost 100 companies hawking home computers and 150 with personal computers—all shooting for market shares of 5 to 15 percent. By the time you read this, probably one in ten of these companies, maybe more, will have dropped out of the market, folded shop, or filed for protection under chapter eleven of the bankruptcy act. The casualty list in little computers already includes Timex, Osborne, Mattel, Franklin, Coleco, and Apricot. But no doubt the dropouts will be replaced by newcomers chasing that proverbial pot at the end of the rainbow. Among the more recent entrants is Sweden's Ericsson.

Everyone hopes to have a time of success like Apple. Its growth curve has looked almost like a straight line pointing north. Expanding at an average compound rate of over 150 percent a year, Apple has zoomed to the billion-dollar level in just eight years. And had IBM not waded into the market in 1981, Apple would have joined that inner circle of companies at least a year earlier. Steven Jobs, Apple's youthful cofounder and chairman (he just turned 30), says that "IBM wants to wipe us off the face of the earth."

But Apple doesn't relish being crushed into applesauce. To ensure long-term growth, the company has devised a devilishly clever marketing strategy: classroom "collusion." If the first computer someone learns to use is an Apple in a classroom, odds are that when he or she is ready to buy a computer, it will be an Apple. So Jobs's company offers deep discounts to schools and has placed more Apples in local school classrooms than all other brands combined. In addition, the Apple University Consortium, a group of twenty-four prestigious colleges and universities—including Stanford, the University of Michigan, and the entire Ivy League—is buying $50 million worth of Apple's remarkably easy-to-use Macintosh computer for student use.

However, IBM is by no means a rival to trifle with, as Apple keenly knows. Although Big Blue has been in the PC business only half as long as Apple, it already has grabbed the leading share of current sales. IBM's disk operating system (DOS), the fundamental program that must be fed to the microprocessor before any other software will work, has become the de facto standard for virtually all new personal computers.

Even mighty AT&T went with IBM's DOS when it jumped into PCs. AT&T has been building big computers for years, of course, but only for its own use. The switching systems in telephone company central offices, which tie local exchanges together and hook into long-distance lines to form a vast nationwide network, are nothing more than special-purpose computers. That's why Bell Labs invented the transistor. But as a regulated monopoly, AT&T had been barred from the open market for computers until the mammoth Bell System was broken up.

AT&T now sells a family of big and small computers, but "the personal computer is a key to our office automation strategy," says

Robert J. Casale, head of marketing and sales at AT&T Information Systems. He told *Business Week* that AT&T's strategy is to offer an integrated office system that links its PCs, its larger computers, and the telephone system—a sort of microcosm of the empire that once was the Bell System. Recognizing the need to move rapidly, since IBM is chasing a similar strategy, AT&T didn't attempt to design its own machine. Instead, it imports a PC from Olivetti, an Italian electronics and office equipment manufacturer that is one-quarter owned by AT&T. The Olivetti machine runs the IBM DOS, but it does so 30 to 80 percent faster than IBM's own PC.

Japan seems to be caught on the horns of a dilemma in personal computers. Practically every big Japanese electronics company—NEC, Fujitsu, Sony, Panasonic, and so on—is selling a PC, but so far they haven't tried to swamp the U.S. market with low-ball pricing. One reason is that Japan invested considerable time and money in developing its own disk operating standard, called MSX, and all PCs sold in Japan conform to this standard. Thus, customers have no trouble using the same software in any brand of computer (unlike the situation here, where the programs written for Apple, Commodore, CP/M, Tandy, and IBM machines are mutually incompatible).

In Japan, the role of the personal computer in office automation is quite possibly even more vital than in America. That's because Japanese executives reach decisions through an elaborate, consensus-making ritual, and nothing occurs until all parties involved are satisfied. This entails an endless series of meetings that can drag out the decision-making process for months and months. The Japanese recognize this is a weakness. It also is probably a factor in Japan's lackluster record in invention, which is ordinarily done best by lone individuals or small teams who pursue a private vision that, on the basis of conventional wisdom, is ridiculed by other people. On the other hand, the group-think mode of operation may be at the root of Japan's penchant for long-range planning: The Japanese have to plan that way because it's so difficult to get agreement on turn-on-a-dime decisions.

Early experiments with PCs in executive suites, linked together in a local network and tied into the company's mainframe computer, indicate that consensus decision making can be speeded up considerably. Position papers and reports can be computer generated by Japanese language word-processing software in a fraction of the time that it now takes to laboriously write such documents by hand (typewriters are almost unknown in Japan because of that country's unusual "alphabet"). In addition, some meetings can be convened electronically, requiring only a time when all parties can physically gather around a conference table.

For the vast U.S. market, the Japanese can't seem to make up their minds whether to go all out and butt heads with IBM by trying to establish MSX as an alternative DOS standard, or whether they, too, should ride IBM's coattails. However, with PCs soon to be the biggest segment of the entire computer industry—bigger even than mainframes—an aggressive Japanese drive is inevitable. Look for it in 1986 or 1987.

So far, there is little interest in Japan's MSX among American software companies, and without software the MSX standard doesn't stand a chance. While the Japanese try to drum up support, they are keeping their options open by making IBM-compatible machines, usually. These are sold under their own brand names (but with an uncharacteristic lack of zeal) and through so-called OEM agreements. Under an original equipment manufacturer (OEM) strategy, a Japanese firm simply puts different brand names on the same equipment, and different American companies then resell it as their own. The advantage is that the Japanese supplier can quickly attain economies of scale in production and doesn't have to bother much with marketing costs, since the U.S. resellers bear the risks of establishing the product. For their part, the American companies avoid having to invest capital in a production line.

The danger in these OEM arrangements is that once it's clear what is and isn't succeeding, the Japanese can charge in and undercut the prices of their reseller customers. Even if that doesn't happen, America's manufacturing resources and its pool of skilled workers continue to erode.

Of course, the U.S. companies can build a factory and yank back production whenever they wish, but that hasn't happened very often— although there are some encouraging signs in this regard. IBM feels that, by using automation to minimize the need for expensive American labor, products can be made in the United States as cheaply as in Asia. To prove the point, last year IBM cut the ribbon on a fully automated plant in Lexington, Kentucky, that makes computer printers which feature a novel method of transferring ink from a ribbon onto paper without the chatter of impact printers. While these letter-quality printers were never built anywhere else, IBM is also reported ready to build another totally automated plant to make conventional dot-matrix printers, which it now buys overseas. Similarly, a few semiconductor companies are constructing fully automated plants to bring back the chip assembly work now done at labor-intensive plants in southeast Asia.

Waiting for a Smarter PC

The Japanese strategy in personal computers may hinge on development of a 32-bit system that will run both MSX and IBM software, plus offer "natural language interface"—meaning that the user can communicate with the machine by typing words in his or her native language, whatever language it may be. (What a joy it'll be, not having to bother remembering the precise computerese commands now required to make a computer do anything.) All this and more will be possible with the advent of 32-bit microprocessors, which offer the performance of today's minicomputers on a single chip. If Japanese companies are in on the first wave of 32-bit machines, they could rapidly make up for lost time.

Over the next decade, 32-bit PCs will gradually decline in price to the point where they become home computer candidates. Sales of these machines will make the success story of VCRs look pale by comparison. And the home will never be the same again.

Tomorrow's child will do an enormous amount of learning at home, with a zest born of systems that make education seem more play than work. Rather than relying on odious rote memorization, home computers and teaching software will use clever graphics and video-game techniques to compel attention. Each child will be able to learn at his or her own pace, taught by a machine that is infinitely patient, always understanding, and superhumanly well informed. The benefits of having a tutor work with a child one on one, as opposed to stuffing a room with one teacher and a class of twenty-odd personalities, are obvious.

Even before 32-bit computers fall to $1,000, home learning will get a helping hand from the next consumer electronics craze: DAVID players, or turntables that interchangeably play *d*igital *a*udio-*v*ideo-*d*ata disks. Panasonic has already unveiled a machine that plays both video and audio disks. They will be an integral component in future home entertainment systems. Since these turntables don't care whether they play back music or pictures—or computer data—the next round will be even more crucial to home education, functioning as memories for computers as well as repositories of stereo and video programs. Stupendous quantities of information can be stored on DAVID memory disks. The entire contents of *Webster's Unabridged Dictionary*, for example, will fit on a 5-inch disk, and the text of an entire encyclopedia can go on 12-inch disk. The duo of educational DAVID disks and home computers will alter the learning process far more than any previous educational technology.

Just think what it will mean when kids grow up liking education, yearning to learn so much that they spend hours glued to the computer screen, honing their intellectual skills. This will happen when they have access to the global telecom network that will be emerging in the 1990s, along with 32-bit home computers that exhibit rudimentary intelligence and contain graphics-generation chips beyond the power of today's best computer-aided design systems. With these tools, youngsters will be able to retrieve information on virtually any topic. And when a dull statistical table comes in over the fiber optics network, the computer will summon an expert program that will analyze the contents of the table, relate this to the context of what the user has been doing, and generate an appropriate cartoon strip or animated graph.

By the turn of the century, such computer "toys" will be expanding the horizons of kids around the world. These children will grow into adulthood with a deep appreciation of each other and themselves, with a sense of global kinship more profound than any preceding generation, so the twenty-first century could be the age when peace on earth becomes more than a dream.

Thinking About Machines That Think

While U.S. personal computer companies are waiting for the Japanese to drop their PC shoe, there is no such suspense in big computers. As pointed out at last fall's meeting of the Association for Computing Machinery by Edward A. Feigenbaum of Stanford and Michael L. Dertouzos of MIT, Japan well recognizes that economic leadership and international political power in the modern world derives from information-processing technology, so Japan is determined to be a leader, if not the leader, in computing technology. Western Europe also would like to carve out a bigger share of the business.

Today, the United States is the unquestioned *numero uno*. American computer companies make about 55 percent of the world's output of computers and related data-processing equipment, including roughly 45 percent of all computer exports. There are more large computer-system installations in the United States—more than 500,000 systems worth $350 billion—than in Europe and Japan combined. The U.S. market for computing equipment has soared from just under $13 billion in 1975 to more than $60 billion in 1984, including desk-top and other small systems, and should top $135 billion in 1989.

Heading the U.S. industry, of course, is IBM. This behemoth accounts for two-thirds of America's computer production and is eight times the size of the next-biggest producer, Digital Equipment Corporation (DEC). In fact, IBM grows by more than one DEC a year, and IBM's profits equal DEC's total revenues. In the 1984 list of the *Fortune* 500 corporations, IBM ranked first in profits, with $5.5 billion, and fifth in sales, with only two auto companies and two oil companies preceding it. Stacked up below DEC is the so-called bunch—Burroughs, Univac, NCR, Control Data, and Honeywell.

Since 1958, when IBM and the "bunch" shipped barely more than $400 million worth of equipment, the industry's sales have climbed a steady 20 percent annually, adjusted for inflation. Although demand for computing power will keep on increasing, the rise in dollar sales will gradually shrink over the short term due to the combination of intensifying competition from overseas, which will drive down prices, and the decreasing cost/performance of integrated circuits. For the rest of this decade, U.S. computer makers will average about 18 percent annual growth. However, the advent of the next generation of computers (loosely referred to as non–von Neumann machines, for reasons that will be explained momentarily) will unleash a new buying spree that will restore historical sales growth in the mid-1990s.

Exports of computer equipment and parts, an important item in the U.S. balance of payments, rose 20 percent in 1983 to $10.7 billion. But imports were up 35 percent, to nearly $3 billion. Imports have been outpacing exports for the past few years, in part because many U.S. computer companies, like their semiconductor suppliers, have assembly facilities outside of the country. Ireland and Hong Kong recently emerged as major importers of U.S. computer equipment— not because there is a large local market, but because parts and sub-assemblies are shipped there from the United States for assembly, then finished computers are exported from there to various nations, including back to the United States.

IBM has subsidiaries all over the world, and in virtually every country it is the market leader and main exporter. In fact, in all but two free-world nations, American computer makers have sold more than half of all the computers installed. The two exceptions are Japan and Britain, where government subsidies and discriminatory purchasing practices have kept money-losing ICL, Limited, in business. Even in Japan, until 1979, IBM Japan was the biggest computer company in that country; it is still a close second, and it still exports more data-processing equipment than any Japanese producer. Nevertheless, in 1979 Fujitsu climbed to the top of the heap and has been there ever since. By 1983, Fujitsu's computer sales stood at $2.7 billion versus IBM Japan's $2.6 billion.

In addition to Fujitsu, NEC and Hitachi have also become world-class rivals in mainframes. Fujitsu and NEC now do more business in computers than any European supplier, and Japan's computer industry as a whole outshines that of Europe. Moreover, Fujitsu and Hitachi installed their first supercomputer prototypes in November 1983. The performance of these huge number crunchers compares well with all but the biggest U.S. supercomputers from Cray Research and Control Data Corporation.

But what set teeth grinding worldwide was Japan's 1981 decision to go for broke and leapfrog current technology by spending ten years and $425 million to pioneer a quantum jump in technology—a "thinking'' computer, a fifth-generation machine that would in some respects mimic human thought. Using artificial intelligence (AI) techniques, it would be able to analyze masses of raw data and independently derive conclusions, infer relationships, and even synthesize new knowledge. Applications could include decision-support systems for management; expert systems in medicine, computer engineering, manufacturing, and various other disciplines; machines that understand human language and can translate from one language to another; and automated office equipment that can take dictation and automatically find information and organize it meaningfully.

To oversee the ambitious program, in 1982 MITI set up the Institute for New Generation Computer Technolgy, known familiarly as Icot. Currently, the institute has fifty full-time scientists working on new computer designs, a new software language engineered to facilitate logic programming, and AI programs for a variety of applications. Researchers also are attacking these areas in corporate labs at NTT, Fujitsu, NEC, Hitachi, and the other major electronics companies.

Given the almost instantaneous reaction in the United States and Europe, MITI probably wonders whether it was wise to ballyhoo the effort so much. The European community countered with a multinational effort called Esprit, which IBM, ITT, and DEC were recently allowed to join. In addition, France and West Germany launched their own research drives, and Britain waded in with Alvey, a five-year industry-government-university program with the same goals as Icot.

In the United States, Japan's fifth-generation ambitions galvanized both the computer industry and the Defense Department. The MCC co-op, which had been in the talking stage for some time, was quickly ratified. In February 1982, Richard D. DeLauer, then defense undersecretary for research and engineering, made a hastily scheduled appearance at a symposium on cooperative research and pledged Pentagon resources to help American industry ''Keep the information processing market for the next decade.'' He reported that the Defense Advanced Research Projects Agency (DARPA) had just asked Congress for $50 million to launch a five-year, $600 million project to develop a thinking supercomputer that DeLauer dubbed the ''Nth-generation computer.'' ''I don't want to say it's a fifth- or sixth-generation machine,'' he quipped, ''only that it will outperform anything the Japanese develop.''

Add up the U.S. and European budgets for work on AI computers and you get a whopping $3.5 billion, says Mirek Stevenson, chairman of the market research firm of Quantum Science. And because of a budget-cutting mood in Japan, Icot may not even get its full $425 million. As a result, a new sense of realism surrounds Japan's fifth-generation program, and many Western experts assert there is no immediate danger that the Japanese will leapfrog the United States in information technology. But that doesn't mean the United States is about to turn smugly complacent.

DARPA, which has been the premier backer of AI research for three decades, has already handed out more than $40 million—nearly matching Icot's spending to date—to a dozen companies and universities, and the agency has another $40 million in the kitty to pass out during 1985–86. The money will pay for the building of several different computer prototypes based on new operating concepts, some of which are similar to the computers that Japan's Icot is working on.

Virtually all computers now process data using the "architecture" that mathematician John von Neumann first outlined in the late 1940s: A central processing unit (CPU) is here, memory banks are there, and a pathway in between connects the two elements. The trouble with this scheme is that everything happens in one CPU, so it can only operate in a serial, step-by-step fashion.

The CPU fetches the first program step from memory, determines what data are needed to execute that step, then sits idle while an electron messenger goes to get the information and brings it from memory to the CPU; after executing the first instruction, the CPU dispatches the results back into storage, again twiddling its thumbs while the data move through the CPU-to-memory funnel. Only after the connection is clear can the CPU summon the next program step to repeat the cycle. The constricted passage between the CPU and the memory, which causes the processor to sit inactive much of the time, has become infamous as the von Neumann bottleneck.

To attempt to build a practical AI system based on a von Neumann computer is an exercise in futility, simply because astronomical volumes of data must be processed to imitate human reasoning, and it would take way too long to find the answer to most problems. For example: Suppose you're running a small factory with ten different key manufacturing operations that are used in various combinations for turning out different products. You've got nine orders in the shop when suddenly your best customer hits you with a rush order that takes priority over everything else. What is the most expeditious production schedule, the one that will get the rush order done as fast as possible with as little disruption as possible to the work already in progress?

The problem involves juggling ten tiers of ten variables each. That may not seem terribly complicated at first blush, but in fact it means there are 10 billion possible combinations. The computer doesn't have the foggiest notion of how to attack the problem, other than grinding away and examining each and every possibility. If it can make 1 million calculations per second, it's going to take 10 million seconds to find the solution. That's roughly three months.

Indeed, the problem is so tough that not even the human brain can cope with it in detail. The shop manager probably analyzes only one or maybe two tiers, then guesses at the remainder. Although such intuitive guesses rarely hit the most optimum solution, a human expert faced with such a problem comes remarkably close most of the time. Providing the computer with that sort of intuitive grasp of how to attack the problem, especially which possibilities to ignore, is one of the prime goals of AI research.

To avoid the von Neumann bottleneck, the Japanese—and more than fifty U.S. universities and companies—propose to build computers with multiple processors. One "non-von" architecture would string numerous microprocessors together in chains, with multiple side-by-side chains each nibbling away at different parts of a problem. Japan's Icot is one proponent of that method. It has built a prototype computer with four parallel processing paths, has designed an upgrade with eight parallel processors, and hopes to develop 16- and finally 64-path systems. At the California Institute of Technology, computer scientist Charles Seitz and his students have already built a prototype of another "concurrent" computer with 64 processors. Successive versions of CalTech's Cosmic Cube will shrink in a few years to desk-top size, predicts Seitz, yet offer the power of fifty closet-size Cray supercomputers.

Another idea is to create tree-shaped hierarchies of microprocessors, with a boss chip at the top, four underbosses under it, four subbosses under each underboss, and so on. In contrast to this federalist design, still another proposal is a republic consisting of a governor processor directing as many as one million microprocessor chips, all interconnected by a complex grid so that any one processor could communicate with any other. The intent is to create a unified array that could assault problems collectively across a broad front. Some of the processors might be particularly proficient at various tasks, such as doing math or making logical inferences. When a logic chip encountered a situation involving vexing math, it would pass that part of the problem to a math specialist.

One uncertainty surrounding these new architectures is that no one yet knows how to program them. Jacob L. Schwartz, a computer scientist at New York University who hopes to get DARPA backing for his non-von concept, told *Business Week* that the difference between producing software for von Neumann and for non-von machines is at least as great as that between writing music for a guitar versus composing a concerto for a symphony orchestra.

A Conversation with a Machine Expert

While a full-blown thinking computer is still years in the future, AI research is flowering in the more limited area of expert systems. As documented by *Business Week* and *Fortune* and other major magazines, expert-systems programs developed for traditional computers have become a very hot market. DM Data, one of several market research firms following this emerging technology, reports that sales of commercial expert systems exploded from $1 million in 1981 to $34 million in 1984. Another market watcher, InfoTym, forecasts sales of $2.5 billion in 1993.

And once non-von computers enter the market, sales will really take off. Stanford University's Feigenbaum predicts that the AI business will skyrocket to something between $30 and $70 billion by the year 2000, and could reach $110 billion by 2010. The first four decades of the next century, adds Carl Hammer of Research Consulting Services, will usher in "the cognitive processing era," when AI computers with heuristic reasoning powers will begin pushing the office-automation revolution up into the ranks of top management. These computers will be capable of not just replacing an executive's assistants, but of displacing some managers as well. It will be a time of excruciating trauma, because the computers will then be essential to executive success yet will also pose a growing threat to the manager's own job.

Meanwhile, at least three dozen of the biggest American companies—such giants as IBM, Litton, ITT, General Electric, and Hughes—are already spending huge sums on AI research and budding commercial projects. New firms jump on the bandwagon almost monthly. Sperry did so late in 1984. And over the past three years, venture capitalists have pumped in excess of $100 million into fifty start-up companies, many founded by AI researchers from the academic community. Expert systems are the primary focus of all this activity, although natural-language programs aren't far behind.

In expert systems, says Raj Reddy, a professor at Carnegie-Mellon University, "the primary goal is the creation of intelligent assistants, whether it is an assistant for a banker, a doctor, a geologist, a chemist, a communications expert, or whatever. The issue is to capture the knowledge that a person with a B.S. or M.S. degree might have—and also give the program the fundamental mechanisms that most humans have for problem solving." The hangup with building expert systems, he adds, is that they are totally different from classical computer programs. "You're talking about 'what' rather than 'how' programming. You state what the goal is that you're trying to achieve, not how to actually achieve it," Reddy explains.

Conventional software must stipulate specific, step-by-step instructions on how to solve a problem. For instance, the digital code might say: Go to memory location A and retrieve its contents; add 40; if the result is less than 100, store it in memory location A01 and do the next program step; otherwise, put the result in BB and jump ahead 16 program steps.

Expert systems, by contrast, typically utilize a program divided into two independent parts: a knowledge base of facts, plus a collection of rules that guides the computer in solving the problem at hand by making associations between the data in the knowledge base and the facts available about some current situation or problem. The set of rules is often called the inference engine. The rules can take two forms, which Stanford's Feigenbaum calls "the law" and "the lore." The law includes established relationships of the sort contained in textbooks and reference tables. The lore is much more difficult to obtain and codify, since it often consists of hunches and heuristic judgments evolved by human experts through years of experience. Usually, the rules are "if-then" statements: If conditions a, b, c, and d are satisfied, then execute x.

To cite a hypothetical example, the knowledge base for a medical expert system might contain the following facts:

Reddish swellings of the skin are a symptom of measles.
Reddish swellings of the skin are a symptom of pimples.
Reddish swellings of the skin are a symptom of hives.
Elevated temperature is a symptom of measles.
Measles usually occur over the face and body.
Pimples may occur on the face and body, but usually the face.
Hives can occur on any part of the body, usually localized.

Should a patient call a doctor's office and complain of reddish swellings on the face and chest, that information could be entered into the computer (one day, the computer will just listen to the conversation), which would search its rules and find:

If reddish swellings occur on any part of the body, and if temperature is not elevated, then diagnosis is hives or pimples; to resolve, search for other diagnoses of pimples and hives.

If reddish swellings occur on the face but no other part of the body, and if temperature is not elevated, and if age is 10 to 20, then diagnosis is pimples.

If reddish swellings occur on any part of the body, and if swellings occur in more than one location, and if temperature is elevated, then diagnosis is measles.

In this case, a diagnosis isn't possible because not enough facts are known. So the computer would respond with something like: "Considering diagnosis of pimples, hives, or measles. What is temperature?" If the reply were "101.2," the computer could then state: "Suggested diagnosis is measles."

An actual example of a rule from Prospector, a program developed at SRI International (formerly Stanford Research Institute) for mineral exploration: "If there is hornblende pervasively altered to biotite, then there is strong evidence (320, 0.001) for potassic zone alteration." The numbers in parentheses are statistical data indicating the probability that the if-then association is true. Prospector has 1,600 such rules. The electronic geologist scored an impressive victory a couple of years ago by pinpointing the location of a rich molybdenum deposit in eastern Washington state that had eluded human rock hounds for decades. Ironically, the ore deposit was in an area surrounded by exploratory mines and test borings.

Another real-world example comes from Digital Equipment Corporation, which uses two AI programs, Xsel and Xcon, to help sell and then configure its minicomputer systems. When a customer wants a price on a DEC computer, the salesperson enters the model in a computer. Then Xsel begins asking questions on the video terminal, such as how much memory is needed. Once a DEC customer has settled on one of the supplier's minicomputers and listed specific needs, Xcon identifies the necessary peripherals and accessories and combines them in the most cost-effective manner—something that before could be done with proficiency by only a few human experts at DEC. Even their selections were only 75 percent accurate, whereas Xcon's batting average is .950. Xcon contains 1,200 rules in its knowledge base, and the computer's working memory is generally fed about 500 descriptions of parts, engineering constraints, and customer specifications.

If the descriptions in working memory satisfy each and every condition of a certain rule, says John McDermott, a CMU professor who headed development of Xcon, then that rule "fires." The result is a new working-memory element—perhaps a subsystem consisting of two formerly separate components. Then the procedure repeats. But since at least one element in working memory has been created or changed during the previous cycle, a different set of rules may be satisfied the next time around. The system keeps on cycling in this fashion until all the components and peripherals have been combined into one integrated system. To configure one of DEC's large VAX minicomputers, Xcon generally prances throught 1,000 cycles.

Is Fuzzy Thinking More Accurate?

The present methodology may work fine on relatively simple problems, but to avoid choking a conventional computer with billions of calculations when it attacks a complex situation, Hans Berliner, an AI scientist at Carnegie-Mellon, is developing a new way of representing knowledge that could revolutionize programming. Instead of insisting that everything be either true or false, black or white, to conform to a computer's binary states of 0 or 1, Berliner believes that some knowledge should be represented as percentages and probabilities.

"Take something like medicine," he says. "The larger the chunk of medical knowledge you bite off, the more approximate the rules have to get. Otherwise, if you insist that each variable divide the world into two, as soon as you get beyond a score of variables, you're dealing with billions of discrete little states. That's just impractical."

Another example: Both Carnegie-Mellon and Stanford have built AI computer programs that have discovered new laws of physics and mathematics, concepts that humans had overlooked. They did this by meticulously correlating seemingly random facts and principles to see what relationships might exist. Neither system's discoveries were very earthshaking, however; in fact, they were disappointingly trivial. Before the programs could get to things that might have been important, says Berliner, "they came to a grinding halt because there were just too many things that could be combined" in a black-or-white way.

In Berliner's "fuzzy" approach, "you don't always insist that something is either X or Y before you deal with it. You allow a spectrum between X and Y. Any situation can vary from 0 percent X and 100 percent Y, to 100 percent X and 0 percent Y. The reason is that when you make a binary decision, you cannot afford to be wrong, because when you're wrong, you're completely wrong. The other way is a more forgiving way of looking at the world," he explains. "If you figure that something is 80 percent X but it turns out to be 90 percent X, you're not going to get punished very much. If you have something that's a 50 percent effect and you are forced to make a black-white decision, neither one is going to be very good."

Suppose you have an expert system with a rule that says, "Do

Action A only during the day; do not do it at night." And you have a situation where all the other rules are satisfied, except that it's twilight. "What you'd find," says Berliner, "is that the system would say, 'great, great, great'—until it got to that day-night rule; then all of a sudden it would say, 'stop.' That's a terrible kind of problem-solving system. For most real-life situations, you don't want to strap yourself into a system where you must believe everything is a discrete point, when in fact you're moving along a continuum and things change slowly. Most of the time what you want to do is bring to bear what you know in some sort of fuzzy way, so you can react to the small changes."

The "fuzzy" approach should be especially valuable in medical diagnosis, Berliner believes. "Some medical-diagnosis rules say something like, if a person is over age 25 and under 55, a certain symptom means one thing; under 25, it means something else; and over 55 it means a third thing." These rules tend to be applied blindly, but Berliner asserts that is a mistake, since such age cutoffs are a midpoint on some statistical distribution, and what you really want to do is flag the physician to be cautious when he encounters a patient near the cutoff points. For example, if age 55 is a delineation point, there are going to be some people on either side of the cut-off whose bodies have aged faster or slower than the norm. Statistically, explains Berliner, you know there will be such exceptions—a lot of exceptions among 54- and 56-year-old patients, then fewer and fewer exceptions with increasing distance from the cutoff. But some might be found as far as five years on either side.

Berliner has a lot of work remaining before his fuzzy expert can take on real-world applications in business. Right now, for example, the system only remembers the extremes of all its experiences. "But that probably isn't enough. I think the system will need to remember a distribution of all its experiences," he notes, so the computer knows that in the past the value of a certain variable was, say, thirty times more likely to be 40 percent than 90 percent. When humans work on a problem," Berliner explains, "they bring to bear incredible amounts of knowledge—fundamental concepts and generalized rules of thumb that we somehow apply all over the place. A real learning entity needs to have that ability, that kind of information base, because otherwise there are just too many alternatives to test.''

Japan Takes a "Second-Best" Approach

Patrick Henry Winston, director of MIT's AI laboratory, sees the ultimate goal as a computer that thinks the way people do, by reasoning from analogy and using experience gained from one situation to apply to a new, unfamiliar situation—in the process formulating new insights and knowledge, and learning. This level of flexibility should enable computers to make hunches, to keep to unsupported conclusions, then analyze the issue "backward" in an effort to prove or disprove the hunch. That is what distinguishes truly creative minds from the plodding, stuffy train of thought evident in most academic research.

Such leaps of insight are way beyond the scope of today's two-part, rule-based systems. It will presumably require, instead, some type of model of the cognitive process. This model need not parallel the mechanics of how the brain functions during cognition, though. "It's clear that all biological organisms are jerry-built, the end result of a series of random capitalizations on the existing organic structure that in a given environment allowed it to better adapt to that environment," asserts Allen Newell of CMU, one of the early AI pioneers. "Therefore, it follows that anything a biological organism does is *not* the best way of doing it." In other words, organisms wander toward environmental compatibility; they do not take a direct route.

What a better way of thinking might be is so far unclear, but Newell is confident that one will be found. "It's certainly the case that humans are not the last stage in evolution. Everything we know about evolution says that it will continue." The question is, will the next uptick in intelligence occur naturally and result in a new species, perhaps with double the cranial capacity of *Homo sapiens*, or will it instead be fashioned by mankind from silicon, bioengineered circuits, or a technology now wholly unforeseen? If it is to be man-made, then whatever shape this future sentient progeny takes, Newell believes that AI scientists will first need to construct a catholic theory of thinking that will apply to it as well as to the brain and any other intelligent entity.

Japan's Fifth Generation Project lacks this cognitive thrust, this attempt to understand how thinking happens, and for that reason some AI scientists believe the much-touted program is unlikely to attain its most ambitious goals. "They're trying to catch up," says Marvin Minsky, an MIT scientist who has been an IA guru for thirty years, but "they're taking the second-best approach"—namely tried-and-true logic programming, with superfast computers that can do the billions of calculations that will be necessary. Minsky allows that this brute-force approach is "a simple, good way to train beginners—something the Japanese need to do. But," he adds, "the way to do common-sense reasoning is by analogy, not by deduction."

Logic programming, Minsky declares, "breaks down very fast" when presented with complex problems. To illustrate why, he cites the problem of packing a suitcase: You have a certain space to fill and a bunch of clothes that you need to put into it. A logical approach requires the precise geometry of the suitcase and of the folded clothes. Then the computer spins through all possible combinations of packing patterns to find the best fit between the folded clothes and the space available for them. No matter how fast the computer is, this tactic inherently limits applications to comparatively simple problems. But it is a technique that the AI community now knows how to implement.

On the other hand, a computer using analogy would tackle the suitcase problem by asking, "What is most like this that I already know how to do?" The computer would search its memory for similar knowledge (just as a child might realize that packing a suitcase is more like packing a lunch box than stuffing soiled clothes into a hamper, despite the fact that the latter also involves putting clothes into a given space) and extract the appropriate parallels. Trouble is, AI scientists don't yet have the know-how to construct such a system. They lack satisfactory techniques for categorizing knowledge and identifying parallelisms between dissimilar situations; moreover, no computer has the huge collection of knowledge and experience that would be needed.

Because of the difficulties and uncertainties involved, less than a score of scientists worldwide are working to develop systems that would use analogy to reason, Minsky notes.

Consulting with a Computer

Despite current limitations, expert systems are currently the rage in business and professional circles. The principal attraction is that, like the computer, synthetic experts can exert enormous "leverage," producing a multiplier effect on productivity. For exmple, AT&T last year adopted a troubleshooting expert system called Ace. In an hour or so, this program can locate a fault in a telephone cable—a job that takes as much as a week to do manually.

And a system for hospitals, called Help, has in fact helped trim paperwork and costs while improving care and safety at a hospital in Salt Lake City, Utah, and in Elmira, New York. Among other things, Help keeps track of all data on a patient and alerts the doctor if, say, a specialist who was called in prescribes a medicine that may produce a negative reaction with another drug the patient is already receiving. Roughly one of every seven hospital days is caused either by such untoward drug interactions or by a patient's being given a medication to which he or she is known to be allergic. The Ogden Memorial Hospital in Elmira bought Help for $1.5 million in 1983 and reports the system saved $1.8 million in the doctors' time and paperwork in its first year of use.

Medical applications are among the hottest areas of AI research. Two of the oldest AI systems are Puff and Mycin. Puff analyzes pulmonary (lung function) data for doctors at Pacific Medical Center in San Francisco. Mycin assists in the diagnosis of blood infections at Stanford University Hospital, and that hospital also uses another software package called Oncocin to help administer treatment of certain cancers. MIT, Rutgers, and the University of Pittsburgh are developing new computer experts in medicine.

One reason for all the activity in medicine is that, after the Defense Department, the National Institutes of Health has been the most consistent provider of research dollars. "By the turn of the century," predicts William R. Baker, "every physician will be dealing with some kind of computer expert." Baker recently left the NIH, where he was in charge of AI research funding, to form a company that will market various medical systems, including AI/Rheum, an expert system for diagnosing rheumatism and arthritis that was developed at Rutgers and the University of Missouri. He also hopes to peddle Caduceus, a system embodying a lifetime of expertise in internal medicine.

Caduceus is to be the legacy of Dr. Jack D. Myers, the curmudgeonly former chairman of the medical school at the University of Pittsburgh and now professor-at-large. "I've had long experience in the field of internal medicine—four decades' worth, with massive numbers of patients, because I've always been in large institutions," says Dr. Myers. "I've acquired quite a bit of information from seeing these many patients over the years, and I wanted to capture this. But I didn't want to write another textbook." So he hooked up with Harry E. Pople, associate professor of business administration in the university's Graduate School of Business. Pople studied under AI pioneer Allen Newell at CMU, which sits atop an adjacent hill northeast of downtown Pittsburgh. The result of their collaboration is an expert system that, with a dash of wry gallows humor, has been nicknamed "Jack in the box."

The system features a novel approach to decision making that could have broad application in expert systems for other fields, including business and economics. "In fact," says Pople, "one of the reasons why they continue to tolerate my presence in the business program is the evidence that what we're learning does impact some of the fundamental notions about how people deal with the tasks of building conceptual models within which they go about doing their business."

Pople explains that in business and economics—and medicine—making a decision isn't just a matter of finding one optimum choice among alternatives. "The physician can't assume that he has to make only a single judgment, because the patient may have disease X plus complications from old disease Y and maybe the beginning of disease Z. So the usual decision-making model excludes a very important activity that a physician engages in." This activity is defining the problem that he (or she) will consider.

Problem formulation is an iterative process, Pople notes, because the first concept of what the problem is—not the patient's problem but the physician's problem—is often highly speculative. "So the physician constantly gathers new information that may feed back on the problem-formulation process. As time goes on, his concept of the problem may change quite radically," he adds. "It's fascinating to observe—and almost impossible to figure out how to model. It really was the most challenging aspect of this whole thing.

"The problem-formulation activity is the real key," he emphasizes. "That's what allows Caduceus to ignore nonrelevant data, the red herring data. I don't know of anything like this in any other program. Yet I think it's fundamental to what people do in theory formation in many fields." The AI world has not had to come to grips with this aspect of the problem because most of the work on expert systems has been aimed at methods of solving problems after the problem has been formulated. "For example," says Dr. Myers, "you only use Puff if the patient has something wrong with lung function, so the program only addresses an extremely narrow area. Similarly, the original Mycin system was for individuals with meningitis, and it's fine—if you know the patient has meningitis. But you have to make that decision first."

The primary activity that happens in the problem-formulation stage is that the computer scans a mass of data entered by the physician, picks out what seem to be the relevant facts, then ignores everything else while it tries to find a tentative diagnosis. This process of selection is based on weighting factors attached to the symptoms in Caduceus' knowledge base. Under rheumatoid arthritis, for example, is a list of more than one hundred symptoms, including:

JOINT(S), MORNING STIFFNESS LONGER THAN 30 MINUTES . . . 34
KNEE(S), PAIN . . . 23
SKIN, SUBCUTANEOUS NODULE(S) . . . 42

The first digit of the number on each line indicates, on a scale of 1 to 5, the likelihood that, given this symptom, the patient has rheumatoid arthritis. "This number has to be based on experience," Dr. Myers points out. "You're not going to find it in the library."

The second digit indicates the inverse: Among patients with rheumatoid arthritis, what is the frequency of this symptom? This information is widely available in texts and other medical literature.

So, in the problem-formulation step, the computer looks at the symptoms the doctor has entered in working memory and attempts to find a disease or set of diseases with high correlation. It tries to explain as many symptoms as possible with one model. The computer displays the symptoms it is working on and may ask for additional data. "It may be narrowing the gap, converging on a solution," says Pople, "or things may be getting worse, so it will change its focus entirely. Its behavior is very similar to what I've seen Dr. Myers go through."

To demonstrate how Caduceus works, Dr. Myers picked up an issue of the *New England Journal of Medicine* relating an actual case history of a woman with rheumatoid arthritis. He typed in the pertinent facts:

SEX FEMALE
AGE GREATER THAN 55
ARTHRITIS HISTORY
RHEUMATOID FACTOR POSITIVE
HYPERTENSION HISTORY
CHEST X-RAY INTERSTITIAL MARKINGS INCREASED
(A total of 59 symptoms and test results)

"After the computer weeds through the data," Dr. Myers explained, "it'll set up umpteen models of the diseases that the data have evoked, as we call it. Certain disease models will be supported by more findings than others, so after it puts all of the appropriate findings under each hypothesis and determines which model is the strongest, it picks that as the initial subject on which to work. This set of data will probably evoke fifty to one hundred models," he observed. "Now, a person can't deal with that many alternatives; we can only evaluate about seven models at one time—and that often isn't enough."

The computer's screen then flashed a message:

DISREGARDING:
  HEART SOUND(S) P2 INCREASED,
  JOINT(S) INVOLVEMENT POLYARTICULAR SYMMETRICAL,
  (and several other symptoms).

CONSIDERING:
  AGE GREATER THAN 55,
  SEX FEMALE,
  DYSPHEA AT REST,
  COUGH,
  CYANOSIS,
  CHEST X-RAY INTERSTITIAL MARKINGS INCREASED,
  (etc.)

"Now it's telling us that, for the time being, it's disregarding the joints. It's having a problem in that, while the two things this woman has—rheumatoid arthritis and pulmonary interstitial fibrosis—are connected, the machine doesn't recognize that." Shortly, though, the computer did realize that it was working on the wrong problem, set aside that model, and began working on another set of symptoms.

After another minute or so, the video screen blinked with a diagnosis. "Okay," said Dr. Myers, "it's concluded the rheumatoid arthritis, which gives it the opportunity to recognize that this does cause interstitial fibrosis. Now we'll see if it can solve the second problem." Moments later, that diagnosis appeared on the screen. "It solved the problem, but it did it in sort of a left-handed fashion," Dr. Myers admitted. "But it didn't make a mistake."

To some physicians, the advent of computer consultants seems at best a mixed blessing. But Dr. Myers is convinced that expert systems will become indispensible. "The human memory is just not big enough to deal with the modern medical-knowledge base; everybody admits this. Because the human brain is not capable of entertaining an adequate number of simultaneous hypotheses, the physician has to have a crutch.

"Today, with the growth of medical knowledge, the physician's brain has, to a great degree, become a filing cabinet. If he has ten patients in the hospital, a lot of his thought processes are remembering which data belong to which patient—and not analyzing the data." That's a terrible misuse of brainpower, Dr. Myers feels. "So we'll take that load off him and thereby give him more time to think about problems and spend more time with each individual patient."

Dr. Myers also believes computer experts will force doctors to practice more careful medicine. The data that a doctor feeds a computer must be precise; otherwise, the old garbage-in, garbage-out dictum will apply. "I hope it's going to make the physician more cognizant of the value of the patient's history and the physical exam. Physicians have gotten into sloppy habits," he charges. "They depend too much on laboratory tests. The careful taking of a patient's history and the good physical examination have, to an extent, been downgraded. That's wrong. You don't send the patient for a CAT scan of the brain until you've done a very good neurologic exam."

So, while Caduceus and its relatives will transform the medical profession, perhaps radically, Dr. Myers is all for it. "Personally, I say three cheers!"

Expert Help for Smokestack America

Industrialists also cheer the promise of medical AI systems and their counterparts for the insurance business. They see computer experts helping to stabilize and possibly trim overhead costs. For example, the cost of workers' medical benefits now adds almost $500 to the price of a U.S.-built car. That is one-third of the disparity between the cost of an auto made in the United States and the "landed" cost of building a comparable model in Japan and shipping it to the United States. So, Detroit's car makers could be more competitive to whatever extent artificial intelligence techniques can reduce the need for workers with their attendant medical costs. Similar benefits would accrue from expert systems in banking and financial services, another area of concerted AI activity. At least eight start-up companies are vying to develop expert systems for bankers and venture capitalists.

While some AI scientists are sure to become wealthy from expert systems, the real winner will be the whole country. As the American Electronics Association has often pointed out, the crucial role that technology plays is to provide new tools that boost productivity and competitiveness in other sectors of the U.S. economy. The main beneficiaries of high-tech innovation are thus not the relatively few electronics companies that furnish the new tools, but the much larger number of companies and organizations that puts them to work. One sign of just how essential high-tech tools have become: Investments in electronics capital equipment have climbed dramatically, from 25 percent of all capital spending a decade ago to 50 percent today.

Now computers and expert systems stand poised to breathe new life into America's factories. By the turn of the century, a product designer will be able to sit down at a computer-aided engineering terminal and create a *three-dimensional* model of a new product. When he or she finishes, the computer in the CAE system will forward the design data to the central manufacturing computer, which will be able to check that the company has the necessary machine tools to produce the components from the materials specified. Next, the manufacturing computer would access its data base to determine the cost of the materials and the machining time required and display these economic data on the CAE screen, in some instances, perhaps, recommending that certain parts be purchased rather than produced internally. The designer could then modify his or her model to trim production costs.

As this happens, the central manufacturing computer would also be "talking" to the shop-floor computer that handles production planning. These two machines would work out an optimum schedule for making the product. Based on that schedule, the materials-supply computer would dispatch electronic orders for materials, supplies, and purchased parts. At the designated moment, as robot-driven materials handling carts bring the needed supplies and proper machining tools to the flexible manufacturing system (FMS), the central computer would "download" to the FMS computer the dimensions, tolerances, machining speeds and sequences, et cetera for each part.

Throughout actual production, the FMS would monitor its processes and relay that data to the central computer. If anything went awry, the central computer would make adjustments "on the fly" to maintain quality. When the FMS was ready to assemble a certain component, robotic carts would return with purchased parts. The FMS computer would also be able to detect when its own parts need maintenance and call for a robot repairman.

This degree of factory automation is not just blue-sky pipe dreaming. At the IEEE Centennial Technical Convocation in October 1984, celebrating the one hundredth anniversary of the Institute of Electrical and Electronics Engineers, several high-level speakers asserted that the coming of such an entirely new genre of factory is inevitable. One speaker also suggested a new name for the totally automated factory: microfactory. The "micro" reflects both their eventual size and their fundamental reliance on microelectronics.

Koji Kobayashi, chairman of Japan's NEC, said the logical extension of today's trends in automation and computer control will be unmanned plants that can rapidly switch from making one product to almost any other. Raj Reddy, director of the Robotics Institute at Carnegie-Mellon, mirrored Kobayashi's vision and added that such factories should be technically and economically viable by the turn of the century. The microfactory will have various modules for working with different materials—steel, nonferrous metals, plastics, glass, semiconductor chips, and so forth. Each of these, plus assembly and software-writing modules, will be regulated by a small local computer linked to a larger central computer that coordinates operations. In the case of the metalworking cells, the raw material will be rods and bars and sheets, which will be transformed by highly flexible machinery into nuts and bolts and washers, gears and shafts, motors and bearings, and all of the myriad other metal components in a product.

Such factories will be able to make TV sets one day and computers the next, Reddy noted. Eventually, they may be so versatile that they can turn out products one at a time: a single TV followed by a single bicycle, a radio followed by a food processor. Everything will be produced on demand, one at a time, in response to an individual consumer's order; there will be no inventories of finished parts, let alone finished products, lying about in a warehouse. Kobayashi envisions neighborhood factories that will literally be controlled by the customer. With their home computer, Joe and Janet consumer will call into the factory's computer and be led by videoscreens of multiple-choice menus to the product they want, then they will be given a list of options and even be allowed to specify modifications and features not on the standard menu.

Perhaps the ultimate factory of the future was described at the IEEE meeting by Robert A. Frosch, vice president of research at General Motors and a former administrator of NASA. He foresees autonomous, intelligent plants capable of self-diagnosis and -repair, even self-replication. Such factories could be sent to the moon and the asteroid belt, where they would exploit local resources and ease the drain on the earth's natural resources. They could produce the steel rods, bars, and sheets needed by the microfactories back on earth, and they might also disgorge the finished products needed to colonize the solar system—and then send self-replicating probes into deeper and deeper reaches of the universe. What this amounts to, says Reddy, whose Robotics Institute has been helping NASA study the implications of self-reproducing machines, is "dropping an electronic DNA on the surface of the moon and having it make whole factories out of nothing."

Both Reddy and Kobayashi concede that such technology will mean the loss of millions of factory jobs and massive dislocation. In fact, by the year 2010 or 2020, factory jobs will have virtually vanished. But these traumatic effects will be temporary. "Look at the ways things have happened historically," says Reddy. "Those countries that have used technology to the fullest have always had more employment than countries that didn't use techology or did not use it as extensively. Look at Japan, which is more automated than the United States. Who is losing jobs? Not Japan. They have the lowest unemployment in the world."

The analogy to consider is the difference that technology has made in our way of life since the nineteenth century. Then, people worked twelve- to fourteen-hour days, seven days a week, and still went hungry much of the time. Today, people don't have any trouble filling in the extra nonworking hours with avocations and hobbies and all manner of leisure activities; whole new industries and service opportunities have arisen to help—and to provide new employment for other people. Why should it be any different if autonomous factories can produce goods so cheaply that people can provide for their needs by working only four hours a week or maybe only one week per month?

"There is no way," says Allen Newell of CMU, "in which any economy could produce a technological revolution that would create this fabulous amount of goods and at the same time put everybody out of work and on welfare. It can't happen that way. You've got to have consumers for the goods. The economic world is a closed loop."

The autonomous factory's greatest benefits will rain on the Third World. If one automated plant can turn out electrical motors on one shift, refrigerators the next, and personal computers on the third, then today's economies-of-scale justification for capital investments cease to apply. Factories won't need a substantial local demand for one specific product or product family. The autonomous factory will build whatever is needed when it is needed. That means such factories can be constructed anywhere. And as they can clone themselves, the successive generations will become progressively cheaper and will be erected in more and more remote corners of the globe, ultimately bringing dramatic gains in living standards to even jungle tribes and Arctic Eskimos.

Efforts to help developing nations now are often agonizingly slow because the workers in Third World countries lack even the rudimentary skills needed to use modern machinery. Anecdotes abound. In the 1950s, for instance, an American institution sent a tractor, cultivator, and other implements to a small village in Mexico. An agricultural expert stayed in the village for one growing season, showing the peasants how to use the tractor to boost the number of acres planted and then to reap the biggest harvest in the village's history. Five years later, another expert was sent back to the village to see how much the tractor had improved living conditions. Nothing had changed. Except that the tractor and its implements, broken down and rusting, were enshrined in the village square.

But suppose the tractor, produced locally by an autonomous factory, came with its own artificial intelligence, an expert system capable of not only teaching a beginner how to drive and maintain it but also how to apply modern agricultural methods. "Building that kind of intelligence into machinery makes a whole range of things possible," says Reddy. "Think of AI as a mechanism for improving mental abilities. Anything you know how to do you can do better. Anything you don't know how to do you may suddenly be able to do. That will have a major impact on people with low and marginal skill levels. People will suddenly have the means to become extremely productive."

There will be some limitations on autonomous factories, of course. For example, it would make little sense to outfit every microfactory with equipment that could bore auto and truck engine blocks or fabricate the huge turbine blades used in hydroelectric generators. But every country could have at least one plant with these capabilities.

Tearing Down the Fences Around Markets

Although most of the debate over automated factories has focused on their impact on jobs, the implications for management are no less profound. For example, the capital-investment barriers to entering new markets will fall by the wayside. Today, manufacturers tend to specialize in particular products because the capital equipment used to produce washing machines is unsuitable for making motorcycles. Before GE would consider funding a diversification into motorcycles, it would want to be fairly sure that it could win enough market share to recoup the cost of building a motorcycle factory within a reasonable time.

Over the next twenty to thirty years, though, such considerations will become less and less of a factor. As GE and other companies put in flexible manufacturing systems, they will be able to go after wider and wider markets with impunity. Indeed, part of the economic justification for the move to FMS will be the opportunities afforded to generate revenues from new markets. Integration will spread both vertically and horizontally.

Manufacturing technology won't leap overnight from present constraints to a level where one plant can switch from washing machines to motorcycles. The transition will be gradual. But whereas GE likely wouldn't risk investing in a motorcycle factory now, five or ten years hence it might consider building a plant that could make motorcycles and golf carts, irrigation pumps and portable generators, snowmobiles and airport baggage-transport vehicles. This degree of versatility is coming soon.

In other words, we are heading for a time when manufacturing technology for extremely diverse mixes of products is a given, available to any firm that has the purchase price—and the cost of such technology will rapidly plunge. So how will one company distinguish itself from all the others? Better product design, better quality, better reliability, better service. Even the most recalcitrant manufacturer will be forced to emphasize marketing in order to survive. The consumer will be in the driver's seat as never before.

TELECOMMUNICATIONS: PUTTING IT ALL TOGETHER

A computer in every pot, computer experts that help doctors diagnose illness, microfactories that make products on demand—these and other wonders of the information age will depend upon effective telecommunications. Once a tool for simple voice phone calls, telecommunications is rapidly emerging as the linchpin of the information society. It is the "glue" that links computers in the home, the office, and the factory. The amount of traffic pouring through phone lines and satellite relays by the end of the century, perhaps even by the end of this decade, would inundate today's system. At a forum last year, Archie McGill, chairman of Rothschild Ventures and former Vice President for Business Marketing, TK-TITLE of AT&T, said that by 1990 the telecom switches that now route calls "will be architecturally or functionally inadequate to handle the huge volumes of information."

Fortunately, telecom companies in the United States and around the world are already preparing for that flood of data and are installing digital systems that can handle the vastly increased traffic. Tap into a typical phone call carried by analog equipment and you'll hear actual voices. Do the same for a digital link and you'll need a computer to decipher the bits and bytes pulsating through the system, representing human voices, computer-to-computer information and electronic funds exchanges, facsimile transmissions, video teleconferencing images, remote-control commands, video games, hi-fi music, and network TV signals.

The phone system is changing from primarily a means for people to keep in touch with other people to one for putting people in touch with "a larger intelligence—whether human intelligence, singly or in groups—or computer intelligence. What we're talking about," says Robert Lucky, executive director of communications science research at AT&T Bell Laboratories, "is accessing intelligence."

As the pathway to intelligence, telecommunications is the cornerstone of the modern world's electronic infrastructure. Without an up-to-date telecom system, any country would be in real danger of clamping a lid on business growth. Michael Tyler, chairman of CSP International, a consulting firm, put it this way to a *Washington Post* reporter: "Telecommunications technology is as fundamental to the information age as the automobile and the highway system have been over the past fifty years."

Many of the world's developing nations, recognizing the strategic importance of a modern telecom system, have launched multimillion-dollar projects to modernize and expand their communications infrastructures. These include South Korea, Mexico, Brazil, Argentina, and Saudi Arabia. They realize that telecom facilities and policies can make or break a business deal.

A case in point: Ford Motor Company built a communications center in Britain rather than on the Continent because British Telecom permitted Ford to set up its own electronic mail facilities to serve its offices elsewhere in Europe; the phone companies on the Continent refused to allow such an independent operation to use their transmission lines. Ford wanted its own facility because of the advent of the so-called world car. With different parts being made in different countries and shipped to several assembly plants around the world, the auto maker decided that better communications were vital to coordinating these far-flung activities. So, instead of letting each of its four regions (North America, Latin America, Europe, and Asia) do the best job possible with local phone companies, Ford put in its own hub in each of the regions.

Not since the early days of telephone service nearly a century ago have national telecom markets been open to competition. In every industrialized country, monopolies were annointed long ago to provide telephone and telegraph service. In Europe, the same agency—called the PTT—also handles postal services. The PTTs formed comfortable working relationships with a handful of local equipment makers that supplied standardized telephones, switching systems, and sundry other hardware that was engineered to last twenty, thirty, or forty years. Typically, a PTT buys 70 to 80 percent of its equipment from three or four large suppliers, whose managements have tended to grow fat and lazy. In Europe, in particular, telecommunications fell woefully behind developments in the United States.

Now, however, those cozy arrangements are being torn apart by the relentless pace of new technology. The life cycle of today's telecom equipment is rarely more than the four to six years that's typical of computer hardware, and the demand for new services arising from the burgeoning use of computers outruns the ability of even state-supported PTTs to fund new systems and set new standards. The dynamics of the market are forcing many telecom authorities to lift exclusionary regulations and permit at least a trickle of competition—a trickle that many companies believe will soon become a flood, as it has in America, Japan, Britain, and Canada, where telecommunications is now relatively deregulated.

The worldwide market for telecom equipment is huge: almost $60 billion in 1983 and heading for nearly $90 billion by 1988, according to Arthur D. Little, Inc. The business is split roughly one-third for equipment sold to users—phones, private branch exchange (PBX) systems, telex terminals, et cetera—and two-thirds for hardware sold to telephone companies, or "telcos." Practically every major manufacturer of telecom equipment in the world is focusing its attention on America; some 1,100 companies are now competing for a slice of the U.S. business. That's understandable. The United States is the world's largest and fastest-growing single market. Hardware sales in 1983 topped $23 billion and should increase 8 percent annually through 1988. By comparison, all of western Europe fell short of $14 billion and the combined market there is growing only 5 percent per year; Japan's market barely squeaked past $5 billion in 1983, and ADL predicts it will increase 6 percent yearly until 1988.

Spurred by continuing deregulation of the U.S. market, imports of telecom equipment in 1983 jumped 60 percent above 1982 figures to more than $1 billion. That knocked the U.S. balance of trade into the red for the first time since 1974. The $200 million surplus in 1982 gave way to an even bigger deficit, largely because exports barely moved—up less than 1 percent, to $835 million—because of exclusionary buying practices in most foreign countries. Japan not only became the leading offshore supplier to the United States, with roughly 40 percent of 1983 imports, but also displaced the United States as number one in world sales of telecom equipment. It grabbed 20 percent of the $5 billion in world trade. The United States came in second, with 17 percent of total exports, just a point or so ahead of West Germany and Sweden.

The demand for services is even bigger and gaining still faster than the equipment market. Estimates of the total bill for voice, telex, data, and other transmissions run anywhere from triple to quadruple the spending on equipment. Spending on telecom services is growing about 10 percent a year in the United States and as much as double that in some industrial nations where the telephone isn't quite the household fixture that it is in America, where there are eighty phones per one hundred people.

A Strategic Weapon in Global Markets

The newest, computer-related services are among the most explosive. Sales in the United States of information delivered electronically via phone lines will mushroom 23 percent annually, from $1.2 million in 1983 to $3.5 million in 1988, predicts Link Resources Corporation, a market research firm. The bulk of this is, and will continue to be, business information such as stock quotes from Quotron Systems' financial data base, legal and business information from Mead Corporation's Lexis and Nexis data bases, and credit checks with TRW's credit information service. A subscription to Lexis is considered indispensible for law firms, else an adversary gain the upper hand in court, and increasing numbers of multinationals regard the latest telecom facilities as an essential strategic weapon for doing business in world markets. Among the globe-straddling corporations, it's not uncommon for telecom expenses to represent 5 to 10 percent of revenues.

First National of Boston, for example, has installed a data communications system linking its banking offices in Boston, New York, Hong Kong, and London. Where once it took days to send a loan application from London to Boston for review, then back to London, the transmission process now takes a minute in each direction. When several banks are bidding on the same loan, that difference can be crucial.

Despite the preponderance of business services, by far the highest growth rate is coming from consumers. Link Resources sees consumer demand for electronically delivered information compounding 60 percent a year and reaching $192.5 million in 1988, with the number of users mushrooming from less than 500,000 last year to more than 5.5 million in 1989. The consumer market is served by such text-only videotex systems as Source Telecomputing and CompuServe, banks and stock brokers that allow teletransactions from home computers, and graphics-oriented videotex systems such as Knight-Ridder's Viewtron service and Trintex, a new joint venture of IBM, Sears, and CBS (a similar effort is being studied by another consortium: RCA, J. C. Penney, and Citicorp). These systems deliver text-and-graphics "screens" of information by phone lines for display on a TV set or home computer. With Viewtron, consumers also can order merchandise from a local department store, buy airline tickets, and send and receive electronic mail.

In the wake of deregulation, the traditional AT&T rivals—contenders such as GTE, Harris, ITT, MCI, Northern Telecom, RCA, and Rolm—have brought forth a cornucopia of new long-distance networks, services, and products. In the process, old business lines are blurring everywhere. It used to be that once a common or specialized carrier had made a hardware decision, it was locked into a particular mode of communications. But now a company that used to carry only text messages, like Western Union, can offer other services as well. Technically, that's because all digital transmissions look the same to the carrier. The signal coming out of, say, a digital facsimile machine is a series of zeros and ones which are, for most intents, indistinguishable from those representing a human voice or any other type of message. These zeros and ones can be transmitted as electrical pulses over copper wires or as blips of light through optical fibers, then reconstructed at the receiving end.

The battle among common carriers predates AT&T's breakup by several years. Back in 1981, Washington eradicated the regulations that had blocked so-called international record carriers, like RCA Global Communications, from providing domestic services; until then, these carriers had been limited to telex and low-speed computer communications between a seacoast or border point and some other country.

To play fair, Washington at the same time unlocked the shackles that had bound Western Union to domestic service.

Deregulation also opened the doors to foreign carriers. Britain's Cable and Wireless acquired TDX Systems, a long-distance phone company that offers low rates. And France Cables and Radio bought a share of Argo Communications Corporation, a common carrier start-up. The latest competition is coming from big-time users themselves: McDonnell Douglas, Eastman Kodak, and Sears, Roebuck are among the companies that are building their own telecom networks, including transmission facilities (wires, microwave relays, or satellite links). In some cases they are selling surplus capacity to other users.

But the real struggle with foreign suppliers dates from the Federal Communications commissions' 1968 ruling that customers could hook non-Bell equipment into the Bell System. That lured droves of overseas producers of user equipment. A dozen or so foreign giants have been beating the bushes for new business in the United States, including Siemens of West Germany, NEC and Fujitsu of Japan, CIT-Alcatel and Thomson of France, Plessey of Britain, and L.M. Ericsson of Sweden. Recent moves include Plessey's late-1982 purchase of Stromberg-Carlson Corporation and the installation of a PBX production line at a Stromberg plant in Florida. With computer and telecom technology merging, Ericsson figured it could benefit from having access to American computer know-how, so in 1983 it negotiated a deal with Honeywell, which will market the Swedish firm's PBX switchboards in the United States. And as if to dispel any last, lingering doubts about the blurring of computer and telecom technologies, IBM last year bought Rolm, a leading producer of PBXs.

PBXs are currently the hottest segment of the transnational telecom market, since most PTTs still hesitate to buy their own big-ticket equipment from foreign manufacturers. PBX sales in the United States reached $2.8 billion in 1983, double the figure in 1977, and climbed to $3.5 million (40,000 units) last year. Half of the business went to a handful of Japanese and European companies plus two Canadian suppliers, Mitel Corporation and Northern Telecom Ltd. But this offshore competition may now be the least of the American companies' troubles.

More worrisome, the PBX business may have peaked and could now begin contracting. That's the pessimistic forecast from Eastern Management Group. Rolm's president, M. Kenneth Oshman, explained to *Business Week* that "the beauty of telecommunications systems is that everybody needs one. The problem is that they only need one."

To compensate, AT&T *et alia* are eyeing overseas markets for the first time, and several American manufacturers are hitching up with foreign partners that can help them navigate the unfamiliar politics with PTTs or provide access to local markets. Examples: AT&T in 1983 signed a cooperative pact with Philips of the Netherlands, Europe's biggest electronics company; and ITT has joined with China's National Postal & Telecommunications Industry Corporation to make switching gear for the Chinese market. The U.S. companies scrambling to boost offshore PBX sales face familiar hurdles—local content rules, high tariffs, and bureaucratic foot dragging. Despite all the noise about the more-competitive nature of foreign telecom markets, in France the only American PBX company that's visible is IBM, and only because it builds its switchboards in France; and in Japan, local suppliers still control 90 percent or more of the market.

Even without the first whiffs of a more open-competition climate in customer equipment, economic factors almost surely will work their magic and force more PTTs to go to competitive bidding even for their own capital items. Reason: The cost of developing new central-office and exchange switches, which are essentially special-purpose mainframe computers, has swollen so large that producers need the extra business that exports bring to recoup the investment. Despite the fact that in 1985 switching systems should top $15 billion in sales—the single biggest market in the telecom industry—no national market, other than America's, is large enough to keep up with the spiraling cost of developing electronic switches.

To forestall chaos in the open markets that are coming, since the various national telecom systems have to mesh together, the world's PTTs are striving to formulate universal standards. The Integrated Services Digital Network (ISDN) will be an intelligent system providing not only a broad range of services and transmission speeds, but also internal data-processing capabilities. First generation systems could emerge as early as 1986, and by 1990 full-blown ISDN services should be available.

In addition to the expected services (voice, telex, electronic funds transfer, facsimile, videotex, et cetera), the ISDN will have special high-speed facilities for digital music, TV conferencing, cable TV distribution, and, of course, computer communications. It also will integrate certain low-speed services like remote meter reading (special transmitters mounted on utility meters can be polled by telephone so electric and gas companies won't have to send people to read the meters), video surveillance of sensitive rooms and plant perimeters, burglar alarms, and signals for doing remote control of energy management and other systems.

The most dramatic advances will appear in the post-1990 years. Then it will be possible to pick up a phone and retrieve information from data bases by voice, with the ISDN converting the caller's voice commands into computer code, and then converting the data-base output into a synthetic voice. Phones hooked into the ISDN will also respond to voice commands; for example, to transfer a call to another number, instead of hitting a command string of one or two buttons and then punching in the new number, you would just hit the "star" button and tell the system, "Transfer. 685-2717."

Other features to watch for: Executives will have so-called national numbers that follow them wherever they travel. A 1990s phone will be able to display the number of the person calling you. ISDN will enable you to program your phone to reject calls from certain numbers or to allow only calls from specified numbers to ring through. Nippon Telegraph and Telephone even plans to offer two-way (talkback) TV and simultaneous translation of foreign languages into Japanese and vice versa.

The ISDN also will provide European users with many services that U.S. phone customers take for granted, such as itemized bills. European PTTs simply send out lump-sum bills every quarter to homes and business, and the user has no way of verifying the bill's accuracy. Given the present archaic level of service, ISDN features like call forwarding, user-initiated conference calls, call holding, and abbreviated dialing will seem remarkable enough, not to mention the capabilities cited above.

"Next Comes the Optical Age"

While ISDN standards will establish protocols for communications signals to ensure compatibility among the digital telecom systems in different countries, they won't close the door on new techniques for generating and transmitting those signals. Even if the PTTs wanted to nail down such specifications to aid domestic manufacturers, they know that the frantic pace of fiber optics technology makes it impractical. The entire industrial world is now in the throes of an upheaval to replace all copper phone lines with hair-thin optical fibers over the next twenty or thirty years.

The stakes are mind-boggling. The United States alone has more than a billion miles of copper telecom wire installed, or nearly 2 trillion meters. Assuming that the price of the wispy fibers of glass plummets from today's 50¢-per-meter level to NTT's optimistic 5¢ projection by 1990, and that every mile of copper is replaced with a mile of fiber, the cumulative U.S. market for optical fibers alone will top $100 billion. And fibers represent less than half the total cost of a fiber optics system. The bulk of the investment goes to electronic and optoelectronic components, such as switches, transmitters, and receivers. Japan estimates its total cost of converting to fiber optics will be $80 billion over the next twenty years. It expects to be the first nation to string optical fibers into every home.

The United States and Japan are also racing to develop optoelectronic switches—computers—that will process photons (pulses of light) the way that today's integrated circuits process electronic signals. The successful fabrication of integrated-optic circuits (IOCs) that come anywhere near the size and cost of present semiconductor chips would likely trigger as much of a revolution in computing technology as did Bell Lab's original invention of the transistor. An optical computer could be at least 1,000 times faster, maybe 10,000 times faster, than any electronic computer. "Now we are in the microelectronics age," says Mikio Ohtsuki, who directs fiber optics transmission research at Japan's Fujitsu. "Next comes the optical age."

So far the fiber optics contest between Japan and the United States looks like a replay of the situation in semiconductors: The United States leads the way in technology, but Japan takes over the commercial market. A U.S. trade official told *Business Week*: "It looks like another classic case of what we find unacceptable about Japanese industrial policies: They shut us out while they build an export launch pad, often using our patents and technology, then bombard us in our own and third markets.'' With subsidies from MITI and NTT, Japan's production capacity for optical fibers and associated electronics hardware is expected to zoom from $200 million in 1983 to $2 billion by 1990. That will be nearly triple the country's domestic needs. Michael K. Barnoski, a consultant with ten years of fiber optics experience in industry, warns that the United States had better move quickly to match Japan's push into commercial production, else "the Japanese are going to do to us in fiber optics what they've already done to us in autos.''

Turning the tables, several U.S. giants are getting in on the ground floor of Japan's now-deregulated telecom business. AT&T, the world's largest telecom manufacturer with estimated sales last year of $24 billion, is prepared to make an initial investment of $85 million in joint investment with Mitsui and Company to offer nationwide ''smart'' networks. IBM is expected to develop a nationwide network with Mitsubishi and Cosmo-80, a small Japanese software company. GE plans to offer communications services over a network it runs jointly with Dentsu, a major advertising firm.

For telephone companies, fiber optics technology delivers two important benefits: more communications capacity and longer transmission distances. One strand of glass can carry up to 500 times more calls than a copper wire. Today, as many as 6,000 calls can be piped through a fiber, and Bell Labs is confident that the eventual number will be hundreds of thousands of simultaneous calls.

The blips of light are pumped into a fiber by laser diodes—minuscule lasers so tiny they fit through the eye of a needle. To create a stream of pulses sufficient to carry 6,000 calls, the laser has to turn on and off 400 million times per second. As incredible as that seems, Bell Labs has already tested experimental diodes that pulse 2 billion times a second, and Bell scientists say that 7 to 8 billion pulses per second are feasible. That would be enough to transmit the entire *Encyclopedia Britannica* in about one-half second, something that would take 420 hours (more than two weeks) by copper wire.

Equally important, light pulses travel 20 to 30 miles through optical fibers—and ultimately may go 100 or even 200 miles—before degrading into unintelligible "noise." Before that happens, the signals are processed by a so-called repeater that receives, amplifies, and retransmits the flashes of light. With copper wire, by comparison, electrical signals degrade so fast that repeaters are needed every mile. Today's repeaters are not only expensive, they are also prone to failure (which is why metropolitan telcos are constantly working down in manholes or digging up the streets), and they sometimes make a mistake when processing high-speed computer data. By extending the distance between repeaters to many miles, the costly and time-consuming chore of repairing repeaters will be alleviated, because they will all be located aboveground, in switching centers.

Boxing the Country in Fiber

As a result, most telecom companies have stopped installing new copper lines. By the end of the decade, says Robert W. Kleinert, president of AT&T Communications, "AT&T will have constructed the world's largest fiber optic telecommunications network." Currently the company has laid 3,700 miles of optical-fiber cables (more than 100,000 "fiber miles," since a cable typically contains around thirty fibers), running along much of the East and West Coasts and from Philadelphia to Chicago. By 1988, it will add 5,000 more miles, including a Sun Belt route from Atlanta to Tucson. Come 1990, the westward spurs in the north and south will be extended to connect up with the West Coast trunk, and the United States will be boxed by optical fibers. The total fiber routes that AT&T plans to install by the mid-1990s, including transatlantic and transpacific cables, add up to 21,000 miles.

AT&T is hardly the only company with fiber optic ambitions. Nine other firms are installing or planning to install regional or nationwide optical-fiber trunks. Southern New England Telephone, for example, is laying 5,000 miles along CSX Corporation's railroad tracks to link forty-three cities in twenty-four eastern states. MCI Communications is spending $200 million on a 4,250-mile system along Amtrak routes east of the Mississippi. West of the Mississippi, United Telecommunications is installing 23,000 miles of fiber cable. When all of these systems are up and running, notes consultant Robert E.

LaBlanc, "we will have about twenty times the carrying capacity that exists today."

In addition, phone companies serving large metropolitan areas are putting in local optical-fiber loops to satisfy business demands for data communications. There is a "Ring around Manhattan," for example, plus ten office buildings that are "wired" with fibers. Pacific Bell has 2,000 miles of optical cable in urban loops in Los Angeles and Bakersfield, and a Bay Area Ring in San Francisco. Chicago, Miami, Boston, and Stamford, Connecticut, also have local loops.

Last year, sales of optical fibers and electronic components in the United States totaled nearly $500 million—more than half of the world-wide market. And Information Gatekeeps, a Boston market researcher, predicts that the fiber optics market will grow at a rate of 40 percent or more annually for at least the remainder of this decade.

The Japanese are lapping up a good share of this business. Fujitsu of Japan is supplying most of the lasers and electronic components for MCI's system. NEC boasts that its optoelectronic hardware already has won more than 10 percent of the U.S. market not subject to AT&T's buy-American guidelines. Even AT&T turned to a Japanese company, Hitachi Ltd., for the laser diodes in the transatlantic cable it is now laying. This 3,600-mile, $450 million cable will enter service in 1988.

But scientists at Bell Labs assert that Japan's lead in electronic devices is temporary. Lawrence K. Anderson, director of electronic components research at Bell Labs, says that his staff is working to "head off the Japanese with forward-looking, manufacturable technology." AT&T's selection of Hitachi lasers for the transatlantic cable, he adds, was a matter of necessity: They were the only suitable laser diodes that were available when AT&T was planning its bid for the job. Since then, AT&T Technologies (formerly Western Electric) has been rapidly catching up.

The acid test will come in the Pacific. Once the transatlantic cable is operational and demonstrates that fiber optics is adaptable to undersea environments, everyone expects huge demand from the island nations along the Asian Rim—and in the Caribbean and Mediterranean seas. While few of these countries need the extra carrying capacity, a fiber optics system can be justified just on the basis of eliminating the need to repair repeaters spotted along the bottom of the ocean. With undersea copper cables, there is a repeater every mile; with fiber, repeaters will be unnecessary except for runs of more than 100 or 150 miles.

Some observers, here and in Japan, wonder whether there will be enough demand for services to warrant the expense. Masahiro Hirano, planning director of Japan's Engineering Research Association of Applied Optoelectronics Systems, has a ready answer: "Ten years ago, people wondered whether there was really a demand for all the memory capacity that semiconductor makers were manufacturing. Now we know: The more you have, the more you want." In fact, proponents of Japan's Information Network System, a 1,800-mile optical fiber backbone through the Japanese archipelago, insist that once cheap transmission is available, it too will create demand. They envision a $170 billion market by the year 2000, including both services and equipment ranging from home facsimile machines to videophones.

Hirano's association was formed by MITI in 1981 to spread fiber optics technology beyond the usual telecommunications environment. Its original membership has ballooned from eleven to more than 150 companies, and they have been instrumental in putting fiber optics to work at more than 400 sites. One nontelecom application for fiber optics is to monitor traffic flow on highways. Several other installations carry computer, video, and voice data inside factories. Now the group is working on a factory automation system to make Japan's smokestack industries more competitive. Optical fibers will transport data to and from remote sensors that measure temperatures, detect flaws visually, and gather data on production trends.

"Fiber optics is still young, and the potentials for what it will do for the future are so far-reaching that we are only beginning to grasp them," says Charles K. Kao, the executive scientist at ITT, who first described the concept of fiber optic communications thirty years ago. But before another decade goes by, "the resistance will fall away and we'll realize that we really need to have much more information input into our homes to complement our daily living. Then optical fibers coming into each person's home will indeed be regarded as a necessity instead of a luxury."

Semiconductors, computer experts, fiber optics—three technologies that have just begun to stamp their imprint on business and society. By the end of this century, the United States and the Western world will be caught in the throes of a social revolution without precedent. It will be far more sweeping than the Industrial Revolution. We have only twenty-five to thirty-five years to understand what is happening and formulate the appropriate social, political, and economic responses. Even fervent proponents of AI, intelligent factories, and automated offices admit that that won't be easy. So far, very few leaders in government even begin to grasp the enormity of what's coming.

Clearly, the electronics revolution has only begun.

AEROSPACE: TECHNOLOGY THAT'S FLYING AWAY

Putting Electronics to Work

"Aerospace is the future. If there's one industry that this country can count on being here decades from now, it is our aerospace industry." This optimistic assessment from the fiftieth anniversary issue of *Tooling & Production* reflects a little wishful thinking. It's on target for the military and space side of the business, at least for the present. But for the rest of America's $75 billion aerospace industry, the outlook is pretty glum. And just how competitive even the military segment will be "decades from now" is a matter of growing concern.

The bright spot, though, is that the diverse responses to the industry's troubles are now coalescing into a battle plan that, as we shall see, could well become a grand strategy for the salvation of U.S. manufacturing as a whole. Indeed, the aerospace industry's political clout may be just the stimulant needed to wake up Washington in time for the bureaucrats to realize how crucial it is to safeguard the manufacturing sector, that what matters most is not jobs but the wealth-generating capacity of industry.

The main culprit responsible for today's dour climate, not surprisingly, is rising competition from foreign companies that are highly subsidized—and not just by their own governments. Indirect props also come from the U.S. government and cash-strapped American companies. The United States almost seems determined to give away its once-unassailable lead in aerospace technology.

Foreign countries, NATO members and Japan in particular, acquire considerable advanced U.S. military aerospace technology through mutual defense agreements. "Co-production" is the latest buzz word; to sell a squadron of fighters, the Pentagon is all too ready to hand part of the production job even to second- and third-tier countries such as Brazil, Spain, or Indonesia. Such "offset" arrangements include a multibillion-dollar contract with Turkey, which is buying 160 of General Dynamics' F-16 fighters. Naturally, that means the U.S. developer is compelled to cede advanced know-how to the foreign "partner"— in manufacturing techniques, composite materials, powder metallurgy, or maybe sophisticated electronics. Every such agreement only hastens the day when subsidized foreign companies can match U.S. technology at lower prices and compound the mounting competition from Sweden, Israel, Germany, and Britain.

Co-production also plays to the short-term interests of some aerospace companies, by lowering their development and/or manufacturing expenses. The concept of voluntary co-production is akin to the auto industry's "world car" strategy of spreading the risks and costs of new product development. Cost-cutting appeals to the companies because, surprisingly, profits as a percent of sales in the aerospace industry have been consistently lower than the average of all manufacturers. In fact, during most of the 1970s, profitability was 25 to 50 percent under that average. Industry profits have topped 4.5 percent of sales only once since 1970—although, expressed as return on equity, aerospace profits since 1978 have been slightly higher than the all-manufacturing average.

For national security reasons, Washington would never permit prime military contractors to go under. But unless corrective steps are taken, the Pentagon could end up having to subsidize some "metal-bending" aerospace suppliers. And the U.S. would lose part or all of the export revenues that aerospace generates. In 1984 the industry's exports came to about $15.4 billion, for a trade surplus of almost $13 billion, a tad below 1983's figure. Still, that was the biggest positive balance of any manufacturing industry.

The two most significant steps that Washington could take would be, first, to relax antitrust regulations to encourage collaborative research projects, along the lines of what the semiconductor and computer industries are doing. The business is getting so capital intensive that the industry suffers for lack of R&D funds. The cost of developing a new passenger jet, for example, now runs $1.5 billion and up. Second, Congress might also put a formal stamp of approval on cooperative engineering and production arrangements—if you will, co-production within the United States.

For civilian aircraft, there's a rocky runway ahead. And once the industry clears the short-term obstacles, sales will climb only moderately—5 percent or so per year—from 1988 through 1995. The problem in commercial jet transports, the bulk of the civilian business, is the financial plight of the world's airlines. During 1982 and 1983 airlines canceled more than fifty orders for big transports—worth $2 billion, or nearly one-quarter of actual shipments in 1983—and the delivery dates for many more orders were postponed. Since the lead time on large airliners is more than a year, some of those cancellations and delays continue to affect business in 1985. A further drag on sales comes from a surplus supply of used jetliners.

On the other hand, the Federal Aviation Administration's new noise-control regulations took effect on January 1, 1985, and similar rules will be applied by several European countries over the next year or two. The FAA reports that some 15 percent of the passenger and cargo planes now flying will need to be replaced or modified to muffle noise during takeoffs and landings. Because of those pending rules and the airlines' demand for more fuel-efficient aircraft, manufacturers are gradually phasing out older models. In 1983 Lockheed dropped production of its L-1011 wide-body, and in 1984 Boeing rolled out the last 727 airliner.

For U.S. firms, Boeing in particular, the chief rival is Airbus Industrie, the government-backed French-German-British-Dutch consortium. Airbus entered the business with two medium-range, wide-body jets, designed expressly for intra-European routes. The planes have also proved very popular in the Middle East and Africa, and the consortium's share of the market for such planes has expanded alarmingly, to 42 percent in 1982 from 24 percent in 1980. Airbus has even snatched one-third of America's domestic market. Just ten years ago,

U.S. manufacturers attracted 95 percent of the world's orders for such airliners.

Politics have contributed significantly to America's downfall. The Export-Import Bank has cut its financing help to U.S. firms, so Boeing is unable to offer packages as attractive as those that Airbus can put together. While the United States persists in its unwaivering support of Israel, France courts the Arab states; the upshot is that Airbus has seized a major position in the Middle East. And while trying to slug it out with a subsidized competitor, Boeing not only doesn't get much sympathy from the federal government, but more often than not finds Washington actively hindering its plans.

Many legislators and regulators in Washington don't seem to realize the grave damage their antibusiness attitudes and platitudes do to America's overseas competitiveness—and worse, don't even seem to care. This country has no divine mandate to lead the world in technology forever. Unless Washington wakes up soon, the aerospace industry will be only the first of a succession of industries that will fall to second-class status, thanks to federal ignorance and stupidity.

Airbus has no intention of braking its momentum now, with the United States on the defensive. It wants 40 percent of the whole world market, including the jumbo-jet area where Boeing still reigns supreme. The consortium reckons that worldwide demand over the next twenty years for jet liners with 100 or more seats will amount to 8,000 planes. Airbus plans to grab more of that business by expanding its offerings at both ends of the scale, smaller and bigger, longer-range designs. The new aircraft will be built with many of the same components and parts used for the original A300 and A310 models. That should be a powerful inducement to its customers to convert to all-Airbus fleets, in order to realize savings in maintenance and training costs by eliminating duplication in equipment and parts inventories. Airbus unveiled its third plane, the 150-seat "new technology" A320, last year.

To counter the A320, Boeing has entered a joint venture with three major Japanese firms—Mitsubishi Heavy Industries, Kawasaki Heavy Industries, and Fuji Heavy Industries—to develop an advanced-technology passenger jet for introduction near the end of this decade. Boeing will retain at least a 51 percent controlling interest in the venture; the Japanese firms, combined, have 25 percent, and other manufacturers own the remaining 24 percent. The Japanese trio is already helping co-produce Boeing's 767 passenger jet in return for 15 percent of the profits. With the new plane, they are getting a bigger stake because they are sharing the risks of development as well.

In small aircraft for corporate and recreational aviation, the market has been in a slump since 1980. From the 1979 high of 16,500 planes worth $14 billion, the so-called general aviation business plummeted by 1983 to about 2,600 units worth $1.5 billion. The fortunes of this market will pick up as the economy improves and as a new generation of lightweight, high-performance, yet fuel-stingy planes—such as the nearly all-plastics Avtek and LearFan—are certified by the FAA. Another composite-plastics airframe, the oblique-wing design by Burt Rutan (its wing pivots at the center of the fuselage, so that at cruising speed one side is swept forward, the other swept back by as much as 60 degrees), has been chosen by the air force as a trainer. Fairchild Industries is producing 650 of these unusual trainers for use through 1995.

The switch from aluminum to composites—plastics reinforced with such new materials as graphite and boron fibers—already well advanced in military planes, will spread rapidly. Currently, the mythical average airframe is 75 percent or more aluminum and only about 3 percent plastics; titanium, high-strength steel alloys, and other metals account for the remainder. But because the latest composites trim considerable weight without sacrificing performance—1 pound of plastics can replace up to 3 pounds of aluminum—the average airframe will be 40 percent plastic by 1995.

Into the Wild Blue Yonder

Aside from aircraft, the heftiest items in the aerospace industry's catalog are engines and missiles. In fact, these two product areas each generate more revenues than do either military planes or civilian planes separately.

Jet engines are big-ticket items. Those mounted on large passenger jets typically run between $2 and $4 million each, and total 1983 sales amounted to $13.6 billion. Pratt & Whitney, a division of United Technologies, has the lion's share of the airliner business, with GE and Rolls-Royce splitting just 20 percent. Pratt & Whitney also dominated the market for military fighter jet engines until 1984, when the air force decided to stimulate competitive juices a bit by tipping the scales in favor of GE. Between 1985 and 1990, the air force plans to buy nearly 2,000 engines for its fighters, at a projected cost of $8 billion.

With two-engine passenger jetliners now approved by the FAA for even transatlantic routes, the trend away from three- and four-engine passenger planes will accelerate, propelled by concerns for fuel efficiency and easier maintenance. This obviously will depress the market for engines. And since the cost of developing a new engine can easily match the $1.5 billion for a new aircraft, U.S. engine makers are also seeking relief through shared production. GE, for example, builds engines in conjunction with Snecma of France. Even mighty Pratt & Whitney has joined International Aero Engines, a consortium of European and Japanese companies headed by Rolls-Royce.

Guided missiles are one product category that has posted steady and substantial gains for the past decade. Shipments have been rising more than 9 percent annually since 1972, and this will continue at least through the rest of the 1980s. The Falkland Islands crisis and the ongoing Iran-Iraq war have demonstrated the effectiveness of modern missiles, and their acquisition has become a priority for many governments.

Now the frontier of space beckons. Here, the United States will retain its technical leadership, although competition will increase markedly by 1995. The European Space Agency has made substantial progress with its Ariane launch vehicle, and while it has nothing comparable to the American space shuttle, the eleven member nations of the European Space Agency and the fifty shareholders of Arianespace are shooting for a 25 percent share of space missions by 1990. (The major investors in Arianespace are: France's space agency, 34 percent; French companies, 25 percent; and German firms, 20 percent.)

Japan's Space Activities Commission oversees that nation's various space programs, with a budget only about one-tenth the size of NASA's. The National Space Development Agency now serves only domestic needs, but its satellites are generally acknowledged to be first-rate. Japan will no doubt emerge as a competitor for commercial launches around 1990, with the ability to boost multi-ton space platforms into orbit. In the late 1990s, Japan may commence independent manned space-flight operations.

From now to the year 2000, about 500 satellites—for communications, navigation, weather, resource sensing, and surveillance activities—will be lifted into orbit. This will take an estimated $50 billion worth of launching hardware, both expendable and reusable. However, notwithstanding today's heavy demand for space missions, the need for civilian communications satellites could decline in the late 1990s because of the burgeoning capacity of fiber optic telecom systems here on earth. Whether the growing interest in zero-gravity manufacturing will take up that slack remains to be seen. But for the next ten years, there should be no reason for NASA to whittle back plans to increase the number of shuttle missions to roughly one per month.

For small payloads, NASA and Arianespace may even get some competition from the private sector: Two totally unsubsidized ventures, Ortag of West Germany and Space Services in Texas, hope that a tight-belt, small-company approach will provide space launching services for budget-conscious customers. Ortag is having problems, though, because its launch-test sites are in politically unstable areas in Africa. Space Services hopes to begin commercial service in the near future.

GIVING A BOOST TO SMOKESTACK AMERICA

To help justify its huge, $7 billion budget, NASA has been trying for years to foster commercial spin-offs of technology developed for the space program. One of the agency's goals is to be "a leader in the development and application of advanced technology and management practices" that contribute to significant increases in U.S. productivity. But so far the results have been meager. It's not that good technology isn't available, but companies have been reluctant to pick up NASA technology and use it for commercial products because the basic technology is public property. They had no way to protect an application from me-too copycats.

Recently, though, NASA hit upon an idea that will have sweeping effects on the entire manufacturing community: The space agency will spearhead the drive to bring computer-integrated manufacturing, or CIM, to full fruition.

The thrust of CIM is to link together the "islands of automation" that exist in the most progressive companies, creating a comprehensive approach to manufacturing that embraces everything from the original conception of a new product through design, development, production, distribution and marketing, to customer support and field maintenance.

Today, each of these activities is automated to some extent, but the data bases used are incompatible. For example, the text and graphics information in a computer-aided design (CAD) system cannot be transferred to a computer-aided manufacturing (CAM) system. Nor are either of these data bases understandable to the computer used by the purchasing or marketing departments. So what happens, typically, is that CAD data on a new product are printed out, hand carried to a CAM operator who laboriously translates everything into the codes and conventions of his or her system, then retypes this data into the computer. Needless to say, the duplication of effort and inevitable errors are quite costly. At one company, systems designers spent 60 percent of their time reconciling data bases.

NASA, concerned about launching its manned space station by 1992 while staying within the project's $8 billion budget, wants to eradicate that waste and foster development of standards that will enable the same data to be shared among all types of computer-based systems. To gauge the feasibility of such an effort, NASA asked the National Research Council, an arm of the National Academy of Sciences and the National Academy of Engineering, to investigate the current status of CIM and propose measures that NASA could sponsor to further advance the technology. The result was a study—*Computer Integration of Engineering Design and Production: A National Opportunity*—that is must reading for the entire manufacturing community, not just the aerospace industry.

The study team concentrated on CIM efforts at five companies of diverse size and style, making a variety of products: Deere, General Motors, Ingersol Milling Machine, McDonnell Douglas Aircraft, and Westinghouse Defense & Electronics. It soon became clear why progress in CIM has come so slowly. Not only is the task of integrating CAD and CAM difficult and costly, but the benefits are so pervasive that they are tough to assess by traditional accounting methods. The most important payoffs come not in terms of labor reductions or enhanced productivity—although both certainly result—but in better quality, flexibility, responsiveness, and design excellence.

In fact, not one of the companies studied cited return on investment as an important factor in deciding to work toward integrating CAD and CAM. The main motivator among all five companies was a fear that they would lose market share to foreign competition. All of the managements recognized that if they waited until their share began slipping, it would be too late to respond by improving manufacturing technology. The process simply takes too long. All five have made substantial progress already, yet not one expects to be finished, to achieve full CIM, for at least five more years.

Still, an impressive record of achievement has been attained already:

BENEFIT	PERCENT
Lead-time reduction	30–60
Improved product quality	300–600
Increased overall productivity	40–70
Gains in utilizing capital equipment	300–400
Work-in-progress reduction	30–60
Design cost reduction	15–30
Personnel cost reduction	5–20

Further gains are on the horizon, thanks to work on artificial intelligence systems that should also have wide utility outside the aerospace industry. For example, Lockheed-Georgia is perfecting an AI expert system called Genplan, for generative process planning. It helps manufacturing engineers formulate comprehensive production plans. Genplan contains rules for making so-called detail parts and a knowledge base with various specifications. Automating the process planning task, says Joseph Tulkoff, director of manufacturing technology, has drastically upgraded quality by virtually eliminating inaccuracies while slashing the lead time between design and production. In a CIM environment where Genplan has direct access to the company's engineering data base, Lockheed-Georgia expects an enhanced version of the system to process engineering design data without human intervention and forward appropriate instructions directly to numerically controlled machine tools and flexible manufacturing systems.

Several expert systems are being developed by Northrop Corporation, including five aimed at sheet-metal manufacturing. Boeing is working on computer experts to help select the best plastic for a given reinforced-composite application; another expert system identifies what type of rivet, bolt, or other fastener would be most cost effective.

The National Research Council study recommends that NASA adopt CIM, develop the necessary standards—in data definition, formats, languages, and communications protocols—to enable all brands of computers to share the same data, and then help spread the technology among all contractors involved in the manned space station. The NRC study team points out that the Apollo and space shuttle programs show how effective NASA can be at diffusing new technology into industry.

Because integration will be so expensive, even with NASA funding part of the bill, the study team recommends that contractors form research co-ops to share the costs. Only the very largest corporations have the resources to go it alone, the study notes; yet without CIM the vast majority of American manufacturers won't remain competitive in product quality, response time, or production costs. If these proposals are adopted, the aerospace industry will become the trailblazer for America's manufacturers.

Based on findings by Harbor Research, a Boston consulting firm specializing in manufacturing technology, progressive manufacturers in other industries would readily follow NASA's lead. Harbor president Glen Allmendinger says "forward-thinking" companies are making major investments in automation, on a scale that cannot be supported by traditional ROI formulas, because management has come to realize that CIM has many hidden justifications which outweigh the more apparent ones.

Unless someone takes the lead, another recent report—*Factories of the Future: Defining the Target*—funded by the National Science Foundation and published by the Computer Integrated Design, Manufacturing and Automation Center at Purdue University, warns that "it is no exaggeration to say that the American way of life is at risk."

The health of the entire U.S. economy relies upon manufacturing, stresses James J. Solberg, the Purdue University professor who headed the NSF study team. Manufacturing produces 85 percent of the country's physical wealth, he adds, and directly or indirectly creates many service jobs as well.

"There are two possible scenarios," says Professor Solberg. "One is that there will be no manufacturing in the United States in about ten years—and that's the direction we're going in now," with so much manufacturing moving offshore. "Each company may need to do that in its own self-interest," he concedes, "but the collective impact is pretty serious for the country as a whole."

The other scenario requires that the country make whatever technological breakthroughs are needed to save manufacturing. The ultimate objective would be CIM factories where it is economical to make products in runs of just single units, "where you can innovate a new product today and deliver it tomorrow."

If that occurs, the results might go far beyond simply rescuing American manufacturing. It could very well vault the United States ahead of Japan and restore many lost markets. The reason is that Japan has made tremendous investments in mass production, and replacing those investments with small-lot production facilities would be economically difficult and require massive retraining of the work force—plus a radical reorientation in management philosophy. The latter would be inordinately trying. Japan's culturally bound management style rewards seniority, not creativity, which would put Japanese manufacturers at a severe disadvantage in a market where overnight innovation would be the norm.

Will CIM Save Detroit?

THE AUTOMOBILE'S FUTURE.   Computer-integrated manufacturing is America's best hope for keeping a domestic automotive production capability in the twenty-first century—but only if CIM happens in a big way within the next five years. The odds that this will happen soon enough, pervasively enough are, frankly, only about 50-50. Otherwise, look for essentially all production to have shifted to foreign plants in low-wage-rate countries by the turn of the century, certainly by 2015.

Even Japan's auto makers will be forced to make similar moves, and the next century's auto industry will consolidate more and more in three locales: the Asian mainland (Korea, perhaps supplanted by China in the distant future), Europe (probably Italy), and Latin America (Mexico and Brazil being the two most likely candidates).

Each region will be dominated by one or, at most, two giant offshoots of the present surge in cross-investments. With almost everybody buying pieces of other companies, the industry is already well on its way to becoming one vast interlocking cartel. By 2005, a few nameplates are all that will be left of Chrysler's U.S. operations, and the U.S. assets of Ford also will be well along the road to absorption or liquidation. General Motors will remain the world's leading car maker, reigning supreme in the Americas, with a 25 percent stake in Europe's major auto company and a 35 percent interest in the leading Asian producer; conversely, GM will be 40 percent or 45 percent foreign owned.

On the other hand, if CIM does take hold and preserve the competitiveness of American manufacturing, GM will no doubt deserve much of the credit. The auto king is mounting the industry's most vigorous integration campaign, investing billions to establish its Manufacturing Automation Protocol (MAP) as a CIM standard. The company will demand that its suppliers adopt the concept, and GM hopes that MAP will spread to the rest of the auto industry and even beyond.

But MAP could turn out to be a mixed blessing at best, says Professor Solberg. While he grants that GM has to do something to "sort out a mess," he insists that it's too early to cast MAP in concrete as *the* manufacturing standard. GM's approach to CIM is too narrow and too much of a stopgap measure. If GM does foist MAP on the entire auto industry—which is to say approximately 10 percent of U.S. manufacturing plants—Solberg worries that "it may inhibit the kind of innovation that's really needed."

Whichever way the CIM matter goes, the United States will continue to be the largest market (Americans now buy one-third of the world's production). And it's safe to predict that twenty-first-century cars will be made primarily from petrochemicals rather than steel, for several reasons: Plastics are lighter and hence will improve fuel economy, it's easier to automate the production of plastic parts, and they don't rust. The average car now lasts nearly eight years; by 2000 you can expect a new car to be on the road for twenty years. The prototype is GM's new Spartan venture.

Where tomorrow's cars will be built is of vital importance. Today, making autos is the backbone of this country's business fabric. The auto industry directly or indirectly supports one of every six Americans working in the private sector. For every $1 million worth of car production, fifty jobs are created—fifteen in the auto industry and more than double that number at independent contractors, suppliers, and myriad other firms and service organizations that cater to the independent suppliers and their employees.

Only yesterday, it seems, U.S. auto makers dominated the world's output of motor vehicles. In 1950 nearly 80 percent of all motor vehicles were produced in the United States. In 1960 America's share still approached 50 percent, and Japan was way back with a measley 3 percent, just 500,000 cars and trucks.

Then came 1980. Detroit turned out 8 million vehicles, the same number as in 1960. But Japan's output multiplied twenty-three-fold, to 11.3 million units. It was the first time any nation had outproduced America since 1903, when France did it, 13,000 vehicles to 11,200 for the United States.

Two other dubious records were notched in 1980: For the first time, imports took more than one-quarter of the U.S. market—at a cost of some 400,000 domestic jobs, 125,000 in the auto industry and the rest in fields ranging from steel and machine tools to printing and tree harvesting. In addition, a single U.S. industry posted a loss of more than $4.2 billion. The flood of red ink was partly due to unprecedented investments in capital equipment—$11.2 billion, which was hiked to $12.3 billion in 1981—or more than twice the spending in any previous year. Cumulatively, spending from 1978 through 1985 will come to a stupifying $65 billion. Servicing that debt will put heavy burdens on profits for years to come, especially since the industry will also need to maintain a reduced level of investment, restore stockholder dividends, and rebuild working capital. So the upswing in sales in 1983 and 1984 by no means signals a return to prosperity.

TOWARD CHEAPER PRODUCTION. In reaction to the Japanese challenge, says Roger B. Smith, chairman of General Motors, "We took our industry apart and put it back together again." The auto makers' wrenching metamorphosis is perhaps the most profound shift of human, capital, and technological resources that any industry has endured during peace time, notes Ralph Landau, vice president of the National Academy of Engineering and consulting professor of economics at Stanford University. Detroit laid off 40,000 managers plus a quarter-million union workers, squeezed suppliers for millions of dollars in concessions, canceled or delayed over a dozen new products, and closed enough plant space to house a small city. All told, the Big Three chopped more than $10 billion off their annual overhead costs. The industry that has emerged can break even on one-third fewer sales.

The next challenge is cutting production costs. It will be rough to pare costs down enough to offset the $1,500 per-car cost advantage that Japanese imports now enjoy. The single biggest factor mitigating against the United States stems from the success of the United Auto Workers in pushing U.S. wage rates so far above those of foreign rivals—to the point where no near-term change in technology or management practice can fully compensate.

The futility of just throwing more microchips and robots at the situation is highlighted by this datum: $1,500 was two-thirds of GM's average per-vehicle labor cost in 1982, when production was at 60 percent of capacity. Consequently, to achieve cost parity with Japan through automation alone would take huge investments beyond the money already spent and committed. But that may not be necessary. A close look at the Japanese auto industry reveals that despite its use of advanced robotic assembly, it is less automated than many U.S. auto plants.

In search of the magic ingredients in Japan's success, the car companies are borrowing pages from Japan's management manual. Gone are the minions of assembly-line workers who once were Detroit's hallmark, mechanically repeating the same narrow task in an alloted period of time as partly finished cars trundled by. To make the work interesting, job definitions have been expanded so workers can share various jobs within a work "module." In addition, decision making has been pushed down to lower levels, so decisions are quickly translated into practice. Roger Smith told the *Wall Street Journal* that people now have "a very exciting sense that they are participating—and that what they do really matters." This sense of personal worth is an essential precursor to improving the quality of American cars by boosting the pride that workers take in their jobs. Poor quality is a needless drain on resources that can add an astonishing 15 to 25 percent to the cost of doing business.

Another cost-saving tactic is "just-in-time" delivery, an adaptation of Toyota's *kanban* methodology for expunging the hidden costs of excessive inventories and work-in-progress defects. Under JIT, the auto makers rely on suppliers to deliver small batches of high-quality parts and subassemblies on some prescribed schedule—every couple of hours or every shift, just in time to avoid a shortage on the shop floor. "Buick City," a new manufacturing complex near Detroit where the assembly plant is surrounded by JIT suppliers, will be GM's test of the extent to which the Toyota example can be emulated in this country.

In a related trend, the auto makers are forging computer linkups with their principal suppliers to reduce lead times. Ultimately, design data will be fed directly to a supplier's numerically controlled tools. "We have an aggressive program to bring our suppliers into more of a partnership relationship," says Paul Guy, director of Ford's Manufacturing Engineering and Systems Office. Ford wants its suppliers to feel like they are an extension of the company's own manufacturing operations. "This means linking them electronically with many of our engineering systems," adds Guy, "so they can communicate with us quicker and more accurately than the old [way] of shipping bundles of blueprints back and forth, which introduced all kinds of opportunities for error, misunderstanding, and miscommunication."

Although European auto markets are under substantially less pressure from Japanese imports—most governments have imposed quotas to limit Japan's total market share to 10 percent or less—car makers there now face the trauma of reallocating resources. The European industry figures that, to be viable internationally, it needs to spend $85 billion from 1984 to 1988 to modernize and automate its plants.

And the big crunch will come when the companies try to trim the work force. It's not unusual for mandatory severance payments to come to a year's wages or more, plus retraining expenses; the cost is so dear that companies will do almost anything to avoid laying off workers, including postponing needed capital investments. But the time is fast approaching when European auto companies will have to bite the bullet.

In France, for example, Peugeot would like to cut its domestic work force drastically, by 6,000 jobs. But economic realities have so far limited job reductions to its foreign operations. In Spain, Peugeot's Talbot division cut its payroll by 9,000 workers, or 60 percent, and its British subsidiary slashed 20,000 jobs, fully 78 percent of the payroll. In France itself, the first cuts will likely fall on the ranks of immigrant workers from Algeria, because Peugeot's financial liabilities will be relatively modest: a stipend to cover each worker's cost of returning home.

With the handwriting on the wall, the labor climate throughout Europe has grown testy. Last year, workers struck I. B. Metall, Germany's major parts supplier to the auto industry, demanding a thirty-five-hour week. They hope the shorter hours will create additional jobs and help offset the coming losses to automation.

The auto maker farthest along in solving its problems is Fiat. It chalked up a profit in 1983, the first black ink in more than four years. That feat can be attributed at least in part to the fact that Fiat is Italy's largest single user of robotic technology. In addition, Fiat got rid of less-profitable ventures, selling its steel plants and backing out of money-losing operations in Argentina, Chile, Uruguay, and the United States. In Europe, Fiat maintained its number one market position, with a 12.8 percent share that kept it a nose ahead of its nearest rival, Renault.

Steel: Less Smoke Up the Stack

Over the long haul, the U.S. steel industry will occupy a position of declining economic importance. Burdened by very high wage rates ($22.50 per hour, including fringes, or more than double those of producers in Japan and Europe, and several times the going rate for such newcomers as South Korea and Brazil), America's steelmakers cannot compete in international markets. And as the production of autos, aircraft, and machine tools migrates to foreign countries—and U.S. manufacturers replace more and more steel with engineering plastics and other alternative materials—domestic demand will fall, so the U.S. steel industry must surely deteriorate.

Thus far in the 1980s annual U.S. steel consumption has averaged 12 to 13 million tons below the 108 million–ton average figure for the 1970s. The down-sizing of autos is a major cause, together with decreased demand from the construction and aerospace industries. In fact, the U.S. economy as a whole will go on becoming less and less steel intensive unless this country reverses the trend of exporting manufacturing jobs and relying increasingly on services and high tech. For thirty years steel consumption as a percentage of gross national product has been steadily slipping by 2 percent a year, on average, and for nearly a decade the erosion has been running at double that rate.

Now that the reformation in car size is nearly complete and the economy is on the upswing again, there will be a brief respite from the gradual decline in steel demand. U.S. consumption should edge above 100 million tons in the late 1980s, and domestic steel companies could chart a 10 percent or even a 15 percent rise in production from the current 83 million–ton level. But the downward trend will return by 1990 or shortly thereafter and continue for the foreseeable future. The impact on industry employment, which has plunged 40 percent since the onset of the latest recession in 1980 and shows no signs of rising during the present recovery, will be still more severe as American steelmakers strive to improve productivity and trim costs.

Hit by the recession and competition from U.S. minimills and foreign producers, steelworker employment in northeastern Ohio plummeted a wrenching 43 percent, to 27,000 from 47,400, between 1980 and 1983. Once the rolling Monongahela Valley east of Pittsburgh was choked with smoke from dozens of plants that lined the river. U.S. Steel's six plants employed 50,000 workers during World War II; just six years ago there were 30,000 workers. Now this formerly thriving industrial pocket has about 9,000 union hands. The sign that greets visitors to Homestead, Pennsylvania—"Steel Center of the World"— is as rusty as the town's shuttered plant.

Overall, membership in the United Steelworkers of America has fallen 25 percent from 1.25 million in 1979, and only 750,000 of those members employed. The union was runner-up to the Teamsters as America's largest union a decade ago. Now it trails in fourth place.

This dire picture has parallels in western Europe. The Lorraine region is France's Monongahela Valley. The grimy towns along the Moselle River north of Metz were "the cradle of steel," producing 44 percent of France's iron and almost as much steel. Now Lorraine's plants have been upstaged by more modern French mills built on the seacoasts. The French steel industry lost $1.25 billion in 1983. The government plans to economize by eliminating 20,000 or more of the industry's 90,000 jobs by 1987 and cutting output by 23 percent, to 18.5 metric tons. The Mitterand government has established a fund to encourage new industries to move into Lorraine.

Germany's Monongahela is the Ruhr River valley, where post–World War II mills have been hard hit by the decline in steel orders. Unemployment is rampant, and the typical German steelworker now clocks only 1,773 hours a year, compared to 1,900 hours in the United States and 2,100 in Japan.

Even Japan is feeling the pinch—from Korea. In 1983 Korea's output of crude steel was 12 million metric tons, of which virtually half was exported. The United States took 29 percent of Korea's exports, while Japan accounted for 25 percent. A decade ago, most Korean steel was made from scrap in electric arc furnaces. Then the government set up Pohan Iron & Steel Co. (Posco), the country's first integrated steel mill, using Japanese technology and Japanese financing. Posco produces about two-thirds of Korea's steel, utilizing the latest continuous-casting technology.

Japan figures there's no point in beating a dead horse. Steel is now deemed a sunset industry, and the country is cutting back on capacity and shedding 2,400 jobs to concentrate on fewer but bigger and more modern plants. Nippon Steel, for example, is the world's biggest producer, accounting for a third of Japan's output. Fujitsu recently installed a factory automation system at Kawasaki Steel's Chiba Works to automate such tasks as quality control, inventory control, and billing and shipping. The Fujitsu system is engineered around three large mainframe computers and hundreds of terminals linked together by a fiber optics local-area network.

The European Economic Community also takes the view that steel should be allowed to migrate to lower-cost countries. But the hard-pressed members of the EEC are loathe to lose the jobs involved, even if it means absorbing part of the industry's losses. In 1982 the Commerce Department ruled that some European governments, as well as those of Brazil and South Africa, had been unfairly subsidizing steel exports to the United States. Nationalized British Steel, for instance, in 1981 was subsidized to the tune of 40 percent of the average price it charged in the United States.

When the United States applied restrictive duties on Brazilian steel in 1984, Brazilian officials accused Reagan of protectionism—discriminating against foreign steel to protect against further job losses in the depressed U.S. steel industry in an election year. Brazil's commerce and industry minister retorted that if the United States doesn't buy a certain amount of Brazilian steel, U.S. creditors won't get paid, since Brazil must sell steel to help pay its debts. American banks hold about one-third of Brazil's $100 billion foreign debt.

STILL ROOM FOR NEW IDEAS.   The steel business here is also consolidating. National Steel didn't innovate, automate, or emigrate, so it evaporated. It sold its tinplate plant in Weirton, West Virginia, to the employees, and its steel operations to U.S. Steel. Phoenix Steel filed for chapter eleven protection, and Connors Steel was closed down by its parent company. "It's a world economy," says management consultant Peter Drucker. "The Mexicans can make steel and the Japanese can make cars. We have to automate industry or lose it."

Inland Steel has clipped its main product lines to just four in order to minimize the costs of updating its technology. The company has purchased two continuous casters—from Hitachi Zosen of Japan and Mannesmann Demag of West Germany—and has also added a continuous-annealing line to turn out new types of high-strength automotive steels. Now the company is building another cold-rolling mill patterned on Nippon Steel's state-of-the-art Hirohata Works. Amrco Steel dropped the word "steel" from its name and quietly exited the industry.

U.S. Steel chairman David Roderick, explaining his diversification moves, has said that "we are not in business to make steel, we are in business to make money.'' In 1980, nearly half of U.S. Steel's assets were in nonsteel areas—and that was before it bought Marathon Oil for $6.2 billion. By 1983 more than half of U.S. Steel's revenues came from oil and gas, and the company announced that it is getting rid of 15,400 steelworkers.

Yet the American steel industry isn't rolling over just yet. ''Imagination is the ingredient that can reinvigorate American steel,'' declares LTV Corporation's chairman, Raymond A. Hay. LTV's Jones & Laughlin Steel has joined forces with Republic Steel, the biggest merger in steel industry history, to form LTV Steel, the nation's number two producer, marginally smaller than U.S. Steel. Hay believes that by reevaluating the fundamentals—ignoring the old business precepts and emphasizing efficiencies and advanced technology—LTV Steel can cut costs and improve productivity enough to compete with overseas rivals.

Surprisingly, the steel industry still has entrepreneurs. Four executives frustrated in their positions at large steelmakers have resigned and purchased a mill of their own. G. Watts Humphrey, Jr., grandson of National Steel's founder, and Edwin Gott, Jr., son of a former U.S. Steel chairman, joined with two other partners to form Metaltech. It will produce zinc-coated (galvanized) steel sheets to tap the burgeoning demand for rust-resistant metal. Its nonunion workers are encouraged to participate in decision making and broadening work roles, and they receive an annual salary plus an incentive tied to the company's overall financial performance.

Ministeel plants are another imaginative way to compete in today's markets. Minimills have captured 20 percent of U.S. steel shipments and their share should rise to 35 percent by 2000. Nucor is an example of how successful the ministeel companies can be. When F. Kenneth Iverson took over Nucor in 1965, it was a small and battered miniconglomerate. But Iverson soon transformed Nucor into a successful, $540 million enterprise. While the company is a mere tenth the size of U.S. Steel in revenues, Nucor is a possible guide for the future of the steel business.

The turnabout Iverson engineered was based on three strategies: First, he avoided the huge capital investment needed for an iron-ore furnace by using steel scrap as his raw material; it can be melted in small electric-arc furnaces. Second, he focused on a few specialty markets and exploited the newest continuous-casting and automation techniques. Third, he structured the company so employees determine their own pay through an incentive arrangement designed to assure maximum productivity: Workers receive low wages, but they can double or triple their take-home paychecks through incentive bonuses. Iverson enthusiastically competes head-on with the Japanese and other foreign steelmakers. And he routinely undercuts them.

So the United States needn't fear being denuded of a steel industry—and with any luck it will be a livelier, more responsive, albeit smaller one. The jobs that have gone to Korea and Brazil won't ever come back.

Robot Tailors Are Coming
The fiber-textile-apparel industry is coming full circle. Once again, it is applying advanced technology to traditionally labor-intensive jobs—"again" because the very first use of IBM punch cards, a century before there was an IBM, was for controlling looms. Now that heritage is finally moving "downstream" to the apparel business, the largest and most labor-intensive segment of the industry. Computer-controlled lasers are already cutting cloth patterns, and soon a robot sewer will be helping to stitch together suit jackets.

The Charles Stark Draper Laboratories in Cambridge, Massachusetts—which designs guidance systems for missiles—has developed a much more plebian guidance system: an artificial vision system for robotic sewing machines. This sewing robit, expected to clock in on its first job in 1986, will be able to fold and sew pieces of limp fabric to make the sleeves and the backs of suit coats, as well as vests, with a speed and precision that few human workers could manage.

Murray Finey, president of the Amalgamated Clothing and Textile Workers Union, told the *Washington Post*, "If that happens, we'll have 15 to 20 percent less people. But if it enables us to become more competitive, we could make up that loss in jobs. If we don't do it," he adds, "I'm convinced we'll lose the jobs anyway." Mauro Defazio, an ACTWU manager in eastern Pennsylvania, shares that conviction after watching seven apparel companies shut down in recent years. "If we don't start competing," he declares, "we won't have an industry."

Development of the robot sewing system was funded by a cooperative research venture involving apparel and textile companies, the ACTWU, and the Commerce Department, and was set in motion by John T. Dunlop, a Harvard University professor and former secretary of labor. "We're still at the beginning stages," he notes, "but there has come to be an enormous interest and support from industry. You have the private sector, labor, and government working on a major problem, bringing in a private lab, and paving the way for the introduction of new technology in the workplace. It's a policy for modernization of the industry."

The ultimate result of this beginning will be robot tailors. In the twenty-first century, the local dry cleaner will have a fully automated clothes-making system that turns out customized dresses and suits while you wait. After picking a fabric and the styling features you prefer, you'll step into a measurement booth, about the size of a phone booth, and sophisticated computer sensors will precisely map the contours of your body. These data will be used by robots that cut the fabric, "drape" it on an imaginary mathematical model of your body, then seam and stitch the garment to produce a perfect fit.

That will cap a revolution even more profound than the one the Luddites challenged a century ago. And like back then, the industry has little choice.

Today, the $103 billion fiber-textile-apparel complex is the biggest industrial employer in the United States. More than 10 percent of all American workers in manufacturing, including a disproportionately large number of women and minorities, are employed in some phase of making cloth or clothes at 27,000 companies—at least one in every state. Textile mills tend to congregate in the Carolinas and Georgia, while the majority of apparel houses are in New York, New Jersey, Pennsylvania, and California.

But these plants are caught in a squeeze. From one side, developing nations are rapidly expanding fabric and apparel production, because it is so easy to enter these downstream segments of the business. Production machinery—such as looms and knitters that are extremely simple to operate—comes mainly from a few European suppliers. As a result, new technology becomes available to all nations at the same time and at the same cost. In contrast, U.S. rug companies developed proprietary tufting processes for making carpets and consequently have been able to hold onto leadership in this market.

Pinching from the top side, demand for synthetic fibers has peaked. The United States is the leading producer of synthetic fibers, accounting for about one-fourth of the world's total production. During the glory decade of the 1970s, shipments of man-made fibers doubled. Since 1979, however, domestic production has declined. And imports have been increasing at double the rate of exports.

International competition is keenest in apparel. America's share of world production is declining steadily in most product lines, giving ground primarily to companies in Asia and eastern Europe. In the last half of the 1970s, the value of apparel imports leaped 240 percent, while the value of domestic shipments gained only 50 percent. As a result, the U.S. trade deficit soared thirteenfold, from $623 million in 1968 to $8 billion in 1983. The value of apparel imports now exceeds exports by fifteen times, and in some products the multiple is much higher: 35 to 1 for women's coats, for example.

Harvard professor Elisabeth Allison studied the competition in clothing and found that in 1965 the wardrobe of the average American male was almost 100 percent U.S.-made. But by 1976, nearly one-third of his shirts and sportcoats, and 28 percent of his trousers, came from overseas. During the same period, employment in the U.S. apparel industry fell by 25 percent. Professor Allison estimates that half of all men's clothing will be foreign-made by 1987.

New technology, preferably proprietary, offers virtually the only hope of arresting this trend. One reason why Levi Strauss has been able to grow into a $3 billion operation is that it constantly searches for better and cheaper production methods. For example, the company developed a $9,000 machine that seams the leg bottoms of jeans—and pays for itself in two to five years. Levi Strauss spent $5.5 million on R&D in 1983, and president Peter Thigpen says he expects that investment to generate savings worth $7 million.

In fabric production, research in new yarn-spinning techniques holds promise for increasing productivity. The most impressive gains, though, are being posted by the rapidly emerging nonwoven sector. Nonwoven fabrics are made by what might be called the Jackson Pollock technique: Drippings of synthetic fiber (not paint) are randomly laid down in layers until a solid sheet of the desired thickness is achieved. The output of nonwoven production lines typically runs 10,000 feet per minute, in widths of 15 feet or more. That compares to 5 feet per minute for knitting looms and even slower rates for weaving machines. Nonwoven materials are used for such things as disposable diapers, furniture fabrics, wall coverings, luggage, disposable medical gowns and surgical drapes, and household and industrial wipes.

Much more automation and innovation will be essential to blunt the surge in foreign competition. Unfortunately, relatively few apparel firms are big enough to afford such capital-intensive gadgets, let alone the R&D investment that has to be committed up front, so the U.S. industry is bound to suffer attrition. Even if a way were found to rescue small companies with the needed capital, jobs would still be lost to automation, though probably not so rapidly. Either way, employment in the textile business is going to suffer.

John A. Young, president of Hewlett-Packard, has said there's only one way that American manufacturing workers can continue to enjoy the high standard of living to which they've grown accustomed: They must be equipped and continually reequipped with advanced tools that enhance productivity and make the workers worth what they are paid.

3

WHAT FUTURE WILL WE BIOENGINEER?

THE NEW BIOTECHNOLOGIES

Science is now mounting its most audacious assault ever attempted on the gods of Mount Olympus: a quest for the key to life itself. Scientists can now extract genes from the heart of a living cell, pull them apart to alter or add genetic information, then put them back into the cell. Since genes hold the blueprints of life—determining such fundamental characteristics as eye and hair and skin color, influencing longevity, personality traits, level of intelligence, and susceptibility to disease— this technology will literally make it possible for people to redesign humankind, to abrogate evolution and tamper with the very core of existence. Beside this technological revolution, even the development of the computer will seem pale stuff.

Through genetic engineering techniques, scientists have already created new life forms, such as a virus that consumes spilled oil; even the Supreme Court recognized the uniqueness of this achievement and decreed that it could be patented. Gene splicing promises a new green revolution: plants that make their own fertilizer, crops that grow in seawater, corn and tomatoes that ripen faster and resist disease and insects. Under development are hormones that will cause pigs and chickens to grow fatter faster, cows to grow much larger and give much more milk.

Gene-splicing methods are coaxing viruses implanted with human genes to manufacture human insulin. This form of insulin is safer and more effective than the animal-derived insulin that diabetics formerly had to use. Other strains of viruses have been developed to produce a human growth hormone and a clotting factor, secreting these precious substances in sufficient quantities so that widespread treatment of dwarfism and hemophilia is possible and affordable.

Most spectacular of all, genetic engineering promises a whole arsenal of "magic bullet" cures and vaccines that will vanquish most of humankind's age-old scourges. With these new wonder drugs, influenza and other viral infections, tooth decay, arthritis, emphysema, cancer, and even the process of aging itself will be treatable. Whole new classes of drugs will come into general use. Therapy will be designed around immunomodulators, natural substances that maintain proper functioning of the body's immune system. Neurotransmitters, chemicals that transmit nerve-cell impulses, may control and perhaps even correct afflictions caused by deterioration of or chemical imbalances in the nervous system—such as Parkinson's disease, senility, amyotrophic lateral sclerosis, Huntington's disease, and some types of schizophrenia. And mood-altering drugs may be helpful in relieving pain or depression.

Since 1980, interferon—a protein produced by cells that are fighting a viral infection—has been in clinical tests and shows great potential in combating the common cold and a host of other viral diseases. Previously, this substance was available in only infinitesimal quantities at enormous cost. As science learns more about the microchemistry of the body's immune system, similar substances will be synthesized for treating herpes infections and AIDS (acquired immune-deficiency syndrome).

Exciting progress is finally being made against cancer. Researchers have recently found a half-dozen genes—a new class called oncongenes—implicated in such common malignancies as lung, intestinal, and bladder cancer. The discovery could lead to vaccines or drugs that attack cancerous cells. "There's no doubt about it, this is the biggest single breakthrough in cancer research of all time," says virologist Frank J. Rauscher, Jr., a senior vice president of the American Cancer Society. Centocor, a small gene-splicing start-up, last year raised $15 million for an R&D partnership to explore the anticancer prospects of oncongenes.

The remaining fifteen years of this century will probably bring more improvement in disease prevention and control than any other fifteen years of this century, says Dr. William Foeg, former director of the Centers for Disease Control.

And around the turn of the century, researchers will crack the genetic code that determines how and why the body ages. That will usher in drugs to retard aging. The first antiaging drugs will double the years remaining in one's normal life span, and eventually they will extend average longevity to 150 years, with some people crossing the two-century mark.

Genetic engineering also has applications outside medicine. On the energy front, scientists are splicing together the genes for a bacteria that digests garbage and can be harvested as fuel and petrochemical feed stocks. Another microorganism makes petroleum from nothing more than sunlight and airborne carbon dioxide; genetic engineers hope to increase its efficiency to the point where the "bugs" can supply the world with oil when crude oil reserves are exhausted.

Genex Corporation has developed a drain unclogger based on a gene-spliced enzyme that gobbles up hair. Researchers say there's no reason why other strains couldn't thrive on toxic wastes such as dioxin or PCBs, reducing these into their harmless elements. Bacteria are being designed to help refine ores and to purge sulfur from coal. Another bacterium, which catalyzes the formation of frost at slightly higher than normal temperatures, is being marketed by Advanced Genetic Sciences to help protect citrus crops and to produce snow on ski slopes.

Tote up all the business potentials and some market researchers peg the cumulative worldwide market between now and 2000 at $40 billion. Anticancer drugs alone will quickly climb to $2 billion, maybe even $4 billion, a year in the late 1990s.

Filling Thirteen Encyclopedias

Ever since James Watson and Francis Crick unlocked the secret of DNA's double helix three decades ago, bioscientists have been engaged in a frenzy of discovery. It has been just a dozen years since Paul Berg of Stanford University astounded the scientific world by splicing genes, earning the Nobel prize. Dr. Leroy E. Hood of the California Institute of Technology says that "we're doing things we would have thought impossible five years ago." In fact, the painstaking process of recombinant DNA—extracting the deoxyribonucleic acid and breaking it down so new material can be inserted before the DNA is recombined—is now done by technicians using automated "gene machines." Cloning has become "sort of boring," says David W. Martin, Jr., research vice president at Genentech, Inc., a pioneer in the new field of biotechnology.

Yet researchers have barely scratched the surface. "We're just beginning to learn the rules" for reading DNA, observes Kevin M. Ulmer, a scientist at Genex. "We are still reading at a 'See Spot run' level. We won't be truly creative until we are fluent. And that is still an arduous task." It's easy to understand why. Dr. Victor A. McKusick, director of medicine at John Hopkins, draws this comparison: If a gene's four building blocks, called nucleotides, were each a letter, and each gene were a word, the genetic contents of a human cell would fill thirteen sets of the *Encyclopaedia Britannica*.

The DNA that genes carry is neatly packaged in forty-six chromosomes within the nucleus of each human cell. Scientists are now busy "mapping" the location of various DNA sequences. So far, more than 1,700 genes, most of which can produce disease, have been mapped. "Mapping places genetics on a firm ground for diagnosis and therapy," says Dr. McKusick. Scientists believe that his information is the key to finding cures for such genetic disorders as sickle-cell anemia, Huntington's disease, and chlamydia—a little-known but widespread disease that can cause infertility in women.

Geneticists predict that by 1990 the genes responsible for most congenital disorders will have been identified, and DNA probes for precisely diagnosing these afflictions will be available. Eventually, counselors will be able to provide a complete "genetic profile" of a person's susceptibility to disease so that preventive measures can be taken before a disease is contracted. Already, about 600 centers in the United States offer some form of genetic counseling.

Once this knowledge is codified and assimilated, our ability to play God will be essentially boundless. "We are going to have genetically engineered people," predicts John H. Kreisher, president of International Biotechnologies. Futurists such as Joel de Rosnay foresee the creation of gene libraries and computerized equipment that manipulates the contents of genetic encyclopedias with all the facility of a modern word-processing system that deals with English text.

The Business of Biotechnology

Obviously, a whale of a lot of money is going to be made in the process of transforming bioscience and biotechnology into commercial products and services. In fact, by 1990 the revenue stream from genetically engineered medicines will easily top $1 billion a year in the United States. And during the 1990s the biotech business is going to be bigger than the entire chemical industry has been for the past ten years. Which explains why venture capitalists, private investors, and established corporations have been falling over themselves, rushing to put up more than $2.5 billion to nurture some 200 start-up ventures in biotechnology.

When Genentech went public in late 1980, its stock rocketed from $35 to $89 in the space of just twenty minutes—Wall Street's fastest price rise ever. Early in 1981, Cetus offered its first shares to the public and investors eagerly plunked down $107 million, then the fattest initial stock offering in the annals of corporate America.

Genentech has used gene splicing to develop a variety of products, including human insulin, human growth hormone, and human interferon, and it is working on products for industry and agriculture. In 1984 the start-up marketed its first commercial recombinant product—a vaccine against pig disease—and launched clinical tests of interferon and t-PA, a substance that dissolves blood clots in the arteries of people suffering from heart disease or at risk of a heart attack. President Robert A. Swanson and university scientist Herbert W. Boyer put up $500 each to form the company in 1976. Genentech had 1983 sales of almost $50 million.

Biogen, formed in 1979 (with headquarters split between Cambridge, Massachusetts, and Geneva, Switzerland), got a lucrative contract from SmithKline Beckman Corporation in 1984 to develop an anticlotting agent. In Europe, Biogen is testing alpha-type interferon for treating several kinds of cancer and hopes to win FDA approval to test and then market the drug here. In June 1984 the company began tests of recombinant interleukin-2 on AIDS patients. These are the first such human tests in Europe. And late in 1984, Biogen licensed Wellcome Foundation Ltd. to market its hepatitis-B vaccine in major world markets. The vaccine has been tested successfully with chipanzees, and Wellcome plans to begin human clinical trials in 1985.

In the future, gene splicers say that new insights into the body's immune system and of the incredible complexity of body chemistry at the inter- and intracellular levels will lead to innovative pharmaceuticals. Once the details of these interactions are understood, concoctions such as monoclonal antibodies can be prepared. So far, however, of the 50,000 proteins that any human cell can produce to fight antigens, only about 100 have been cloned.

The "monoclonal" preface comes from the fact that gene-splicing techniques yield antibodies that are pure, single-purpose substances— magnificently well designed to destroy a particular virus, protozoa, or other invading cell. That's in contrast to older antibodies, which are derived by infecting rabbits, mice, goats, or sheep with a mild form of a particular disease and extracting from their blood any new proteins produced by the animals' white blood cells. Not all of the new antibodies in the animals' bloodstream are targeted specifically at the disease in question, so these antibodies are now known as polyclonals. They have "impurities" and may trigger allergic reactions in some people.

The first monoclonal antibody was produced in 1975 by a pair of British scientists who fused a spleen cell that was producing antibodies against a specific antigen with a cancer cell. The hybrid cell continued to produce the same single-minded antibody—and continued to grow and divide like its cancerous parent. Using that technique, monoclonal antibodies are now produced in large quantities against specific microorganisms, even against the malignant cells in children with one type of leukemia.

In the United States, monoclonals are perhaps most widely used as diagnostic tools, since they react to one and only one antigen. Hybritech, Inc. is the oldest (seven years) and biggest ($16 million in 1984 revenues, 300 employees) American company specializing in monoclonal antibodies. Its most publicized product is a pregnancy-test kit, but the San Diego company is also working on cancer treatments. Last year it raised $70 million from a private placement of stock and signed a $1.6 million deal with Baker Instruments, a subsidiary of Richardson-Vicks, to develop new diagnostic tools. Hybritech has other joint-venture agreements with Japanese and German companies, as well. "We've rapidly taken the company to break-even operations," says vice president Ronald Taylor, "and product revenues were one of the main sources."

Yearly sales of monoclonal antibodies—$57 million in 1984, quadruple the 1983 figure—will likely top $1 billion by 1990. By then, 90 percent of all *in vitro* immunological tests will use one or more monoclonal diagnostic aids.

U.S. Drug Industry Needs a Shot in the Arm

Because of all the venture capital that has been pumped into biotech start-ups, the United States is now clearly the world's front-runner in gene splicing. But genetic engineering is far from a U.S. monopoly. Growing competition is coming from both Japan and Europe.

While the United States is counting on start-up companies, most of which have yet to earn a profit, Japan's research is in the hands of some 160 established companies, many with very deep pockets. These firms spent more than $200 million on gene-splicing research in 1983. Since 1980, spending on biotech R&D in Japan has more than doubled and the number of scientists working in this field has quadrupled. In one year (1982) the number of companies doing recombinant-DNA research zoomed from ten to fifty-two. Several Japanese companies, in addition to developing their own products and techniques, have technology-transfer associations with U.S. companies; to gain entry to the Japanese market, fifteen American drug firms regularly pass technology to their Japanese partners in return for royalties on Japanese sales.

Just how serious Japan's intentions are in genetic engineering is pointed up by this fact: Japan has the world's only Department of Molecular Engineering at a major university. It was established in 1983 at Kyoto University. Japan is already recognized as the world leader in certain areas of bioprocessing technology, especially fermentation and enzyme technology. In fact, Japanese companies are the sole source of twenty-one of the twenty-six enzymes that were produced commercially in 1980. Japan's large, integrated companies dominate world markets for synthetic amino acids, and they developed more that 20 percent of all the new antibiotics introduced since 1980.

Japan's remarkable gains trace back to government initiatives in the mid-1970s to prod the Japanese drug industry into more innovation and, coincidentally, curb the rise in the nation's health-care bill—of which drugs then accounted for 40 percent. In 1975 the patent law was revised to discourage drug copying and to reward investments in research. In 1979 the Ministry of Health and Welfare revised the price guidelines for drugs: High prices were permitted for new drugs, while prices for old drugs were cut. This severely handicapped many small Japanese pharmaceutical firms that relied on copycat products, and many have since closed down or been acquired. The result is a stronger, more profitable, more concentrated Japanese drug industry.

The European Economic Community, worried that it may fall behind in biotechnology as badly as it has in microelectronics, wants to spend up to $175 million over the next five years to stimulate research. Part of this money would be used to create a "bioinformatics network" to coordinate the torrent of data pouring in from academic labs, research institutions, and industry. The French are anxious to set up a new domestic drug research center, and the West German Ministry of Technology is plowing more money into basic research in bioengineering. Britain is especially interested in gene-splicing methods of making proteins and monoclonal antibodies.

Unfortunately, there are grave questions about the ability of the United States pharmaceuticals industry to meet this competitive challenge and exploit the opportunities proferred by the bright new world of wonder drugs.

For decades, the United States pharmaceuticals industry has been one of the most successful sectors of the economy. It has consistently expanded output and productivity, generating not only export and trade surpluses but also new jobs and a steadily rising standard of health for this nation. But a recent study by the National Academy of Engineering ticks off a long list of less-than-hopeful indicators for the industry's future. Examples:

- In a very research-intensive business, where more than 6 percent of sales has traditionally been plowed back into R&D, the United States share of world spending on pharmaceutical R&D has dropped to 30 percent, or half of what it was in the 1960s. The significance of this trend was also emphasized in a study by the National Research Council: "United States-based pharmaceutical firms remain in a strong position with research efforts that are large and growing, but the U.S. research efforts are not growing enough to match the exceptional expansion of foreign-owned research efforts. The upshot is a significant decline in the United States' share of R&D—the foundation of a competitive position in this industry."
- The number of new drugs that American firms have placed in clinical trials has steadily declined to about twenty-five per year, down from sixty per year two decades ago. There has been no parallel decline in the number of new drugs from foreign companies. Japan's share of new drugs has climbed from 23 percent in 1980 to 35 percent in 1983. Since 1981, Japan has ranked first in the number of new drugs placed on the market, with the United States in second place, followed by West Germany and Switzerland.
- The percentage of world drug production occurring in the United States has fallen from 50 percent in 1962 to only 24 percent in 1983. Over the same period, America's share of pharmaceutical exports has been cut in half, to about 15 percent.
- Innovation among the smaller drug companies is slower now than in 1960, and these firms are increasingly dependent on licenses from foreign rivals. But future licenses will be harder to come by. During the 1970s, the big European drug houses established a broad-based presence in the U.S. market, and they will increasingly market direct to American consumers.
- Both Japanese and European rivals are investing in American

companies. As foreign producers tap into U.S. brainpower, they wll be increasingly competitive in such emerging technologies as gene splicing.

The prime culprit behind these dismal statistics, charges the NAE, is heavy-handed federal regulation, abetted by pervasive nontariff barriers erected by foreign governments that have gone virtually unchallenged by U.S. trade representatives.

In the early 1950s competition in the pharmaceutical business was largely national in scope—with the significant exception of the Swiss multinationals, such as Ciba-Geigy, Roche, and Sandoz. Later in the fifties, American firms began to emulate the Swiss, setting up sizable multinational operations. Because of tariff and regulatory barriers, particularly the latter, exports had become less viable and profitable. In France, for example, all imported drugs must be packaged locally, and before they can be marketed the producer must obtain a "visa." Getting it means that someone from a designated list of experts must approve the safety and efficacy of a product—which in practice means that a visa is granted only for drugs produced and clinically tested in France.

More important, even business in the domestic U.S. market became less tenable. To escape the spiraling costs of complying with this country's tough screening laws and regulations, not to mention lengthy delays in getting the Food and Drug Administration to act on submitted test results—partly the result of antibusiness attitudes infecting Washington bureaucrats—the pharmaceutical industry began transferring its stock of technology abroad. There, a new drug could be tested and marketed sooner, generating revenues, and the results of public use cited in support of the drug's safety. And since federal law prohibits exporting drugs that have not been fully tested and approved in the United States, American companies had to establish international production operations as well. U.S. drug producers commonly reap 40 to 50 percent of their revenues overseas.

Restoring the industry's rate of innovation will be no mean feat. Because lead times in the pharmaceutical business are so lengthy—twenty to thirty years from research to marketing, twelve to fifteen years between synthesis of a drug and its use by the public—there is slim chance of a major improvement before 2000. Meanwhile, at the same time that market shares are slipping, costs continue to rise. Today, developing a new drug costs between $75 and $95 million. The bill for clinical tests alone can run up to $20 million.

The drug companies are counting on innovations from genetic engineering to help turn the trick. Abbot Labs, Bayer, Eli Lilly— essentially all of the big drug producers—are quietly expanding their biotech programs. But they are also getting new competition. In late 1984 new heavyweight domestic companies jumped into the biotech ring. DuPont and Monsanto, two giant chemical makers, cut the ribbon on megabuck biotech R&D labs. Indeed, the $150 million facility that Monsanto inaugurated in October represents the company's biggest single R&D investment ever, and about half of Monsanto's R&D budget—$380 million in 1984—is being rechanneled into gene splicing. As Luther H. Smithson, manager of SRI International's biotech program, remarked to *Business Week*: "It's becoming the waltz of the elephants, and the fleas are going to get squashed."

Monsanto expects to be on the market in 1987 with a growth hormone for cattle. That will be followed by products to improve animal and plant health—and pharmaceuticals. DuPont, which in 1981 acquired New England Nuclear, a leader in monoclonal antibodies, is likewise aiming for agricultural markets—and treatments for cancer and arthritis. Both of the chemical makers are shopping for a drug company to buy. DuPont's goal is to be in the "top tier of pharmaceutical companies," says David D. Mooberry, vice president of the biomedical products department.

While there will surely be a shakeout among the 200 biotech startups by the early 1990s, no one is ready to write off the majority of these firms. In fact, many of them are owned in part by chemical or pharmaceutical giants or have close working relationships with those corporations. For example, Koppers Company owns 30 percent of Genex, and on the eve of opening its own lab, DuPont acquired 7 percent of Biotech Research Laboratories. Dow Chemical has entered into several agreements with biotech firms, the most publicized with Collaborative Research to produce rennin. In 1981, Dow purchased Richardson-Vicks and renamed the unit Merrel Dow Pharmaceuticals.

"It's hard to find a chemical company that's not involved in genetic engineering," says Sarah K. Bayles, vice president and biotech analyst at Wall Street's Oppenheimer & Company. "Genetic engineering is the most important technical development to hit the chemical industry since the development of polymers."

REALIGNING THE CHEMICALS TEAM

The moves into biotechnology by DuPont and Monsanto are indicative of the changes overtaking the chemical industry. After years of ever-fatter trade surpluses, the industry has recently been hit with a double whammy: growing competition from oil-rich countries, which crimped profits, and then the strong dollar, which squeezed exports. As a result, America's share of the worldwide export business in chemicals has slipped to nearly half of the 26 percent–plus position it held two decades ago, and the plastics-and-rubber segment of the industry has fared even worse, despite the technological leaderships of polymer producers such as Union Carbide, Phillips, General Electric, Borg-Warner, and others.

Petrochemicals pervade every corner of modern life. They provide the fertilizers for American agribusiness. They are the foundation for several manufacturing industries, ranging from plastics and synthetic rubber and textile fibers to paints and adhesives. The prime industrial markets are transportation, construction, packaging, and electronics. Consumer products made from petrochemicals include pharmaceuticals, cosmetics, detergents, shoes, furniture and furnishings, phonograph records, Scotch tape, and telephone housings.

The metamorphosis of the U.S. chemical industry began twelve years ago, in response to political factors. In October 1973 the Organization of Petroleum Exporting Countries (OPEC) raised the price of crude oil by 70 percent. Later that month, OPEC nations cut their oil production rate by 25 percent and clamped an embargo on shipments to the United States. "The industry was built on a raw material—oil—and they suddenly shut off the valve," recalls Alexander F. Giacco, chairman of Hercules, Inc.

Then the outlook turned rosy again. Briefly. To compensate for the rising cost of oil, Dow Chemical led the industry in pushing added costs through to customers. The result was an astonishing climb in profits in the mid-1970s.

Much of those new-found riches were plowed back into new plants—so much, in fact, that in some product areas there is enough overcapacity to last for decades. Because, as the 1970s wound down, so did the rate of growth in U.S. demand for chemicals. Inflation took its toll in key housing and automotive markets, and sales to the U.S. auto industry eroded further as a tide of Japanese cars rolled in. During the 1981–82 recession, chemicals nose-dived. (In Europe, the industry was losing $200 million every month.) One grim humorist quipped that "even customers who don't pay quit ordering."

Although 1983 brought improvement, with industry-wide net income jumping 15.5 percent over the previous year, it was clearly only a respite that masked underlying decay. U.S. exports declined 11 percent, in part due to the dollar's strength and lagging recovery overseas, while imports increased almost 24 percent.

But by then even the most reluctant chemical-company managements had been forced to get off their duffs and face up to reality: The future will be very different from the past. Chemical imports are here to stay, and growing, and the U.S. share of exports will continue to decline. And despite the fact that the chemical industry has some of America's best-managed companies, there's little they can do to thwart further erosion.

The reasons aren't hard to divine. Chemicals are high-volume, relatively low-priced products that are easy to make, given the capital to build modern, automated plants. And since refining chemicals from the two main raw materials, crude oil and natural gas, generally adds profits as well as value, production has gradually shifted to locations closer to those resources—especially in Canada and the Middle East, where giant, multibillion-dollar chemical plants have been, and continue to be, built.

Will OPEC Become OCPEC?

Within the next few years—perhaps as few as five, certainly no more than ten—OPEC will have almost as tight a stranglehold on chemicals as it does on crude oil. One industry wag suggests that if

OPEC members can't agree on oil pricing and production quotas at their next meeting, "maybe they'll get down to some serious business and change the name to the Organization of Chemical and Petroleum Exporting Countries." It would be apt.

Saudi Arabia, Kuwait, Mexico, and Indonesia—these oil-rich countries are building huge, world-scale plants to convert their oil and gas resources into petrochemicals. They see no reason why they should continue to ship crude oil abroad so foreign companies can turn their black gold into higher-value products, such as gasoline, chemicals, and plastics. So more and more refining will be done in OPEC nations. By 1990, we estimate that OPEC will control 90 percent of world ethylene supplies, 60 percent of its ammonia, and 40 percent of the methane supply. These are three of the largest-volume chemicals.

Currently, 91 percent of the world's chemical production—$775 billion annually—is consumed in the same region where it is refined (North America, Europe, or Japan). This won't change overnight. But competition from the new production centers is beginning to be felt in world markets. Refined chemicals from Saudi Arabia and Kuwait are already entering the nearby European market, and a shakeout has begun. Union Carbide and Monsanto have walked away from their European petrochemical operations. And it's just a matter of time until Middle East chemicals are exported in volume to the United States, too.

The unnerving aspect of this is that almost all of the OPEC refineries are owned or controlled by the country's government, and governments are notorious for having slender to zero concern about the bottom line. The bureaucrats in the Mideast will have no compunction about running their refineries at a loss, if that's what it takes to sell the output and keep the plant running at peak capacity and employment levels. "None of us understands the ramifications of competing with state-owned producers," says Giacco of Hercules.

While American chemical makers are facing rough times, Japan's industry is in deep trouble. Japan considers chemicals to be approaching "sunset" status, so the chemical industry has gotten little new investment. Its refineries, designed to serve primarily domestic demand, are just too small to compete with the vast scale of the complexes rising in the Mideast.

Sensing that soft underbelly, Asia appears high on the priority list of several oil-rich states. Saudi Arabia is already making fertilizer in Taiwan, a joint venture with that island nation; also, the Saudis are engaged in another joint project, a methanol facility that's being built by a consortium of five Japanese companies. But the Arabs are just getting their feet wet in unfamiliar territory. The real push will come closer to 1990.

Meanwhile, Mexico is sending so-called feedstocks (intermediate chemicals) for polyester fibers to the Far East. Shipments reached 200,000 metric tons in 1983. And Cydsa, a Mexican fibers producer, is rapidly expanding shipments of acrylic fibers to Japan, Indonesia, Hong Kong, and Australia. "The Far East will continue to be the strongest growing market in the world," says Juan Autrique, director of Pemex, Mexico's state-controlled oil monopoly. Mexico formed Pemex Petrochemical Far East, based in Hong Kong, to promote business in the Orient.

Bracing for Intense Competition

To brace themselves for much more intense competition and reduce the exposure of their capital-intensive infrastructure, U.S. chemical companies are backing away from commodity chemicals and polymers, where competition is keenest and profits meager at best; instead, they are concentrating on higher-margin specialty products. Diversification into other industries, especially biotechnology and pharmaceuticals and occasionally electronics, has also become a frequent strategy. The signs of widespread restructuring are everywhere.

The companies are even streamlining management. Monsanto has stripped away one whole level of middle managers. Union Carbide's corporate staff has been chopped to one-third of its former size, and the firm's domestic operating units have been reorganized into independent divisions responsible for their own research, manufacturing, and marketing.

DuPont, Monsanto, Allied, and Celanese are good indicators of what's happening. Ten years ago, these companies together owned more than half of the total U.S. capacity for synthetic fibers made from polyester, nylon, and acetate filaments, and they were major players in markets for plastic resins, too. They frequently crossed paths in organic chemicals such as formaldehyde, methanol, phenol, vinyl acetate, and acetic acid.

Today, while DuPont is indisputably number one in the chemical industry, only about 40 percent of sales—a total of $35 billion in 1984—come from its traditional businesses. Most of the rest comes from Conoco, America's tenth-largest oil company, which DuPont acquired in 1984. So even this shining star of chemicals feels the need to shelter its assets ($24 billion) with other revenue streams.

The troubles in chemicals are perhaps best reflected in Monsanto. With 1984 sales of $6.3 billion, the number four producer is whittling away the weaker parts of its business and grafting on new ventures in biotech and other product lines. Monsanto has dropped out of polyester fiber and is allowing its overall fibers business to shrink as agrichemical revenues have more than tripled. President R. J. Mahoney's goal is to divide Monsanto into three equal spheres by the early 1990s: chemicals and plastics, biotechnology, and electronic goods such as scientific instruments and industrial process controls. Its first commercial gene-spliced product will probably be a growth hormone for cows that will increase milk output; look for it around 1988.

Allied Chemical grew so disheartened with industry trends that it changed its name in 1981, dropping the word "Chemical." It bought Bendix, a maker of automotive and aerospace equipment, then picked up 39 percent of Martin Marietta Corporation, another aerospace manufacturer. Its old chemical business now contributes less than half of total earnings and will doubtless shrink further as the company strives to spread its activities among five loosely related growth fields: aerospace, automotive, chemicals, industrial technology, and oil and gas.

Celanese is the exception. While it has withdrawn from a few old-line products, such as nylon, it is nonetheless sticking by its core business in fibers—as the base of a thriving empire in fashion fabrics. Although Celanese is playing a big-stakes hand against the Far East's "Gang of Four" (Hong Kong, Taiwan, Singapore, and Malaysia), the company figures it has a trump card in reserve: just-in-time delivery. In the hectic pace of the fashion industry, days and even hours can be critical. So Celanese is going to a JIT posture, offering a standard delivery time of five to six days. By way of contrast, it generally takes at least three months to get fabrics from the Orient. Prices in the Far

East may be cheaper, but Celanese believes the salient point is that fast delivery can reduce a customer's warehousing costs by 90 percent and ensure a minimum reaction time to new fashion flings.

Ethylene provides a good glimpse of what's happening to the U.S. chemical industry. United States output of ethylene, the largest petrochemical feedstock, grew from 3 billion pounds in 1955 to more than 20 billion pounds in 1972—a compound growth rate of 12 percent. This commodity is a starting material for polyethylene and polystyrene, two of the most widely used thermoplastic resins. But maturity has overtaken this premier petrochemical. For the next five years, domestic growth in ethylene consumption will average 4 to 5 percent a year and will gradually drop off after that. And there's no chance of offsetting slower domestic growth with exports, because of competition from Canada and Saudi Arabia.

The commodity producers have billions of dollars of investments tied up in products that may never again grow faster than GNP. Many of these operations are now being run for survival rather than growth. With commodities destined for slow growth, there's a rush into specialty products. The hot markets for chemical specialties change over the years. In the 1960s, the big opportunity was in treating municipal water supplies. In the 1970s it was for oil-field chemicals. Now it's chemicals used in health-care products, pharmaceuticals, electronics, and engineering plastics. Engineering plastics, loosely defined, are those that can compete with metals for use as parts and components in machinery, cars, aircraft, and other demanding applications.

The industry's one bright spot is that some oil companies which, like OPEC, had integrated forward, have now decided to get out of chemicals altogether. This not only will leave some market voids that will take up some of the overcapacity, at least in the short term, but also will rid the industry of some poorly managed operations that have been a drag on prices and profits.

THE GREEN REVOLUTION

A Whole New Meaning for "Hybrid"

Along with the phenomenal promise of genetic engineering in medicine, the agribusiness sector is in for enormous upheaval. Scientists foresee a second "green revolution" from genetic engineering, beside which the first—responsible for 50 percent higher crop yields since just 1960—will seem like a kindergarten exercise. One study projects that plant bioengineering will be the foundation of a $50 to $100 billion worldwide business by the year 2000.

There certainly is a dire need for a new green revolution. By 2000, the U.S. population will add some 20 million persons, Latin America's population could jump by 200 million, and the total world population will be bloated by close to 2 billion more hungry mouths— almost a 50 percent increase since 1980. Yet, at the same time, the world's arable farmland is actually shrinking. Come 2000, as much as one-third of all arable lands will have been farmed out or destroyed by slash-and-burn and other wasteful farming practices in Third World countries. The United States, Canada, Argentina, Brazil, and a handful of other bread-basket nations can modestly increase the amount of cultivated land, but agricultural experts declare it's sheer folly to expect a net worldwide gain of more than 3 to 6 percent.

Bioengineered crops, hence, hold out the best hope of averting a disastrous and chronic famine. Scientists are looking for the genes that will enable plants to improve the efficiency of photosynthesis, to make their own fertilizer, to grow bigger and mature faster, and to resist a gamut of environmental assaults. And the search for these genes isn't limited to just the plant realm.

Producing hybrid plants is taking on a whole new dimension, because it's now possible to insert animal genes into plant cells, creating plants with totally unprecedented characteristics. Perhaps the most compelling concept is to correct nutritional deficiencies in certain staples. Imagine the benefits if cereal grains had a complete balance of proteins, combining the nutritional values of meat and grains. A similar idea for a new type of potato has been dubbed the "meatato" by genetic engineers at the International Plant Research Institute in San Carlos, California.

The problem with subsisting on today's plants is that most are grossly deficient in one or more of the essential amino acids from which the body manufactures proteins. Corn, for instance, has virtually no lysine, one of the vital amino acids. This unfortunate imbalance is why vegetarians must scrupulously eat certain combinations of foods, such as beans with rice, to assure proper nutrition.

German biotechnicians have already produced a "pomato," and scientists at the University of Wisconsin have crossed bean and sunflower cells but haven't yet got their "sunbean" to breed true. "The solutions are coming very fast now," says Mary-Dell Chilton, biotechnology director at Ciba-Geigy's new $7 million plant research facility in North Carolina's Research Triangle Park. "In three years, we'll be able to do anything that our imaginations [can conceive]."

The main push now is aimed at developing more conventional hybrids, particularly of wheat, soybean, and cotton—the major crops exported by the United States. It takes twelve years or more to develop a hybrid using classic cross-pollination technques, notes James E. Windish, director of Monsanto's plant sciences business. "We think we can do the same thing with biotechnology in six years." As a result, he adds, "we feel very strongly that in the 1990s some combination of wheat and soybean breakthroughs will generate $300 to $500 million in annual revenues for Monsanto."

No wonder most major chemical companies and some biotech start-ups have either acquired or are shopping for firms that sell crop seeds. In the past year or so, Monsanto, Upjohn, and Lubrizol snapped up seed companies. Even a French company, Lafarge Coppee, got into the act by buying Wilson Hybrids, an Iowa seed supplier. In all, some one hundred small seed firms have been purchased by large companies.

Indeed, the seed market for hybrid wheat, soybean, and cotton could each be a billion-dollar annual business in the next decade. There is ample evidence to show that farmers will pay top dollar for seed that improves their productivity. For example, the hybrid corns now available are so superior that virtually all commercial crops are planted with hybrid seed, despite the well-known fact that seed suppliers such as Hi-Bred International and Dekalb Agresearch rake in 50 percent profit margins. Hybrid corn grows taller and produces bigger ears with more uniform kernels. It also is healthier and more resistant to drought. For similar reasons, commercially raised onions, sugar beets, tobacco leaves, and wheat tend to be hybrids. Truck farmers who grow tomatoes are willing to pay $450 to $1,500 a pound for hybrid seed, a far cry from the $12 cost of ordinary garden-variety seed. But Campbell Soup Company nonetheless launched a $50 million project three years ago to genetically engineer a better tomato for its soups.

New varieties of rice now in the final development stage will boost yields by more than 25 percent. By 1990 researchers expect to have strains that will produce 300 percent more rice per acre—and the rice will have as much as double the protein of today's grain. The combination of lower production costs, thanks to denser growth, and higher nutritive value will halt, perhaps reverse, the slow slide in U.S. exports of rice.

The number of organizations marshaling resources to work on bioengineered plants is encouraging: most of the petrochemical companies; several new plant specialists, such as Agrigenetics, DNA Plant Tech, and Advanced Genetics Science; and Harvard, Stanford, and Rockefeller universities, in addition to the usual "ag" schools. The challenge has attracted major players overseas, too—including the prestigious Max Planck Institute in West Germany. The major targets are:

PHOTOSYNTHESIS EFFICIENCY. Photosynthesis is the biological process by which the energy of sunlight is used to power the formation of carbohydrates from carbon dioxide and water. This process ultimately supplies the energy for all living organisms. Although much has been learned about many of the steps in the photosynthetic process, large gaps of understanding still remain. For example, only a small percentage of the light that falls on a plant is actually used to synthesize carbohydrates. Scientists hope to find ways to help plants make better use of available energy.

In most food plants, photosynthesis happens most efficiently when the temperature is within certain parameters, which is why most crops that haven't ripened by late summer or early fall, won't. A few plants, however, manage to maintain photosynthesis even at temperatures down to freezing. Others thrive under a glaring desert sun that would wilt less hardy plants. If the genes that allow some plants to tolerate temperature extremes can be transferred to the cereal grains, two-crop growing seasons would be possible in more climates.

SELF-FERTILIZING PLANTS. Nitrogen is essential for all growing things. It is a key ingredient in the amino acids from which proteins are made as well as the nucleic acids that are the building blocks for DNA. While nitrogen is abundant in the air, gaseous nitrogen is virtually inert and therefore useless to plants. In chemical fertilizers, nitrogen is in the form of nitrate (ammonia) or a compound (ammonium phosphate or potassium nitrate) from which plants can extract nitrogen and other nutrients, such as phosphorus and potassium. But manufacturing ammonia fertilizers is expensive and energy-intensive, consuming the equivalent of 750 million barrels of oil, worldwide, in 1984. And by the end of the century, to feed a swelling population, that figure will quadruple to 3 billion barrels yearly. That would mean that, worldwide, refining capacity equal to half of all the petrochemicals consumed last year in the oil-hungry United States would have to be devoted to making fertilizers, unless some alternatives are developed.

The likeliest alternatives are certain strains of bacteria, living in the soil, that are able to absorb gaseous nitrogen and "fix" it so it is usable by plants. Some plants—legumes such as peas, beans, and alfalfa—form symbiotic relationships with these nitrogen-fixing bacteria. Unfortunately, cereal grains don't "know how" to do that, nor do the grasses on which cattle feed. So genetic engineers expect to create self-fertilizing grains either by inserting the bacterial genes that fix nitrogen into the plant cells or by giving grains the legume genes which nitrogen-fixing bacteria find so alluring. Either development would rank as one of the major achievements of the century, says Professor Frederich Ausubel of Harvard University.

STIMULATING AND REGULATING GROWTH. Once bioengineers isolate the genes that regulate plant growth, the genes will be modified so that the plant matures faster while, say, producing larger leaves and grains on shorter stalks. The plant's internal mechanisms will also be fine-tuned so that entire fields ripen at the same time; there will no longer be a need to send pickers back into a tomato or strawberry field on several successive days.

Also, the plant's growth regulators will be tweaked to make the plant more resistant to severe drought. Enabling plants to thrive on salt water is another cherished goal. As one researcher muses, "If we can just teach corn and wheat what salt hay grass already knows." In fact, new varieties of barley produced in India have been grown successfully in saline soil, and Australian researchers have grown vegetables irrigated with brackish water.

The payoff from these and other gene-splicing tactics could easily be a fivefold increase in crop yields. But it will be well into the 1990s before any appreciable gains are notched, and the realistic outlook for the year 2000 is no more than a 350 percent jump in the productivity of American farmers, and less elsewhere. The reason is that scientists still know comparatively little about plant biology on the molecular level. So reaping the harvest of the second green revolution is going to be a photo-finish race with growing population.

"It's now possible in theory to move genes from animals to plants, from plants to bacteria, from bacteria to plants, and so on," says Ralph W. F. Hardy, director of life sciences research at DuPont's Central R&D Lab. "There are no barriers to the transfer of genes using the basic technique of recombinant DNA." But it will take time to implement the theory.

And it will be costly, in terms of both dollars and farm jobs. Farming is already a capital-intensive, high-tech business—more farmers use personal computers than people in any other profession outside of the computer industry itself—and it will become increasingly so. In little more than ten years, robotic farm equipment will till fields without the need of a human hand on the controls. Farmers who can't afford this coming generation of "smart" equipment—and that's the majority—won't be able to compete on price, and the business of growing food will become more and more concentrated among giant agribusiness corporations. Come 2000, the work force down on the farm will be half of its current size.

Farming for Energy

Plant-animal hybrids are opening up some interesting side avenues, as well. This year, for example, genetic engineers at Purdue University took a gene from a bacterium and patched it into yeast. The result is a yeast that, for the first time ever, can digest xylose and convert this plant sugar into ethanol alcohol. About one-third of any dried "biomass," or plant wastes—straw, leaves, corn cobs, corn stalks, sawdust, et cetera—consists of xylose. Another third is glucose, a plant sugar that's readily digested by yeast. But it hasn't been economically feasible to recycle biomass into ethanol when only one-third of the wastes was converted. The "xyeast" could give farmers a new source of income. Ethanol sells for about $1.50 a gallon, and the market for this alcohol will double or triple as lead is removed from gasoline and ethanol takes its place as an octane booster.

One of the richest sources of biomass in the future will be the sea. Kelp farms near the shore could produce 20 to 30 tons of dried biomass per acre. The kelp could be farmed in combination with algae, a potential source of animal feed and fertilizer (techniques for making human foods from algae are also under development). The prototype for the sea farm of the future was established in 1981 on the seabed off Ellwood, California (near Santa Barbara).

At the other extreme is the jojoba (pronounced ho-ho-ba), a desert plant. The jojoba's seed contains a liquid wax with multiple uses. It is an excellent substitute for the whale oil used in some fine lubricants. During World War II, jojoba wax was harvested in some quantity and experimentally made into rubber. If gene-splicing methods could augment the wax content, the jojoba could become an important source of domestic rubber—the plant could even be a renewable source of oil in the twenty-first century.

Another extremely promising research thrust would directly harness the phenomenon of photosynthesis. Given a fuller understanding of the process, scientists believe they can develop artificial systems, perhaps built around plant genes, that will exploit the sun's energy. For example, sunlight may one day be used to break down molecules of water into hydrogen—a source of very concentrated energy—and oxygen.

As with farming, fishing also is becoming a high-tech industry.

Some of today's most productive fishermen don't bother going down to the sea in ships. Their catch is already caught, in a sense. The fish are raised in intensively farmed ponds. In 1983, nearly 10 million tons of fish were produced by 12 million acres of fish-farm ponds, and the take is increasing by more than 5 percent a year. Fish farming is hardly new; a few major corporations have been in the business for as long as two decades. But it will get a decisive boost from biotechnology.

New, more nutritious forms of algae together with bioengineered fish that are healthier and faster-growing will improve yields substantially. Fish already are the most efficient source of animal protein, inasmuch the amount of food required to produce 1 pound of fish meat is considerably less than that for red meat or poultry (30 pounds of feed per pound of red meat and 8 to 1 for poultry). By tinkering with fish genes, scientists believe that it may be possible to produce a pound of fish with just 1 pound of feed.

Healthier people who live twice as long, better crops and farm animals that promise an end to hunger, energy farms that will end the world's dependence on crude oil—all this and more is possible through the magic of genetic engineering. The promise this technology holds out to humankind is so open-ended that even the most cautious scientists are awestruck by its implications.

4

SPREADING
THE SERVICE
ECONOMY

New Importance for the Services Sector

Charting the course of American business for the next two decades would hardly be complete without factoring in the services sector, which accounts for better than 60 percent of the gross national product and seven of every ten nonfarm workers.[*] More important, in the context of this book, the competition in services is increasingly international in scope.

First, let's correct a common misconception about services. Many people connect the rapid rise in services with information processing and fast-food restaurants, so their impression is that it's a relatively recent phenomenon. In fact, going all the way back to 1925, the services sector has contributed almost 80 percent of the total growth in nonfarm jobs. The United States became the world's first services economy at least thirty years ago, and some economists maintain that the threshold (more than half of the work force engaged in producing intangibles) was crossed in 1940. During the past ten years, service

---

[*]Among the bigger services: accounting, advertising, architecture, banking, engineering design, consulting, communications, education, information handling, health care, insurance, legal, shipping, tourism, transportation—and, of course, government.

companies created almost 18 million new jobs, compared with less than 2.5 million jobs by the manufacturing sector.

After World War II, international trade in services began rising steadily. With the spread of computers and information processing, the growth in U.S. services exports picked up dramatically: From $92 billion in 1977, service exports climbed more than 50 percent to $140 billion in 1981. Of that figure, about 40 percent was rung up by companies in transportation, insurance, and construction—fields dominated by large companies. The remaining $85 billion was divvied up among markets in which companies of almost any size can participate.

The total value of the international exchange of services in 1980 was $650 billion—just over one-third of the figure for merchandise trade that year. The United States held the biggest share of the services trade, with 20 percent of the action. Japan was number two, followed by Britain, which has long provided international financial services; France and Germany were next in line.

However, the services exports of several other nations, including Japan and Korea, are growing faster than America's international services. From 1977 to 1981, according to the Commerce Department's Office of U.S. Trade Representatives, Singapore posted the biggest gain—up 171 percent, with services exports representing 65 percent of Singapore's GNP. Mexico's increase was 162 percent, and South Korea was in third place with 112 percent. Japan's services exports jumped 91 percent, compared with a 76 percent rise for the United States.

Since 1981, however, America's services exports have been declining. In fact, some service businesses may now be entering a "smokestack" period. "There is probably a trend away from a U.S. surplus," warns economist Gary R. Saxonhouse of the University of Michigan. "As in everything else, our competitors overseas are becoming more competitive."

Brazil and Korea are beginning to win major construction contracts, for example. Korea's Hyundai Engineering & Construction Company is one of the biggest new sources of construction engineering. India has hundreds of software research and production operations that ship sophisticated computer programs to Japanese and European computer companies.

For the past twenty years, in almost every Third World country, the proportion of the labor force in services has grown much more rapidly than either industry or agriculture. That's why some governments are moving to protect their domestic services markets and encourage local service organizations to exploit their cheap labor by peddling labor-intensive services on the global market. Typically, in Third World economies, the services sector has absorbed most of the recent entrants into the labor force. Wholesale and retail trade are the most important types of new jobs in developing countries; public administration is next.

Categorizing nations as postindustrial (service), industrial, and developing just doesn't reflect reality. The world doesn't divide neatly into highly developed countries with service economies and lesser developed countries that don't have much service business. Many less developed countries meet the definition of service economies in that half or more of their GNP and employment are in the service sector.

More Services Than Products by 2000

Two trends will bring services to the forefront of the international marketplace, eclipsing trade in manufactured goods by 2000. The first trend is that more and more services are being sold across national boundaries as firms in advanced countries go hunting for lower costs— the same motives that drive manufacturers offshore. The other need is that not just the West but the entire world is increasingly information-intensive. Communications and information are essential to any business, and as business fans out around the world, the need for information processing and communications rises and the global flow of these services increases.

Washington has shown mounting recognition of the importance of the services during the last decade. The Trade Act of 1974 included services for the first time, and in 1980, a thirty-five-member Industry Sector Advisory Committee on Services was set up to study the implications of services for the world economy. This committee was chaired by Ronald K. Shelp of American International Group, Inc. A comprehensive strategy for promoting trade in services was approved in April 1981 by the cabinet-level Trade Policy Committee. In January 1982 a coalition for service industries was formed to promote public awareness of the services sector's importance to the economy. It seems to be working.

For the past two years, *Fortune* has published a separate listing of the top 500 companies in services, just like its list of the top 500 industrial corporations. In 1984 three companies previously on the industrial list moved to the services listing, because they no longer derive at least 50.1 percent of their revenues from manufacturing and mining. Greyhound Corporation was the largest. The others were Foster Wheeler Corporation, an industrial engineering and construction firm, and GATX Corporation, which leases railcars and operates storage facilities.

For evidence of U.S. dominance in services, one needs look no farther then New York City. "New York is the international capital of the world—the international capital of commerce, communications, finance, and culture," boasts Mayor Ed Koch. New York City has taken the crown away from London and ended 300 years of European dominance of world financial markets. "As the world economy becomes increasingly interdependent, the financial services industry has become more important in providing the fuel," says David Rockefeller, former chairman of Chase Manhattan Bank.

New York is the main pumping station for that financial fuel. The banks and investment brokers on Manhattan Island haven't just accumulated enormous amounts of capital; they also have branched out from money management into electronic information management as well. That has been the key to their stealing the lead from the once-dominant British, German, and Swiss banks. Today, when a corporate treasurer wants, for instance, to perform interest-rate or currency swaps, he or she is more likely to turn to Bankers Trust or Salomon Brothers than to a London or Zurich bank.

On America's balance sheet for international trade, investment income—payments and receipts on investments abroad—is in a very strong position. In 1982 the surplus was $33.2 billion. The United States has been in a net creditor position on direct investment throughout the post–World War II period. Despite the rapid rise of foreign-owned enterprises in this country, direct foreign investments at the end of 1983 totaled only about $100 billion, or 15 percent of total foreign assets—and less than half of America's direct investments in the opposite direction, which represent 27 percent of total U.S. foreign assets. Net U.S. income on portfolio investments abroad has more than tripled over the past five years or so, according to the Conference Board.

In recognition of the growing volume of dollar-based world trade and financing, foreign banks, such as Barclays Bank International, have been actively expanding in the United States. "There has to be a very significant dollar element in any major international bank's balance sheet," notes Brian G. Pearse, chief executive of Barclays' North American operations. More and more overseas banks recognize the necessity of a presence in New York. In 1980 there were 149 foreign banking offices in New York. Today their number surpasses 200.

In 1983, of every $14 in commercial and industrial loans in the United States, $1 came from Japanese banks. More and more American homes are financed by money from Japanese savings accounts. More and more U.S. businesses are covering their risks with policies from People's Insurance Company of China, an aggressive reinsurer with 1,200 offices worldwide. And Canada's Olympia & York Developments Ltd. has jumped to the seat of number two developer in the U.S. real estate market.

The United States Is a Software Lion

Writing the software for the computers that power the financial pipeline—and, for that matter, just about every other business—is one U.S. bastion that looks like it will survive largely unscathed into the twenty-first century. The software market is one of the bigger and faster-growing service areas, with 1984 revenues of $8 billion worldwide, propelled chiefly by the exploding demand for programs for personal computers. The PC software market, which didn't even exist ten years ago, has grown at a rapid rate. For the foreseeable future its growth will continue to outstrip the rate of climb for sales of both PCs themselves and of the software market as a whole. By 1990, in fact, software for PCs will account for more than half of the entire software market, according to InfoCorp, a California market research firm.

Despite intensifying competition from overseas, especially a determined push by Japan with help from programming shops in India set up or supported by Japanese companies, most experts believe that the United States should be able to hold on to most of its current 70 percent lion's share of the world market.

As noted earlier, software comes in two primary forms: operating systems that control the internal functions of a computer, and application programs that enable a user to put a computer to work at certain tasks, such as word processing, managing a data base, accounting, and so forth. Microsoft dominates the market for operating systems, thanks to the disk operating system (DOS) that it developed for the 16-bit personal computers from IBM and the sundry "workalike" IBM-PC clones.

Because the operating systems market is small beside that for applications software, William H. Gates III, the 28-year-old cofounder of Microsoft, wants to make his fledgling company the General Motors of the software business by becoming the dominant player in application programs as well. That market is intensely competitive, so Gates will need every ounce of his legendary drive—he works ninety-hour weeks—to fulfill his towering ambition. There are thousands of basement programmers and hundreds of established software firms, each hoping to come up with the next VisiCalc, Lotus 1-2-3, dBASE II, or WordStar.

When it comes to software for bigger computers, IBM and the "Bunch" are firmly in control. But competition in the international marketplace is as hot as the U.S. market for PC programs. Foreign rivals are determined to recapture their national markets, and their governments are often helping by discriminating against imports while targeting software exports as a national priority that merits subsidies or grants. Japan is considering a regulation that would require imported programs to be accompanied by detailed disclosure of even the secret parts of a program, which would make copying the programs a breeze— especially since Japan doesn't recognize software as being protected by copyright. Japan also has staked out artificial intelligence programs as its special preserve, and Korea's electronics conglomerates are seeking U.S. partners to make a run at the software business. "Software will be a major opportunity for us soon," says Han-Jeng Lee, assistant to the chairman of Daewoo. British and French software houses each earned $100 million on the export market in 1983.

Information services is another business where the United States is far and away the worldwide leader. Here, though, the competition is going to get extremely tough, particularly in international markets, which often are subject to governmental controls.

Information services in the United States generated revenues of more than $2 billion in 1983 and should hit $5 billion in 1988. This rapidly expanding business consists of 700 firms, industrial and professional associations, and government agencies that produce and distribute electronic information. About 350 of these organizations actually maintain the 1,500 data bases now available, four times the number just eight years ago. Half of all data bases focus on business and industry, while 30 percent serve science and technology users. These electronic data bases—which serve some 400,000 online customers, or more than twenty times the customer base in 1977—represent better than three-quarters of total information service revenues.

As a commercial arena, the data-base market is little more than a decade old. The first electronic "libraries" were created by NASA and the old Atomic Energy Commission in the 1960s. Later, the National Science Foundation funded the development of data bases in physics, chemistry, and engineering. But the first for-profit data bases didn't appear until the early seventies. Since then, the number of online electronic data vendors in the United States has grown to seventy-five, several of which are also active in Europe.

But the U.S.-owned data-base vendors doing business in Europe are feeling stiffer competition from the seventy-five European vendors that have cropped up. Europe's online vendors offer many U.S. data bases as well as about 500 locally produced data bases that serve 100,000 European governmental and business customers. Because the U.S. market is so vast and growing much more rapidly—in part due to the relative paucity of restrictions on electronic media here, compared to Europe—most of the big information-service concerns in Europe have designs on the U.S. market.

Continued rapid growth in electronic information is virtually guaranteed at least through the 1990s as the market broadens from businesses into homes, although the bullish outlook for megabuck videotex services carried into most homes with cable TV has dimmed drastically in the past year or two. Early trials such as the experiment in Miami by the Knight-Ridder newspaper chain and in Columbus, Ohio, by

Qube have been disappointing. Videotex will come—the growing popularity of similar services in Europe is evidence of that—but it's going to take a while longer than had been supposed. Still, the physical facilities are being laid every day: Since 1973, by FCC decree, every new TV cable going into a home has had the capability to provide the interactive, or two-way, service that is the core of videotex.

The 7 million homes with computers hooked up to a modem are now recognized as the vanguard of the home information revolution. These homes are "dialing up" such information utilities as CompuServe, Dialog, and Nexis. Using the capabilities offered by these electronic services, users are banking at home, buying and selling stocks through electronic brokerages, and communicating with business partners. These homeowners know the value of online information; they are the model for the electronic home of the future, when interactive cable or fiber-optic phone lines will deliver mail, educational programs, shop-at-home services, and medical diagnoses—even make it possible to vote and participate in town hall meetings from the comfort of one's favorite easy chair.

The Professions Go International

For engineers, architects, advertising executives, and other professionals, the international market can be a lucrative place to do business. For example, several hundred architectural and engineering (A&E) firms operate abroad, planning, designing, and managing the construction of airports, seaports, factories, dams, and power plants. Because the designers of such facilities often specify or select the materials and equipment used in construction—and naturally lean toward sources back home—the contracts won by U.S. A&E firms are frequently only the tip of an iceberg of exports.

Most A&E service companies are latecomers to the international scene. Few have had active overseas offices for more than twelve years. But U.S. industrial designers have certainly come on strong. Today, of the top 150 international A&E companies, 70 are American. And according to annual surveys by *Engineering News Record*, U.S. firms in recent years have typically won 30 to 35 percent of all international jobs, which in 1982 were worth $3.7 billion. Demand for American design services has soared, at the expense of European rivals, in part because U.S. firms have been quicker to adopt computers and advanced management techniques that help hold down project costs. (Unlike the actual construction market, where Japanese competitors are a major factor, the construction services business is a U.S.-Canada-Europe game: The 1983 market-share score went United States, 31%; Britain, 15%; France, 5%; Canada, 7%; Germany, 7%.)

A few U.S. design houses are old hands at international jobs. Louis Berger, an engineering firm in East Orange, New Jersey, started marketing its services overseas in the 1950s. Now, with offices in every major country in the world, it does 85 percent of its business abroad, and its 1983 revenues of $100 million ranked Louis Berger International as the second largest engineering firm in the international sphere, trailing only Resource Sciences Corporation of Tulsa.

Foreign revenues constituted 5 percent of the A&E industry's $33.5 billion in receipts in 1983. Work on Middle East jobs is the main source of overseas billings for architectural and engineering services. Africa is second, with most contracts coming from Nigeria, Algeria, and Libya. The Far East ranks third, with Indonesia, Malaysia, the Philippines, and Thailand being particularly profitable. Latin America has replaced Europe as the number four foreign market.

Overseas demand for design services by U.S. firms is now being adversely affected by the dollar's strength, the debt problems of many underdeveloped countries, and the declining revenues of the oil-exporting countries (which have prompted cutbacks in nonessential construction jobs), and the proliferation of nontariff barriers against foreign design firms. In addition, some governments have been helping their domestic A&E firms to grab more international jobs with low-cost financing and subsidies, hampering the ability of U.S. firms to compete. At the same time, more U.S. companies are chasing foreign contracts, so the American share of the international market should hold fairly steady for the next five to ten years.

If any American profession can sell services internationally, advertising ought to be able to do so. The U.S. training ground is the world's biggest and most competitive. In 1983, 250,000 national companies and 1.75 million local firms spent about $70 billion through 4,000 ad agencies to help sell products and services. Roughly one-quarter of that money came from 100 companies, and 14 percent was funneled through the top ten agencies. And, in fact, the bigger U.S. advertising agencies are doing handsomely in international markets— and will continue strong, despite nontariff trade barriers, even if the only way to gain entry to a new market is to buy a minority stake in a foreign ad agency (a ploy already used on numerous occasions).

The ten biggest U.S. agencies billed foreign clients to the tune of $1.3 billion in 1982, or almost half of their total revenues ($2.7 billion). McCann-Erickson collected the most overseas business for the fifth consecutive year: nearly $200 million, or 70 percent of its total billings. J. Walter Thompson was the runner-up, with $180 million in foreign revenues. Responding to a survey of the fifty biggest ad agencies, thirty-one firms told *Advertising Age* that they earned $1.7 billion in gross income on $11 billion worth of foreign business. On average, the thirty-one agencies derived about 40 percent of their revenues and profits from foreign accounts.

The international scene looks very rosy because of the rapid growth in ownership of TV sets in many Third World countries. Before, the TV audience in these countries wasn't worth an advertiser's consideration. Moreover, as the citizens of developing (and some European) nations demand more variety in TV programming—at a time when TV production costs are climbing faster than government revenues— more and more state-run broadcasters will begin to allow advertising in order to support operations. Advertising is even starting to catch on in parts of the communist bloc.

For U.S. agencies, the main glitch comes from Japan, the second-largest advertising economy. Japan has ten of the fifty biggest ad agencies, including the world's largest, Dentsu, which does twice the business of McCann-Erickson. The best Japanese ads rival (and, some say, occasionally surpass) the most creative efforts of American agencies, and the big Japanese agencies are also looking for new business overseas.

A much more ancient service specialty—franchising—is again catching on rather well overseas. At the end of 1982 some 300 U.S. franchise operations had 24,000 foreign licenses, up from a meager 3,300 foreign franchisees in 1971, and 117 other franchisors were planning to extend their domains into foreign lands by the end of 1985.

The concept of franchising dates from the Middle Ages, when a lord would grant a knight or an abbot the right to govern part of his realm. Markets and fairs were also conducted under franchise. In its modern guise, franchising is distinctive in that, by definition, it is a business that spawns new businesses and helps small enterprises compete with giant corporations. In many countries where venture capital and the infrastructure for nurturing entrepreneurs is lacking or deficient, which includes most European countries and Japan, buying a franchise is one of the few ways that a free-spirited person with limited resources can set himself or herself up in business. That's why, after Canada, the main markets for United States franchisors are in Japan and Europe. Approximately 25 percent of foreign franchisees lease cars and trucks; restaurants such as McDonald's and Kentucky Fried Chicken are the next most prevalent type of foreign franchise.

In the United States, some 450,000 franchised outlets employ 5 million people and in 1983 rang up sales of about $420 billion. That was one-third of all retail sales. The latest fashion in franchising is services ranging from bookkeeping and instant printing to home cleaning and renovation, child care and vocational education, and even some dental and optometry clinics. Computer repair and field maintenance is becoming one of the hottest markets, and among the newer ideas is this: a shopping mall for cars, where various showrooms and maintenance facilities provide drive-in, drive-out convenience for all of a person's automotive needs.

The bottom line in services is that America's trade surplus will go on slipping gradually as the country yields ground in overseas markets to foreign service organizations, mostly in labor-intensive businesses. Even some of the creative and technology-driven services, such as engineering design for overseas projects, will be slowly sapped by foreign rivals. But the United States' grip on international financial services will continue to tighten for the next five years and then remain strong for the next ten years, at least. And America's edge in information processing will survive mainly intact through the end of the century.

CONCLUSION: WRAPPING UP THE SITUATION

It's time to pause briefly and take stock of the situation. We've covered an enormous amount of territory, some of which, no doubt, has been unsettling. Let's quickly review.

The electronics revolution is just beginning, despite the spectacular changes that have already sprung from computers and microchips. Not later than the end of the century, the wizards of electronics will build machines that think and, ultimately, may very well be self-conscious. In other words, they will create a new form of life, the first that isn't based on organic carbon compounds. Intelligent computers will transform human life, taking over the noncreative aspects of work for executives, professional persons, bureaucrats, and finally even the average consumer. Industrial chemists, aided by smart computers, will engineer new plastics and composite materials. Doctors will have computer assistants with perfect recall to help in reaching diagnoses and planning treatments. By 2005, even you and I will have our computer helpers, small enough to carry around in a shirt pocket yet packing more punch than a Cray supercomputer.

Along the way, factories will become increasingly autonomous. Eventually they will be so flexible and efficient that consumers will use home computers to contact the factory computer and order a product tailored to his or her special wishes, and it will be produced within hours. Not long after the turn of the century, NASA will begin designing self-replicating robot miners and basic processing plants that will be set down on the moon and the asteroid belt to assure earth of a continuing supply of raw materials.

Most blue-collar jobs will gradually vanish; ten or so years into the next century, the factory work force will be reduced to the size of today's farm population. The auto industry will consolidate into a handful of global giants, with production centered in Korea, Italy, and Latin America. The U.S. computer and aerospace industries will still be strong, but they won't be spared the intensifying foreign competition that will rattle American executives in every other industry.

The whole education system will have to be revamped. There's little point to training children to be unquestioningly obedient, to use their brains to do rote memorization, when there's no longer a need for industrial serfs for the country's factories. Companies will do a lot of retraining to help blue-collar workers secure other jobs—or to start up their own businesses. A surge in white-collar, creative jobs is coming over the next decade, and the entrepreneurial spirit will flourish as never before.

Culminating the merging of computers and telecommunications, a global fiber optics network will emerge. It will be inherently intelligent. The system itself will provide such sophisticated services as simultaneous translation when the parties at either end of the line don't share a common language.

Yet, as marvelous as these electronic developments may seem, the real wonders are coming in biotechnology. By tinkering with the genetic basis of life, bioengineers will find new "magic bullet" drugs to cure and prevent cancer and most other diseases. Genetic disorders will be corrected. The upshot will be a doubling of human longevity.

To feed twice as many people who'll be living twice as long, genetic engineers will develop new crops that grow almost anywhere, mature rapidly, and afford balanced nutrition. Cows the size of small elephants, chickens as big as turkeys—these and other farm animals, including fish raised in fish farms, will be genetically programmed to grow significantly larger and thus produce more milk, bigger eggs, and more meat.

And when the world's oil reserves begin to run out, we'll turn to renewable oil from energy farms that grow jojoba plants and harvest biomass from the land and the sea, which will be converted into ethanol and other feedstock materials. Today's petrochemical industry will be supplanted by an emerging biochemical industry.

This quick review glosses over the enormous competitive struggle that will wage internationally as nations jockey for economic power in the process of getting from today to tomorrow. American business will be confronted by a host of new competitors. We had better be prepared. The first step is to identify who the adversaries of the 1990s will be, in order to assess their strengths and weaknesses. That's the purpose of Part II.

PART TWO

5

THE
COMPETITION:
GETTING ACQUAINTED

Like it or not, the 160-odd nations of the world are locked in a closed system of economic interdependency. Big or small, almost all have at least one asset that is lacking in some other country; a fortunate few have many such assets coveted by many other countries. But no matter how wealthy a nation is in natural resources, labor, capital, or advanced technology, none is totally self-reliant. Moreover, because the leaders of all countries tend to be ambitious, personally and patriotically, they struggle to wield power and influence by exploiting their countries' native assets through international trade.

For the pragmatic American executive, two primary concerns are hunting down the best foreign-investment opportunities (offensive strategy) and assessing overseas adversaries (defensive). This section can help with both. It looks at two dozen countries, paying particular attention to those on the Pacific Rim—Japan and the so-called Four Dragons of South Korea, Taiwan, Singapore, and Hong Kong—plus the handful of nations that will register surprising gains over the next twenty years. There will be some downside surprises, too—Japan and Italy being the more notable.

Perhaps the most fundamental criterion affecting foreign investment decisions is a country's stability—politically, economically, and socially. A country on the verge of revolution or nationalization of industry is hardly attractive as a market, let alone as an investment candidate. So the first order of business is to gauge each country's ability to absorb both internal and external shocks. For this, Forecasting International, in Arlington, Virginia, has developed a computer model that integrates sixty-four indicators within six elements:

- Political stability: Historically, has the country resolved internal disputes peacefully, and have government transitions been orderly?
- Welfare of citizens: How well the government performs in supplying the basic necessities; the model also looks at the size of the gap between the well-being of the top 10 percent and the bottom 10 percent of the population (if large, this is a prime signal of looming instability).
- Economic base: That's the size and strength of the national economy.
- National security: Can the nation defend itself against either hostile actions by likely enemy countries or insurrections from within?
- International influence: To what extent does the country normally affect the actions of its neighbors, allies, and adversaries?
- National unity: What is the degree of ideological, cultural, and religious schisms among the populace?

Forecasting International used the model to analyze the prospects of most of the countries addressed in this book. Resulting longitudinal stability rankings are shown in the chart on page 157.

Asian nations figure prominently in the following section for obvious reasons. Half of America's trade deficit in manufactured goods ($69.5 billion in 1983) comes from transpacific routes. And that growing imbalance is by no means all smokestack-type merchandise. As this book went to press, preliminary estimates put the U.S.-Japan deficit in high-tech goods even higher than the deficit in autos! Moreover, American industry is increasingly competing for markets in the Third World with the Four Dragons, and this rivalry will dominate the international scene for the next ten years. "The Far East," says Deputy Secretary of State Kenneth W. Dam, "is now America's 'Near West.' "

RANK	COUNTRY	CURRENT	NEAR-TERM	LONG-TERM	COUNTRY	RANK
1	UNITED STATES (US)				AUSTRALIA	1
2	WEST GERMANY (FRG)				UNITED STATES (US)	2
3	JAPAN				CANADA	3
4	AUSTRALIA				UNITED KINGDOM (UK)	4
5	UNITED KINGDOM (UK)				SWEDEN	5
6	FRANCE				WEST GERMANY (FRG)	6
7	SWEDEN				INDONESIA	7
8	FINLAND				FRANCE	8
9	CANADA				SOVIET UNION (USSR)	9
10	SINGAPORE				JAMAICA	10
11	SOVIET UNION (USSR)				SINGAPORE	11
12	ITALY				FINLAND	12
13	SOUTH KOREA (ROK)				VENEZUELA	13
14	MALAYSIA				MALAYSIA	14
15	JAMAICA				ARGENTINA	15
16	VENEZUELA				PANAMA	16
17	THAILAND				YUGOSLAVIA	17
18	MEXICO				THAILAND	18
19	POLAND				SOUTH KOREA (ROK)	19
20	SAUDI ARABIA				BRAZIL	20
21	CHINA (PRC)				EGYPT	21
22	INDONESIA				NIGERIA	22
23	ARGENTINA				ZIMBABWE	23
24	ISRAEL				SOUTH AFRICA	24
25	SPAIN				SAUDI ARABIA	25
26	PANAMA				CHINA (PRC)	26
27	YUGOSLAVIA				MEXICO	27
28	BRAZIL				EL SALVADOR	28
29	LIBYA				PHILIPPINES	29
30	INDIA				JAPAN	30
31	IRAN				POLAND	31
32	EGYPT				COLOMBIA	32
33	SOUTH AFRICA				ISRAEL	33
34	COLOMBIA				ITALY	34
35	NIGERIA				IRAN	35
36	PHILIPPINES				LIBYA	36
37	ZIMBABWE				PAKISTAN	37
38	PAKISTAN				SPAIN	38
39	BOLIVIA				BOLIVIA	39
40	EL SALVADOR				PERU	40
41	PERU				INDIA	41

LONGITUDINAL COUNTRY STABILITY RANKINGS

Perversely, the World Bank is pursuing policies that could foster less, not more, stability. The bank frequently cites the South Korean economy as a model for development. Under the scheme that the bank helped Korea to implement, a country's development targets are based on the principle that each nation has "comparative advantage" in some area. It can export those products at cheaper prices than rival traders, then import its other needs from nations that have a comparative advantage in other fields. In theory, it sounds workable—assuming that most countries have different comparative advantages and that international trade is relatively free of nontariff barriers. Unfortunately, the real world does not always conform to theory.

The leaders in just about every Pacific Rim country, as you might expect, want the prestige that comes with a high-tech image. So most are targeting electronics assembly, hoping to exploit their comparative advantage in low-cost labor as a springboard into more advanced, more profitable technology markets. However, it's by no means clear that there is or will be enough demand to support all of these ambitions, especially as U.S. companies are beginning to build automated factories in this country and retrieve some of the assembly work that has been farmed out to Asian plants. And even for those countries that do leverage their way into a market, the struggle is far from over. Korea, for example, will likely face increasing competition from Indonesia, Malaysia, and other Asian nations that have even more of a comparative advantage in low-cost labor.

Moving beyond job-shop assembly work is inherently capital- and knowledge-intensive, not to mention highly volatile and fast-paced. Because technology "turns over" so quickly, capital requirements are so heavy that few U.S. semiconductor makers can pay dividends. Even Silicon Valley firms regularly raid each other in search of talent; where will a similar pool of talent come from in Korea? Consumer electronics is one big-bucks market that most nations hope to enter, but it is a trendy market where intense competition quickly squeezes margins to the bone—and one that's vulnerable to economic recessions. Countries without very deep pockets for continual R&D might be better advised to stick to more basic commodities for which demand is comparatively steady.

Longer term, after 1995, Africa will emerge as the land of business opportunity. Its natural resources have yet to be exploited fully because the precarious stability of most African countries augurs against long-term investments. But by the turn of the century, many African states will be more attractive to Western investors, and the "dark continent" will likely begin to assume the role of last frontier for low-cost labor. Whether there will be much need for cheap labor by then, however, remains to be seen: It will be a race between native efforts to evolve stable political institutions and Western technologies pointed at creating autonomous factories.

JAPAN: COMPETITORS WHO DON'T NEED TO EAT OR DRINK

Not long ago, the Chicago school board asked for bids on a purchase of a substantial number of electronic typewriters. They got $900 per machine from an American manufacturer. And $450 from a Japanese company.

How could the Japanese manage to undercut the price by 50 percent? The usual platitudes—lower labor costs, lower cost of capital, being satisfied with lower profit margins, and so forth—are all part of the answer. But a deeper look finds an incredibly thorough and pervasive commitment to managing the national system in order to achieve economic superiority. For example, in 1978 the exchange rate was 195 yen to the dollar. Today $1 buys 260 yen. So the yen is worth about 33 percent less now than seven years ago; this single factor accounts for roughly $300 (one-third of $900) of the $450 differential in the Chicago typewriter case.

Yet a decline in the value of the yen flies in the face of all economic reason. In fact, every economic yardstick points in precisely the opposite direction: The yen should have risen in value. Over the past six years Japan's trade balance has continued to grow, accumulating a surplus of $80 billion, while the U.S. trade balance has sunk deeper into the red; its productivity has been rising, America's is stagnant; its unemployment rate is about half of America's, and so forth.

So what has caused the yen to fall relative to the dollar? Simple: The Japanese normally won't accept yen in payment for their exports. Instead, they want dollars. Eighty percent of all Japanese exports are priced in and paid for in dollars. These dollars eventually gather in Japan's central bank, and at the end of every year the bank sweeps them up and invests excess dollars in U.S. Treasury bills. The Japanese bankers bow politely and, good trading partners that they are, say they would like to help the United States finance its federal deficit.

Who's kidding whom? The Bank of Japan invests in U.S. Treasury notes ($7.8 billion at the end of 1984) for the same reason the country prices exports in dollars: because it doesn't want to convert those dollars into yen. Keeping tight reins on the quantity of yen in commercial markets and not converting massive dollar surpluses into yen is the only way Japan has kept the yen from appreciating in value, perhaps reaching a more realistic exchange rate of 150 or 160 per dollar. If that happened, Japanese companies would obviously have much tougher sledding in international markets. So the central bank will do almost anything to avoid that catastrophe. Besides, U.S. Treasury bills pay a handsome dividend over the interest rates that Japanese banks charge for business loans. If the Americans are stupid enough to help subsidize the low-interest rates that are the biggest cost factor favoring Japanese producers—far more important than wage differentials, low inventory costs due to just-in-time operations, or any of the other more commonly cited factors—the Japanese no doubt figure they'd be foolish not to exploit the situation.

Because of the yen's artificially low value, it's difficult to get a true reading of relative manufacturing costs in the United States and Japan. Still, overall productivity statistics are illuminating. Today, the average Japanese worker is about 91 percent as productive as his American counterpart. That figure may be hard to swallow, because almost every U.S. businessperson knows from sad experience that the Japanese seem to be 50, 100, 150 percent more productive. They must be, to clobber competitors so thoroughly in autos, motorcycles, steel, machine tools, watches, cameras, semiconductors, and consumer electronics.

Fact is, both statistics are accurate. Japan is a two-tier economic system. There are certain industries where the Japanese are extremely productive, and there are others where they are woefully inefficient, only 10 to 15 percent as productive as America's industries (agriculture is the premier example). The nonproductive industries rarely make headlines, of course, because there is no way they can compete internationally—and the Japanese government shelters these businesses with prohibitively high tariffs or import restrictions that exclude serious foreign competition. In the agriculture sector, for instance, imported dairy products, beef and pork, fruits and vegetables, and most processed foods are all but banned. The government has had to take extraordinary measures to protect agriculture because of Japan's aging farm population. Nearly 30 percent of all farmers are 65 or older, and their inefficiency is a chief reason why the price of rice in Japan is four times that of the world market.

When it comes to first-tier companies, though, productivity is a way of life. The hallmarks are automation, advanced process technology, economies of scale, vertical integration, and, perhaps most critical, special relationships with other members of its trading group and with second-tier suppliers. None of these factors should seem strange to any American industrialist. Seventy-five years ago Henry Ford framed almost all of the principles that Japan has adopted. He built his own steel and tanned his own leather, for instance, and took Harvey Firestone camping every weekend.

But the rigor with which the Japanese have implemented these principles is frightening to behold. It's often noted that the Japanese will sacrifice profits over the short term for long-term market position. But that's not really accurate. The Japanese will forego profits for any term—short, medium, or long—because they believe in long-term goals rather than instant gratification. Japan's most prosperous year in recent memory was 1979, when the average profit among Japanese manufacturers was a miserly 1 percent return on total assets, versus 8 percent for American manufacturers. If the Japanese can sustain operations indefinitely on such minuscule returns—and indications are that they can—the United States might as well be competing with extraterrestrials who don't need to eat or drink.

How does Japan do it? To answer that question, you have to look beyond low-cost bank loans and trading groups and just-in-time manufacturing. The secret lies in some fundamental precepts of Japanese society that dramatically distinguish it from American society.

The U.S. economy, like Japan's and every other country's, runs on corporate profits. Profits are the primary fount of national disposable income—although American politicians often seem smitten with a death wish and try to kill the goose that lays the golden egg, and many citizens are so poorly educated in how capitalism functions that they turn up their noses at the notion of profits. But the fact remains that taxes on corporate profits are, directly or indirectly, the major source of federal funds, in the form of taxes on company profits and on wages paid to employees. Without business the country couldn't pay the bills for defense and social programs. Defense accounts for 26 percent of U.S. federal spending and 7 percent of GNP. Social Security and medical care gobble up 31 percent of the federal budget. Education takes 3 percent more, and public works, another 4 percent.

Now compare those numbers with Japan's. They spend precious little on defense—less than 6 percent of the government's budget and a niggardly 1 percent of GNP. Even social programs are relatively modest: Social Security represents 19% of federal spending; education, 10%; and public works, 13%. How do they run a society on such skimpy societal programs? They can't. They don't. They just finance them differently. Rather than fund them through the government, the companies furnish employees with housing subsidies, medical benefits, and bonuses that Japanese workers sock away for retirement.

The way Japan handles things has two significant advantages. First, it eliminates the bureaucratic middleman. And second, it provides a powerful incentive to find gainful employment.

Japan's economy operates lean. Only 4 percent of the work force is employed in the public sector (versus 15 percent in the United States). And the benefits that companies pay are distributed at the grass-roots level, whereas in the United States it's not uncommon that half of the monies allocated to various social programs are sopped up as overhead, as government salaries and administrative expenses. In some more notorious cases, such as the CETA program or when funds pass through three layers of bureaucrats (federal, state, and local), as little as 20 percent of the money may actually reach its intended recipients. So the Japanese get more out of every tax dollar.

The Damned Who Toil Down Below

The first thing every Japanese boy learns on his mother's knee is that he must work to survive. Since companies provide so many social benefits, the work ethic in Japan is quite different from that in the United States. How do you get social benefits? In Japan, you work; in the United States, you don't work. And because every worker's long-term security depends on his or her employer's prosperity, the Japanese are fanatically dedicated to assuring their company's survival and success.

The second thing a Japanese boy learns is that he has to work hard to get into the right grade school, the right high school, the right university, and the right company. Children come home from school at 3 P.M., grab a quick snack, then hurry out for eight hours of tutoring. The kids return after 11 P.M., about the same time their fathers get home from work. The reason there is so much emphasis on the right education and the right job is that every mother wants her son to work for a first-tier company. Remember, Japan has a two-tier business hierarchy, and there's a world of difference between first and second layers. With any first-tier firm—Panasonic, Toshiba, Canon, Nissan, and the other familiar names—the pay and benefits are top-notch, working conditions good, lifetime employment the rule, and pension programs certainly adequate.

The bottom tier consists of companies that few Westerners ever hear about, and for good reason. The poor souls who work for these firms do so from necessity, not choice. Wages and benefits are one-third to one-half of top-tier minimums, working conditions can be unbelievably miserable, job security is nonexistent, and retirement programs are inadequate and uncertain, since Japan has had the world's highest rate of bankruptcies for the past thirty-five years—virtually all of them in the second tier. Yet 76 percent of Japan's workers are employed in the bottom tier!

There are three types of second-tier companies, two of which exist purely to help the first-tier giants in minimizing costs. These two kinds of firms are distinguished only by whether they sell their output to just one or to more than one customer company. In either case, the main purpose is the same: trimming costs to the bone. For example, one company supplies 95 percent of all the automobile transmissions used by Japan's car makers. (The third variety of second-tier companies are the few independents, neither a member of one of the trading groups nor a predominantly captive or semicaptive supplier to trading-group members—Sony is the archetype; however, for the moment we are ignoring the independents.)

These second-level workers subsidize the competitiveness of first-tier companies with their sweat, money, and blood—literally. Japan has one of the worst suicide rates in the world. Among the elderly, it's eighteen times higher than in the United States. The prevalence of suicide isn't hard to fathom once you realize that Japan is an anomaly in the Orient. While the sense of family is strong, Japanese children do not feel obligated to care for an aging parent, nor do parents expect them to. The Japanese culture places responsibility for individual well-being on each person's own shoulders. You don't rely on family or government to help you survive, nor do you look to your company if you're one of the 76 percent who work in the second tier.

What you do is save every possible penny. For second-tier workers, the savings rate is frequently 40 percent of disposable income. Most of this money finds its way into the banking system, where interest rates on savings accounts in the 1970s averaged 3 percent—at a time when inflation was running about 9 percent. When a retired person's savings are exhausted, suicide is considered the honorable thing to do. The grand-prize winner at the 1983 Cannes Film Festival was a movie set in a small village in southern Japan. As soon as any villager turned sixty, he or she would say good-bye to friends and relatives, then climb a nearby mountain and commit suicide so as not to siphon resources away from the younger generation or the community.

Ironically, the money that second-tier workers save at 3 percent is likely to get loaned to a first-tier company at something on the order of 5 percent. This source of low-cost capital is one of the more potent weapons that the major companies wield, because it encourages managers to formulate long-term plans and strategies. Reason: If a company can borrow at 5 percent, in ten years $1 will still be worth $.62. The same $1 discounted at 15 percent will be worth only $.24. So when the cost of capital is high, managers will strive to invest in short-range projects that pay off before too much of the capital gets chewed up by interest fees.

Second-class companies also rely heavily on bank loans—the average debt-to-equity ratio in Japan is a hefty 78 percent—although second-tier firms generally pay a slightly higher borrowing rate. But interest points are just the beginning. Most of the debt component among second-tier companies is short-term notes that must be refinanced every year. To see what this means, consider this hypothetical example: Nippoduo Company wins a three-year contract to supply Mitsubishi Aircraft with daiprops. Nippoduo needs $2 million to tool up, and Mitsubishi Bank naturally arranges the loan, no matter that its debt-to-equity ratio is already a whiff about 100 percent. What do you suppose would happen if Nippoduo were to give Mitsubishi Aircraft a hard time about pricing, delivery, quality, or anything else?

Japanese firms also mercilessly exploit second-class workers— women. In Japan, women aren't counted in unemployment statistics. They aren't eligible for retirement benefits. They are expected to join the labor force instead of going to high school, and then to leave the factory by age 24 to raise a family. They are paid about half a man's wages, even less if they continue to work after marriage. Most Westerners on their initial tour of Japanese factories are struck by the contrast of extremes: Either plants are highly automated or they are jammed with young women doing all manner of manual labor.

A Termite Strategy

So, for U.S. executives who will be battling Japan, Inc., it's vital to realize that the Japanese system is different from most other societies. Old-age security does not have high priority. Neither does equal rights. The chief objective is industrial supremacy, particularly in the information technology business. The government believes it is Japan's manifest destiny to attain superiority in this arena, and the Japanese people, by and large, not only don't question this policy but actively support it, even at the cost of comfort in their golden years. The voting population, until now, has apparently condoned the ruthless subjugation of three-quarters of the work force and essentially 100 percent of the female population in order to sustain the members of the thirteen zaibatsu (trading groups) to whom the mission of world domination has been entrusted.

How does a U.S. company compete in such a lopsided contest? Let's be blunt: It usually doesn't. It often can't.

There are two options, micro and macro. The macro is between Washington and Tokyo. The United States has to convince Japan to balance the scales more evenly. Such efforts involve complex issues and will take a long time to resolve (more on this later).

The micro strategy, on the other hand, is simple: Whenever possible, avoid direct confrontations. That's relatively easy, since markets that attract the Japanese are quite predictable. First of all, they look for a high value-added component. Value-added, or revenues minus the cost of materials, is how the Japanese keep score. Given that Japan imports all materials, value-added is the stuff of all export earnings.

Next, in breaking into new markets, the Japanese look for products with high unit prices but low margins; low margins because that indicates chances are good the established suppliers aren't making the capital investments that would enable them to compete. The Japanese also seek products where high reliability is paramount, since products engineered to last for years don't need extensive field service support from the start. And they prefer items where there is at least a possibility of standardization, so they can employ mass-production and mass-distribution techniques.

For example, take a standard floppy disk drive that sells in quantity to computer makers for $100. It costs $80 to produce the drive, so the margin is fairly tight. The Japanese can turn out the same floppy drive for $60—because of foreign-exchange factors, if nothing else. But they won't sell it for $90, or even $80. They'll settle for $70.

Floppy drives and other computer subassemblies, components, and peripherals are in fact the key to Japan's strategy to dominate information technology. Selling these parts to U.S. original equipment manufacturers (OEMs) is a business that meets all the Japanese criteria: high value, low margins, standardized designs, limited need for sales and service support, and price-sensitive purchasing patterns. It's an ideal market—with a devious twist: Every contract won, every American producer that backs out of the market, makes the U.S. computer industry that much more dependent upon Japan.

There was a Chinese military strategist in the fifth century B.C., Sun Su, who wrote in *The Art of War* that the worst form of generalship is to try to take a walled city by frontal assault. The Japanese have taken that advice to heart. Their guiding principle in the struggle for the computer industry might be termed the termite strategy: Out of sight, eat away at the internal integrity of American computers, and sap America's manufacturing base, its ability to make vital components.

Start out by selling microchips, then work up to subassemblies, assemblies, subsystems, then OEM systems where all the U.S. customer does is stick its name on a finished product. By then, the U.S. company will have invested in advertising to soften up the marketplace, and one or more third-party maintenance organizations will have trained its technicians to repair the Japanese product. So virtually all the Japanese company has to do is put its own nameplate on the computer or telecommunications system.

Even knowing the details of this strategy is no help. Few U.S. companies can long afford to buy components and parts that are more expensive than those being purchased by a competitor who buys from Japan. IBM has been gearing up for the Japanese challenge for the past five years. It has spent $12 billion on manufacturing investments and new product strategies. But even that likely won't be enough.

If the U.S. computer, telecommunications, and semiconductor industries are to enter the twenty-first century with any semblance of their current vigor, they will need help from Washington. Career officials there know this. And while the business community is generally cynical about the federal attitude toward business, there are some strange anomalies on the recent record. Three years ago, the Justice Department dropped its antitrust suit against IBM, then turned around and charged some Japanese semiconductor makers—NEC, Hitachi, Fujitsu, Toshiba, and Mitsubishi—with predatory pricing practices. Three weeks later the Federal Trade Commission launched its own suit against the same six chip makers, but this time charging them with monopolistic pricing. Justice says the Japanese charge too little, FTC says they charge too much. The message was impossible to misinterpret, and the Commerce Department had a relatively easy time negotiating a lid on Japanese chip imports (Japan has responded by building chip-making plants in the United States).

Two years ago, AT&T awarded a contract for a fiber optics telephone cable to Fujitsu, after the Japanese company won the usual bidding contest fair and square. Later that afternoon, when AT&T's director of procurement returned to his office from a meeting, his secretary asked him if he knew a certain "Mr. Whitehouse," who had called several times. By the evening of that same day, the award to Fujitsu was withdrawn, and an American winner was announced.

Between 1983 and 1987, the Defense Department plans to increase its annual spending on electronic-systems procurement to $13.2 billion, 2.75 times the figure for 1983. And in January 1984, the Pentagon told its contractors that until further notice, Defense will sock a 50 percent surcharge on foreign components in bids for certain kinds of electronic systems. Again the message is clear: Buy American if you want to compete.

There are more examples. The Internal Revenue Service has criminal tax evasion charges pending against several Japanese companies. The folks at Commerce have even suggested, tongue in cheek, that unless Japan gives U.S. companies access to its capital market and lowers the tariffs on alcohol and lumber (almost all of Japan's lumber is cut from imported North American logs), the United States will insist that Japan allow American lawyers to practice there.

The Juggernaut Will Slow

All things being equal, the Japanese industrial machine might be virtually unstoppable. But things aren't staying equal. Conditions are changing, both domestically and internationally. Whether Japan's institutions have the flexibility to adapt remains to be seen. We believe that Japan will try valiantly to mitigate the stubborn vulnerabilities plaguing the island nation. Still, we predict that the country will experience a period of economic decline during the 1990s. And inasmuch as other Pacific Rim countries (Korea excluded) will manage to raise their status on the chart of forty-one nations—or at least do a better job of holding their own—Japan's slowdown will seem worse than it actually is.

The helter-skelter growth of the 1960s and much of the 1970s masked a number of weaknesses. Virtually all materials and energy are imported, for example, and Japan's national defense is essentially dependent on the United States. In addition, the country is importing more and more food. Now, as growth slows and the Japanese economy takes on more characteristics of developed nations in the West—higher wage rates, higher inflation—the weaknesses demand action.

The OPEC oil crisis taught Japan's leaders what it can mean to get hit with cutoffs or drastic price hikes on almost a moment's whim. Their response has been to try and contain the repercussions of such actions by spreading Japan's vulnerability, shifting from oil to imported coal wherever feasible. Also, recognizing that it is losing its edge in shipbuilding and textiles to less-developed countries, Japan has shifted its sights to high-tech. Nevertheless, the basic dependencies remain.

More important, Japan must come to terms with slower growth and an aging work force—and, at the same time, overhaul at least large portions of the education system and the business environment to stimulate more innovation. Neither will be easy. In the past, men working for first-tier companies could count on steady, automatic advances up the career ladder as they aged. Except for the *crème de la crème*, seniority was directly linked to age.

But slower economic growth and a decline in the number of young people entering the job market will bring an end to this situation. Increasingly, executives and blue-collar workers will find their career momentum stalled. As a result, moving from company to company to gain advancement may become much more accepted. If so, this would certainly affect productivity and product quality. How strong the impact will be is sheer speculation, but Forecasting International believes it will be severe.

While executive mobility is still largely taboo, it is happening with growing regularity. In some cases, a Japanese executive does the unthinkable and joins a U.S. company. Last year, for instance, a senior manager left NEC (formerly Nippon Electric Company) to join Motorola's subsidiary in Japan. More recently, Keiske Yawata, a rising star at NEC, resigned as president of NEC America to become president of Nihon LSI Logic, a Japanese subsidiary of a Silicon Valley company. "When I turned 50 in August '84," he told *Business Week*, "I realized I had ten years left in my career. I wanted to accomplish more than I could dream of accomplishing at NEC." As a child, Yawata lived in China and Manchuria; he took his MBS in electrical engineering at Syracuse University, and his family is among Japan's Christian minority. As a result, he says, "My soul isn't confined to these four small islands."

Significantly, Yawata expects to have little trouble snaring "a few good engineers" from other Japanese semiconductor companies. The lure to join him at Nihon LSI? A superior compensation package, among other things. And, of course, the new company will need to find production workers for the $100 million chip-making plant that it will open in late 1986 or early '87.

There are other signs of change in the wind:

- The Liberal Democratic party, which has dominated Japanese politics with conservative, business-oriented policies since 1955, has seen its majority in the Diet (legislature) gradually dwindle to the point where the current cabinet includes a member of the New Liberal Club, Seiichiu Tagawa, as Home Affairs minister.
- Entrepreneurism is raising its ugly (for the Japanese) head, and the new businesses are less inclined to tow the government's line. For the first time in history, one of Japan's 226 government-sponsored cartels has lost the initiative in a targeted market—computer peripherals—to free-wheeling second-tier companies. The producers that dominate the peripherals business don't sit on the six-company cartel board, don't participate in the usual discussions about standards, and don't share in juicy, government-backed joint research projects. Why should they? They're doing fine as it is.
- Even Japan's remarkable social cohesiveness is starting to fray around the edges. A couple of years ago, a Japanese newspaper asked its readers who their heroes were. The top name was Akio Morita, cofounder of Sony; he was mentioned on 80 percent of all ballots. The number two name, on 78 percent of the ballots,

was Soichiro Honda, founder of Honda Motor Company. What's significant is that both men started their companies in open defiance of traditionalist Japan; neither received favored treatment by the government, and to this day, neither company is a member of one of the established zaibatsu. Next to these two mavericks, the third choice was way down in popularity, cited by only 18 percent of the responses: Yutaka Takeda, president of Nippon Steel.

Sony, by all Japanese standards, is an oddball. It didn't resort to penetration pricing to corral market share; it used premium prices. It doesn't imitate, it innovates. Sony doesn't have a 78 or 100 percent debt-to-capital figure; it's 22 percent. It was the first Japanese company to manufacture in the United States—of its own volition, not because of coercion from Washington—and the first to be listed on the New York Stock Exchange. Even the name "Sony" doesn't mean anything in Japanese; it comes from the American phrase "sunny boy." When one executive first told his mother he was going to work for Sony, she wailed, "Oh, no! You can't mean that American company."

Honda never did anything "right" either. Mr. Honda went to MITI in 1960 and said he wanted to start up a new car company. MITI told him to forget it, that it had carefully nurtured five first-tier producers and the country didn't need another. Of necessity as much as choice, Honda put together an auto company with an extraordinarily low capital intensity—less than one-fourth of Toyota's and even less than that of GM. Honda was the second Japanese company to build a factory in the United States and the second to be listed on the NYSE.

A Pivotal Period Is Here

For Japan, the remainder of this decade will be a crucial time. Its future vitality hinges on how well it reconciles growing pressures from outside with the new strains on the country's postwar economic, political, and ideological traditions. The issue of national security is especially thorny. The United States is pushing Japan to assume more responsibility for its own defense, but the prospect of a revival of Japanese militarism horrifies many of its Asian trading partners. They can't forget the treatment they got from Imperial Japan between the two world wars, and they remain suspicious of Japanese commercial motives. Leaders of southeast Asian countries, in particular, fear that Japan wants only to exploit their resources and will do little to aid their own development.

But even if Japan fails to deal creatively with its problems, the country will continue to be a powerhouse into the early 1990s. The work force won't age overnight. Nor will its productivity and product quality suddenly leap off a cliff.

Japan will give the appearance of relaxing restrictions on imports and direct foreign investments, but U.S. companies will continue to encounter hidden barriers. "Tariffs and regulations are open, but the mentality is still feudal," says Yawata of Nihon LSI. Personal relationships and long-standing business ties generally lead to "buy Japanese" attitudes, he explains. The best near-term opportunities for Westerners to penetrate the Japanese market are leisure-related products and services: sporting goods, entertainment, resort and travel services.

Longer term, Japan faces a serious dilemma. It certainly will end up surrendering some ground to increasingly tough rivals along the Pacific Rim. And if internal conflict over future policy erupts intensely because the economy slows and unemployment rises—or if the military regains a strong voice in Japanese affairs—the country will lose even more momentum in the 1990s. However, if the country grabs the bull by the horns and pulls down some of the societal pillars that hamper innovation and creativity, the trauma of the change is just as likely to impede economic progress in the 1990s. Many Japanese businessmen believe this is essential for long-range prosperity, regardless of near-term damage. As one senior executive notes, "As long as Japan keeps this culture, it will be difficult for us to be at the leading edge of new technology."

SOUTH KOREA SETS ITS SIGHTS ON ELECTRONICS

South Korea pulled off an economic miracle in the 1970s. At the start of that decade, Korea was a small, struggling country with one-third of its 32 million people engaged in agriculture. Because the country imports almost all of its crude oil, it would have seemed highly vulnerable to the havoc wreaked by OPEC's price hikes during the seventies. Instead, Korea was hardly fazed by the oil crisis. Its economy just kept chugging along at around 10 percent growth rates.

As a result, South Korea emerged from the 1970s with one of the world's more robust economies. The global recession at the start of this decade did cause a minor dip in gross national product—the first since the end of the Korean War—but by 1983 per capita GNP had climbed to $1,700 (compared to $9,700 in Japan and $14,000 in the United States), and it jumped 16.5 percent in 1984, to $1,980, as more and more people have moved away from farms. The rural segment of the population has now contracted to less than 25 percent of the country's 42 million citizens.

For the next few years, Korea's economy will continue to blossom. But things will get tougher in the 1990s. Growth will slow as it comes up against increasing competition from other, lower-cost producers along the Pacific Rim. Consequently, South Korea will be forced to shift away from the textile and light-machinery industries that have helped fuel expansion to date; it will need to move into capital- and knowledge-intensive businesses. To fund the transition, the government has revised its latest development plan in order to double R&D spending, which had been a low 1.1 percent of GNP. To help with capital formation, Seoul will encourage more savings, with a goal of adding five points to the current rate of 24.8 percent. These economic strains, plus internal political tensions (military men will stay at the tiller of government, protests notwithstanding) and ongoing tiffs with North Korea, will clamp a 7 percent lid on GNP growth during the 1990s.

Still, come the year 2000, per-person GNP will top $5,000, and total GNP will stand at an impressive $250 billion, more than triple 1984's number. Korea will then rank among the world's top ten traders, with both exports and imports climbing from roughly $27 billion in

1984 to around $120 billion. The Korea Development Institute, a quasi-government think tank, predicts the following realignments in the country's industrial base:

1984 Share of mfg output			2000 Share of mfg output
19%	Textiles	Electronics	19%
11	Machinery	Machinery	15
7	Electronics	Textiles	9
7	Steel	Autos	9
6	Chemicals	Chemicals	7
4	Shipbuilding	Shipbuilding	4
3	Autos	Steel	4
43	Miscellaneous	Miscellaneous	33
$29	Total mfg output, billions		$83

When Korea was partitioned at the end of World War II into U.S. and Soviet occupation zones, liberating Korea from forty years of Japanese colonial rule and economic exploitation, South Korea was a mainly agrarian region that fed the more industrial north. Today, the situation has flip-flopped. In North Korea, more than half of the 19 million people there still live on farms, and an estimated 48 percent of the north's 6 million workers till the soil. The per capita GNP under the communist system is about $1,100.

The south's remarkable progress stems from a consistent policy of stimulating industry through preferential tax incentives plus favorable credit allocations from both state-owned and private banks. In addition, South Korea vigorously shelters targeted industries. For example, to foster development of a domestic automotive industry, the government has imposed stringent local-content requirements; very high tariffs have been erected to protect its synthetic-fiber and textile industry, and imports of steel that would compete with the production of local mills are banned outright.

Since 1962, industrial policy has been embodied in Five-Year

Economic and Social Development Plans. The latest document, for 1982–86, emphasizes more or less in order of priority: machine tools, electronics, steel, shipbuilding, autos, chemicals, and light industries. Machine tools take top billing because government planners recognize that this technology, more than any other, determines which manufacturing industries can be supported internally. To stimulate the purchase of locally made machine tools, the government offers generous credit and tax measures, plus low-cost, long-term financing to foreign buyers.

An Itch to Be in Computers

The most ambitious program, though, is in electronics. In 1981 the Korean legislature passed the Electronics Industry Promotion Law, and a year later the Ministry of Commerce and Industry issued its Criteria for Computer Imports. These regulations ban imports of all personal computers, microcomputers, minicomputers, and most computer peripherals. Imports of bigger computers will be allowed only if the supplier agrees to sell needed know-how and technology to a Korean computer-equipment manufacturer. The government's goals are: to encourage a domestic semiconductor industry capable of designing and producing the latest VLSI chips; to increase the average domestic content of all computers marketed in Korea to 85 percent versus the current 15 percent; and to become the world's largest exporter of peripheral equipment.

As pointed out early in this book, Korea's four big conglomerates, or *chaebol*—Gold Star, Samsung, Hyundai, and Daewoo—are spending prodigious sums on electronics production and R&D. By 1988 or '89, their combined investments since 1983 will exceed $1.75 billion. Gold Star Semiconductor, part of the Lucky-Goldstar Group and Korea's pioneer in integrated circuits, plowed $30 million into expansions last year and has budgeted $160 million for the next five years. Samsung spent $126 million last year and intends to spend $500 million more before the decade ends. The comparable numbers for Daewoo, which already makes almost half of the ICs used worldwide in electronic watches, are $100 million and $200 million. Hyundai Electronics, a newcomer, has already invested more that $150 million and expects to spend another $500 million by 1988.

The Koreans make no bones that their main objective is to take away some of Japan's export business. Many older Korean business-men harbor deep resentment of the treatment accorded Korea under Japanese colonial rule. So they have turned to the United States for help in exacting revenge. Hyundai, for instance, has set up Modern Electrosystems as a listening post and R&D center in Silicon Valley, with a $50 million budget, and has held talks with Intel Corporation about a joint venture in Korea. Samsung seeded Tristar Semiconductor with $8 million ("Tristar" is the English translation of "Samsung") and purchased equipment and technology from Micron Technology. Gold Star has a technology-exchange agreement with VLSI Technology and has purchased chip-making know-how from AT&T Technologies (formerly Western Electric).

To build computers around these chips, Hyundai is getting help from IBM in personal and minicomputers. Samsung has hooked up with Hewlett-Packard, and Daewoo got technical aid from Microsoft. Gold Star, which produced three-quarters of the 110,000 personal computers sold in 1984, has had technical assistance from Honeywell and more recently acquired the technology for AT&T's 16-bit PC.

In addition to the four giants, several smaller firms are making computers. Some examples: Trigem Computer has an IBM-compatible PC developed with help from Personal Computer Products in Los Angeles. Iljin Electronic & Industrial Company, an OEM supplier to Corvus Systems, is making a 32-bit "supermicro" work station, and a similar system has been developed by Koryo Systems, a subsidiary of Korea Explosives Group.

Western experts who have inspected the new crop of computers from South Korea are generally positive about the design and per-formance of the machines. But most experts add that quality tends to be spotty, particularly among the computers from small producers.

While light industry—primarily textiles, apparel, and leather products, but also including processed food, beverages, and tobacco —is still the biggest single slice of Korea's industrial pie, it is less important than it was in the 1950s and '60s. In 1968 the Seoul gov-ernment decided it wanted an integrated steelmaker and established Pohang Iron & Steel, known widely as Posco. The company now has a capacity of 8.5 million metric tons, and a new mill due on-stream in 1988 will boost that by 2.7 million tons. The new plant will eventually be enlarged to 6 million metric tons. Apart from steel, Korea also has developed heavy-industry capabilities in chemicals, plastics, and fertilizers; however, since the raw material for these processes is imported, the fact that petrochemicals is the sixth-largest industry just makes Korea all the more vulnerable to oil price fluctuations.

Offsetting some of the exposure in petrochemicals is South Korea's impressive success in overseas construction. In the 1970s, Korean construction companies won many major contracts, particularly in the Middle East. Recently, though, rising labor costs in Korea have made its construction-for-export business less competitive, and declining oil revenues in Libya, Iraq, and Saudi Arabia—all major construction customers for Korea—have impacted the number of new jobs up for grabs.

Korea's emerging auto industry should more than take up that slack, especially after the government decides to allow Samsung to break into cars, as the company would like to do (probably in cahoots with Chrysler). For now, only two companies, Daewoo and Hyundai, are authorized to make autos. The sanctions are designed to assure that the two firms rapidly reach the 300,000 annual outputs needed to compete effectively in international markets, now expected before the end of 1986. General Motors is already in bed with Daewoo. Both Ford and Chrysler have been wooing Hyundai, but the Korean firm would prefer to do its own thing, if possible. That's unlikely, since Hyundai will need foreign technology. And inasmuch as Ford has an existing business relationship with Hyundai, Ford probably will be the partner of choice.

"I don't know how many years it will take, but I'm afraid the Koreans will account for a very large share of the low-priced U.S. auto market." That's what Shinji Seki, executive vice president of Mitsubishi Motors, told *Forbes* magazine. And a top official of Nissan Motor Company admits "It's very difficult to compete with the Koreans."

Still, the lack of raw materials will remain a chronic problem. South Korea has only limited deposits of coal, tungsten, and iron ore—and no known reserves of oil or natural gas, although it will share in the proceeds or any finds by a joint venture with an Indonesian company. To satisfy future energy needs, Korea has launched an aggressive nuclear power program.

For U.S. companies interested in exports to Korea, the best markets will be medical and scientific instruments, energy-conservation systems, semiconductor production and test equipment, mainframe computers, food processing and packaging machinery, special machine tools, construction equipment, and telecommunications hardware. There will be a continuing demand for such raw materials as coal, chemicals, scrap iron, and timber. South Korea will also be shopping for construction and consulting services bearing on its numerous infrastructure projects, including a subway for Seoul, expanding the harbor facilities at Pusan, sewage treatment plants, et cetera.

One event could forestall the minor decline in stability that we are forecasting: reunification of North and South Korea. That is extremely unlikely, however.

SINGAPORE: CITY OF THE SOFTWARE LION

Singapore Island has only two natural resources: its people, who are industrious and literate, and its location off the tip of the Malay Peninsula, around a superb harbor in the narrow entrance to the Strait of Malacca. Everything must be imported, even the drinking water. So it's abundantly clear that Singaporeans are making excellent use of the resources they have. In just twenty years of independence, this tiny republic has progressed from a poor, backwater country to a bustling center of international economic activity. Singapore is the fourth-busiest port in the world, the third-largest petroleum refinery, and the focal point of regional finance and telecommunications. Its per capita income of nearly $6,000—the highest in southeast Asia—gives Singapore a standard of living on a par with that of Italy.

Singa Pur, which means "city of the lion" in Sanskrit, was the name given to the island by Sumatran settlers in the thirteenth century. Seven centuries later, it is definitely living up to its label.

This city-state—most of the 220 square miles on the main island are urbanized, and only 1 percent of its 2.5 million people engage in fishing or backyard farming—has prospered principally on the strength of foreign investment. It offers a very favorable environment for such investment and will continue to do so over the near and long term. Because of chronic shortages of both unskilled labor and technically trained workers, Singapore has encouraged, and will go on encouraging, overseas firms to build automated factories. Full employment was achieved nearly a decade ago, and the government has had to recruit workers from surrounding countries. These foreign nationals now constitute slightly more than 10 percent of the 1.2 million person work force.

Considering its ethnic diversity, Singapore is remarkably stable. About 76 percent of the population is Chinese (and Buddhist or Taoist), 15 percent Malay (Muslim), and 7 percent Indian (Hindu) and Pakistani (Muslim). Yet the government has always been a one-party affair. Lee Kuan Yew of the People's Action Party has been prime minister since 1959, even before independence. There is only token opposition from such splinter groups as the Malays' National Organization and the Workers' party, which in 1982 managed to elect one member to Parliament—the first non-PAP member ever. That unprecedented event was triggered in part by disillusionment from a severe downturn in two major businesses, ship repairing and oil refining, both resulting from the recession that ravaged the world.

Singapore weathered the early eighties better than most nations, however, because the economy is impressively balanced. Trade (including tourism) contributed 23% of last year's total gross domestic product of $14 billion; finance and business services added 21%; manufacturing, 20%; transport and communication, another 20%; and construction, 8%. Services is the fastest-growing sector, up more than 16% in 1983 and almost 13% in 1984. While the international loan syndication game, which has been spurring much of this growth, is winding down, none of Singapore's financiers expects growth to duck under the 10 percent level during the next five years.

Construction is where the government intervenes most directly. The government puts up tens of thousands of housing units yearly (a record 48,000 were started in 1984), and a $2.3 billion mass-transit system is now being built. Singapore's telecommunications infrastructure is already the second-largest in Asia, behind only Japan. These projects are backed by cash reserves that exceed $10 billion. All employees pay a flat 25 percent of their gross pay to the Central Provident Fund, or old-age fund, and companies match their workers' contributions. The government guarantees an annual return of 6.5 percent on the money in the CPF and invests the funds to prime the economic pump when necessary.

Creating a "Computer Culture"

Over the past ten years, foreign investment in electronics manufacturing has grown by leaps and bounds. One would be hard-pressed to mention a popular U.S. or Japanese brand name in computers or consumer electronics that doesn't have an assembly plant in one of Singapore's free-trade-zone industrial parks. The cumulative total for foreign investment in electronics now stands at about $1 billion and represents one-quarter of all manufacturing output. The island has been dubbed the world's disk-drive capital, since such companies as Tandon do the bulk of their assembly in Singapore. Last year, production of electrical/electronic equipment—semiconductors, printed-circuit boards, subassemblies, computers and peripherals, cassette recorders, TVs, radios, and calculators—jumped more than 26 percent to $3.2 billion, 95 percent of which was exported.

For the future, Singapore wants to add more indigenous high technology. Singaporean leaders aren't kidding themselves about trying to break into the hardware side of high-tech, though. Prime Minister Lee acknowledged to the *Financial Times* last December that "if the Europeans can't muscle in on computers, I don't see how we can." Instead, Singapore aims to become the software and computer services center of Asia during the 1990s, selling programs and integrated systems to governments, banks, stock exchanges, transportation agencies, and factories throughout Asia.

To lay out the strategy and formulate detailed plans for implementation, the government set up the National Computer Board in 1980. The NCB quickly recognized that the biggest hurdle is a paucity of technically trained people. While Singapore's literacy rate is quite high—85 percent—only 60 percent of primary-school students complete secondary school, which isn't mandatory, and not even 4 percent go on to take a university degree. The NCB saw that it had its work cut out. Tan Chin Nam, the board's general manager, put it this way to *Datamation* magazine: "We must create a computer culture that captures the imagination of the whole country."

That ambitious undertaking kicked off in 1983. At the end of 1984 there were just under 3,000 computer professionals in Singapore—engineers, software writers, technicians, programmers, et cetera. The NCB wants to train 8,000 more professionals by the end of 1988, and it is spending $80 million on the crash effort. Computer education is being introduced in secondary and vocational schools, universities, postgraduate institutes, and worker retraining programs. The drive also has established training centers that will turn out a steady supply of 700 new software professionals yearly. Examples:

- All 140 secondary schools now have computer laboratories, and all 13- and 14-year-old students are required to attend classes or take part in an extracurricular activity involving computers.
- A computer science department has been established at the National University, and three vocational training schools emphasizing software were set up in 1984.
- An Institute of Software Technology has been set up at the National University with the help of the Japanese government. IBM is the industrial partner in the university's new Institute for Systems Science. Britain is active in a new Center for Computer Studies at a polytechnic college. Asea of Sweden is participating in a software-oriented project related to robotics, and Computervision Corporation is helping organize an institute focusing on computer-aided design software.
- A Software Technology Center is being built at the New Singapore Science Park, scheduled to open in 1986. The government is using various tax incentives to lure occupants, and DEC, IBM, and Sperry have agreed to set up software development operations at the new park. Hewlett-Packard established a $5 million software center in 1984 and equipped it with 150 personal computers that budding software writers can borrow.
- The island's powerful unions sponsor evening classes at neighborhood centers where adults can learn basic computer skills.

Singapore is hardly alone in identifying the promise of software, though. India and Japan also have designs on the market. So do two of the other "dragons," Hong Kong and Taiwan. But Singapore has proved amazingly adept at mobilizing the forces needed to turn a plan into reality. While the early 1990s will be a period of transition, especially as the old-guard political leaders retire, the success of recent initiatives would seem to assure the island of a prosperous future. Indeed, Singapore's economy should do better in the 1990s, notably the latter half, than in the 1980s.

TAIWAN AND HONG KONG: WILL TWO DRAGONS BE DEFANGED?

Although important, neither Taiwan nor Hong Kong is ranked on the chart on page 158 because they were not included in Forecasting International's multi-client study on which the chart is based. As for Hong Kong, Britain's lease on the land occupied by this crown colony expires in 1997, and it will be returned to Communist China. Britain has extracted promises from Beijing that Hong Kong will be allowed to manage its own affairs and maintain its capitalist economy, but some of the colony's businesses aren't hanging around to see if the pledges will be honored. These firms—including one of the oldest, Jardine Matheson—have begun moving their operations elsewhere. Still, enough may remain that the Hong Kong "dragon" could still scorch the tails of competitors. More important, the know-how residing in Hong Kong could provide a much-needed boost to China's own high-tech ambitions, so it would be premature to write off Hong Kong. But before we explore these implications, let's take a peek at the fading glory of Taiwan.

Located 115 miles off the southeast coast of mainland China, the island of Formosa was ruled by Japan from 1895 to 1945. During this colonial period, the Japanese introduced modern agricultural methods and turned the island into an important exporter of rice as well as bananas, pineapples, and tea—along with such raw materials as coal, oil, and natural gas, plus some gold, copper, and sulfur. Today, about

19 million people live on the island, which is a third the size of Ohio (245 miles long and 90 miles wide). Although 70 percent of the land is too mountainous to farm, Taiwan remains agriculturally self-sufficient, save for some wheat imports, with 20 percent of the labor force engaged in farming and fishing.

But today the island's economic muscle comes from manufacturing and trade. Since 1949, Taiwan has developed into one of the world's fastest-growing industrial and export-oriented economies, and its per capita GNP is approaching $3,000. Foreign trade jumped more than tenfold between 1964 and 1974, and continues to expand. Exports of textiles, clothing, TV and radio sets, plywood, plastics, and cotton fabrics in 1984 surged 25 percent ahead of 1983 levels, when they pulled in $25.2 billion, more than offsetting a $20.3 billion import tab for machinery, basic metals, petroleum, ores, wheat, and cotton. Taiwan's foreign exchange reserves are bloated with more than $16 billion.

However, most factory workers, who represent one-third of the labor force, are employed in labor-intensive jobs in generally small manufacturing plants. Most Taiwan factories are small, family businesses; only ten companies had 1983 revenues of more than $250 million, and the country's biggest companies, such as Formosa Plastics Group ($2.6 billion in 1983 revenues), tend to be in smokestack industries. As a result, the bulk of Taiwan's industrial base is vulnerable to competition from less-developed countries such as Indonesia and Sri Lanka, which can easily do the same work, only cheaper. "We're being squeezed," concedes Chao Yao-tung, chairman of Taiwan's Council for Economic Planning and Development. "On the one hand, we're facing the competitive force of new nations. On the other, our exports are being restricted by protectionism in the United States and Japan."

The Taipei government has seen the handwriting on the wall for a decade, but it has had scant success in persuading industrialists to invest in newer markets. In the early seventies the government decided to start the ball rolling and founded the Electronics Research and Service Organization to spearhead the drive into semiconductors and electronics. When that example didn't catch on, the government intervened again in 1979, setting up the Institute for Information Technology, a software R&D center, and underwriting part of United

Microelectronics Corporation, a maker of integrated circuits. But neither of these initiatives has been a barn-burner, either. Taiwan's business leaders are typically in their sixties and simply scared of the risks entailed in high-tech diversification. Most of the $290 million of computer equipment that Taiwan exported in 1983 came from foreign-owned assembly plants.

So now Taiwan is dangling venture capital in front of expatriate Chinese who came to the United States for a degree in electrical engineering or computer science and stayed on to work in Silicon Valley or along Route 128. Three Silicon Valley companies headed by Chinese managers have risen to the bait and are building chip-making plants in Taiwan. Government officials hope they will be the nucleus of future growth as younger, more adventurous managers take over the reins of business in the 1990s. Unfortunately, the move into microchips comes too little, too late. Taiwan will never be able to compete with the juggernaut building in Korea, and it will need to look to other markets for its slice of the high-tech pie.

Hong Kong's Lease Is Up—Literally

Hong Kong (Cantonese for "fragrant harbor," a name it got when the island city was a center of incense trade in the early 1800s) has a population of close to 5.5 million today. How many will still be crowded into the colony's 400 square miles in 1997, when the land reverts to China, remains to be seen. If the leaders in Beijing continue the economic reforms of recent months, permitting some small companies to be run privately, for profit, most of Hong Kong's industrial infrastructure may be handed over intact.

China would be foolish to tamper with this capitalist enclave on its border. More than one-third of China's foreign income flows in from or through Hong Kong: The colony buys the bulk of its food and water from China, as well as oil and electrical power. And 35 percent of all products exported by Hong Kong are in fact simply reexports of goods destined for the mainland in the first place.

But Hong Kong's chief value is its manufacturing plant. Of a total work force of about 2.5 million, nearly half is engaged in manufacturing. Of those 1.2 million workers, the vast majority are employed in the colony's thriving textile industry, which has turned to high-fashion textiles and clothing in order to compete with lower-cost Asian countries. Roughly 50 percent of manufacturing employees work in fabric plants, and clothing factories account for 33 percent more. Other important light-manufacturing industries include electronics, plastics, toys, and electrical equipment. Heavy industries, such as shipbuilding and repair and aircraft maintenance, are present but insignificant. But for China, the real prize that comes with Hong Kong may be the know-how residing in its handful of semiconductor and electronics companies.

CHINA: THE SLEEPING GIANT STIRS

Despite the westward redirection of China's foreign relations after the Sino-Soviet rift, information about what's really happening inside the People's Republic of China remains skimpy and often contradictory. It's still uncertain exactly how many Chinese people there are, what the standard of living is in the twenty-one provinces and five autonomous regions, and how the populace will respond over time to the Beijing government's new policies and programs, including the capitalistic-type incentives to stimulate productivity championed by Premier Zhao Ziyang.

The news that does emerge, such as *Business Week*'s cover story on "Capitalism in China" (January 14, 1985), tends to focus on the industrial regions and cities along China's eastern coast. But the real China is neither industrialized nor urban. The vast majority—80 percent—of China's estimated 1.1 billion citizens, or nearly one-quarter of the world's total population, are rural peasants.

But there's no mystery about the crucial barriers that any modernization scheme must surmount: The overriding need is for new technology in both agriculture and energy production. The leaders in Beijing can buy all the high-tech manufacturing plants they want, but factories will have negligible impact on the average citizen without reforms in agriculture and energy. The problem with China's earlier, unrealistic plans was that they seemed to promise a quick, high-tech fix, as if buying turnkey technology from the West would somehow eliminate the enduring structural deficiencies and raise the standard of living almost overnight.

There now is a general realization that development must proceed cautiously and deliberately, so that the economy doesn't become unbalanced, so that gains aren't eroded by rampant inflation, so that external debt doesn't mushroom to unmanageable proportions. China is in fact shopping for a lot of high-tech know-how and manufacturing systems, including semiconductor plants and computer technology, and it has enough money to buy up almost anything it can get hold of. China's foreign exchange reserves have ballooned to $19 billion.

Over the next ten years, two factors will probably cause a mild decrease in stability. First, it will be almost impossible to avoid provoking unrealistic expectations among the general public. So much needs to be done to repair the country's infrastructure that the people will become impatient with the lack of gains in their personal standard of living. Second, most of China's top-level rulers are elderly and must begin grooming a new generation of leaders, and it's unclear what the priorities of the new elite will be. Dramatic departures from current policies are not expected but can't be ignored.

China's foreign policy will continue to be sympathetic to the Third World, but the country also will be pushed, however reluctantly, to reenter the larger world community. Increased internationalism will be imperative because the drive to modernize means that China's economy will be less insulated from the world economic situation, and that will affect Beijing's ability to carry out its plans without undue stresses and strains.

Nevertheless, the sheer magnitude of the potential market will continue to lure foreign suppliers and investors. China's GNP is already huge—$350 billion—but the upside potential is enormous: Per capita GNP now comes to less than $350. China will be receptive to Western overtures, but the pace of progress in most dealings will test the patience of businesspersons. Tight controls on imports will persist throughout the period.

By the mid- to late 1990s the effects of modernization will begin to work their way down to lift individual living standards. A stable environment for both domestic and foreign business dealings will evolve, and the influx of imports will accelerate substantially. During this decade, China will place more emphasis on modernizing its military establishment as well, and by the year 2000 China will emerge as a significant force in world affairs, militarily and commercially.

China's Economic Resources

China is well-endowed with vast natural resources, the full extent of which is only partially known. But its mineral riches include the world's largest reserves of antimony and tungsten. China currently produces almost 20 percent of the world's antimony output and about 15 percent of world output of tungsten. It also has considerable reserves of bauxite (from which aluminum is made), iron ore, tin, lead, manganese, mercury, and molybdenum.

On the energy front, China has some of the world's largest coal basins, and it has a huge potential for generating hydroelectric power—as much as 1 billion kilowatts. Currently, it has developed only 10 percent of that potential. China has oil reserves estimated at 19.5 billion barrels, not including offshore deposits, which might be still larger. And much of its land mass remains to be explored by modern oil-prospecting techniques.

The basic instruments of economic development are China's (in)famous five-year plans. The first, covering the 1953–57 period, centered on developing heavy industry, with Soviet assistance. In 1958 the policy of "walking on two legs"—simultaneously developing industry and agriculture—was launched, but that five-year plan was interrupted by the Great Leap Forward. For the fifteen years ending in 1975, agriculture took priority over industry. An overly ambitious ten-year plan for the 1976–85 period called for modernization of all sectors. However, in 1979 this plan was adjusted to decrease the emphasis on steel and heavy industry. And in 1980 the plan was repudiated in favor of new five- and ten-year plans with more realistic targets.

During the Great Leap Forward, hundreds of small "backyard" furnaces supplied an estimated 3 to 4 million metric tons of iron—poor-quality pig iron—from which communes fashioned needed tools, utensils, and machinery. Most of these furnaces have since been abandoned, and industrial production now centers on large, integrated complexes that turn out not only steel but also machinery.

Manufacturing is concentrated in regions near the eastern and southern coasts. In the northeast, a huge iron and steel complex at Anshan is the cornerstone of China's oldest and most industrialized region. Activities there include petroleum refining and petrochemical production, coal mining, motor vehicle production, and logging. The Beijing-Tianjin industrial belt is a coal-mining district that supports iron and steel, machinery manufacturing, chemical, and textile plants. In the east, Shanghai is the center of one-third of China's production capacity in light industry and one-quarter of the machinery industry.

Food processing plants are clustered in south-central China. The southwest is China's principal producer of nonferrous metals, at Chengdu, Kunming, and Chongqing. The northwest, far removed from any ocean, is the region now being industrialized intensively. The rapidly growing industrial cities of Xian and Lanzhou are home to petroleum, petro-chemical, iron and steel, and textile industries.

To generate export revenues, Beijing is stressing light industries, particularly such labor-intensive industries as textiles and the assembly of electronic instruments and equipment. Special foreign-trade zones have been established in Guangdong province near Macao, Xiangong (near Hong Kong), Shantou, and Fujian province near Xiamen. In 1983 exports worth $24.0 billion more than offset imports of $18.4 billion.

Until enough time has passed to repair some of the destruction caused by the Cultural Revolution, China will be heavily dependent on imported technology and foreign experts. China's technological base and educational institutions were essentially obliterated by the Red Guards. And undoing the damage isn't just a matter of reassembling the technicians, scientists, and teachers who were forced onto rural communes, because their skills are a decade out of date. The government admits it will take most of the rest of this century to rebuild the educational system; meanwhile, it is experimenting with private institutes where students pay to learn, with correspondence courses, and with a TV university.

As a result, China has been on a wide-ranging shopping spree for up-to-date technology and know-how. The need for hard currency to pay these bills puts considerable pressure on the Chinese economy. Initially, China succumbed to the credit carrot that many nations eagerly offered to help in acquiring technology and equipment. But Beijing's leaders soon recognized the dangers of overextension and are now more circumspect about accepting credit.

A major policy issue is how to keep a lid on inflation. The government worries that high rates of inflation could undermine its ability to implement the modernization programs, if not to maintain control. The latest figures indicate that inflation is running about 5 percent— not high by world standards, but nearly double the rate of a few years ago. Moreover, this rate sits on top of an extensive system of price controls that keeps the cost of most goods and services artificially low. This system will run into growing trouble as China becomes more integrated into the world economy.

In essence, China is a giant underdeveloped country where superlatives abound. Side by side with incredible market potentials are excruciating problems and exasperating policy swings. For example, after Beijing delegated more investment authority to provincial and local officials, they put a disproportionate amount of funds into heavy industry. Light manufacturing therefore suffered and didn't generate the export revenues that the central government had counted on. At the same time, the surge in heavy industry compounded strains on supplies of energy and raw materials. So look for Beijing to reassert control over all levels of domestic investment, which is bound to slow down the pace of negotiations. Even so, considering the enormity of the promise of business with China, investors and suppliers won't be deterred.

SURPRISING INDONESIA

By 1995, Indonesia will have scored the strongest gains of any Asian nation and will emerge as the most stable political entity in the region, jumping over Singapore, South Korea, Malaysia, Thailand, and China.

Indonesia, the world's fifth most populous country (165 million people on 3,000 islands, a total area about the size of Mexico), is blessed with an abundance of natural resources—oil in particular, but also tin, bauxite, nickel, gold, iron, copper, and timber. Although the recent declines in oil prices have substantially curtailed economic growth, the republic's long-range outlook remains bright.

To diversify and increase its export base, Indonesia is building state-owned petrochemical and other processing plants that will turn crude oil, which accounted for 80 percent of 1983's export revenues of $19.3 billion, and other resources into products with a higher value-added content. Mining and exported ores bring in the next largest chunk of revenues.

Indonesia's historical subsistence economy was altered radically during the 300 years of Dutch rule that ended in 1945. Export crops were emphasized by the administrators of what was then the Netherlands East Indies; in fact, raising such crops was mandatory for most farmers. After independence, a socialistic economic system was devised, but it was replaced in 1969 by the military-backed "New Order" of President Suharto, who promised a return to a mainly free-enterprise system and an end to the 600 percent inflation rate that was playing havoc with the economy.

Suharto's measures have been remarkably successful, thanks in large part to the civilian economists and technocrats at the planning ministry, which enjoys widespread respect. During the 1970s inflation averaged less than 15 percent, real annual growth was 8 percent, the government invested heavily in heavy industry, and the general living standard improved steadily for most Indonesians. Now the government is stressing lighter industry, agriculture, and forestry, plus construction of roads, schools, and irrigation canals. The emphasis on infrastructure projects is designed to create jobs—a serious issue, since nearly 2 million people enter the work force every year.

If the government's new policies address the new situation as successfully as those of the past decade, Indonesia should be well-positioned to benefit from economic recovery. With no serious internal opposition to the military-dominated Golkar party and a central bureaucracy that is comparatively free of corruption, the country should become the most stable as well as one of the more prosperous powers in the region.

The regulations governing foreign investment are perhaps the biggest drag on growth. Foreigners aren't allowed to own or lease land, and since 1980 foreign-owned companies have been required to have a native partner who owns at least 20 percent of the business; foreign companies must also have a plan for selling 31 percent more ownership to Indonesians within ten years. Still, many of the overseas companies that have made recent ventures into Indonesia report that the investments are quite profitable.

MALAYSIA'S RACIAL PROBLEM

Conditions in Malaysia are deceptive. Taken at face value, the statistics indicate it has one of the soundest economies among the developing nations of Asia, with a per capita GNP of more than $2,000 for its 15 million citizens. However, there is a very wide gap between the indigenous Malay peasants and the businessmen of Chinese and Indian descent who dominate commerce and industry. Race riots erupted over the disparity in the late 1960s, a decade after Malaysia acquired independence from Britain.

Since 1969, Malaysia has had a New Economic Policy designed to improve the economic plight of the Malays, or *bumiputras* (sons of the soil). The target of the NEP is to cede 30 percent ownership of all businesses to Malays by 1990, with the government picking up the tab. In fact, Malays now own 15 percent of all corporate equity, and they dominate the large plantations and mines (Malaysia is the world's largest producer of natural rubber and tin). Whether the Chinese and Indian minorities will continue to tolerate the special privileges dictated by the Malay-controlled government remains to be seen. So long as business keeps on expanding, chances of open strife—initiated by the Chinese—are probably low. But there's an ugly threat of new racial conflict from a growing faction of militant Islamic Malays.

And a new destabilizing element could be added in the 1990s: widespread demand for basic welfare services that could strain even the country's newfound wealth in oil. Education has improved substantially since independence, yet it is still fairly primitive in rural areas, where 70 percent of the population and most Malays live. Health care is barely adequate. And there is virtually no provision for Social Security.

Manufacturing now accounts for about 20 percent of GNP, after a drive to attract more foreign investment in the 1970s netted considerable increases in textile and rubber production—and, most important, electronics assembly. For example, several U.S. semiconductor companies ship "naked" chips to Malaysia, where they are put into protective housings and reexported back to America. Indeed, Malaysia is second only to Japan in the quantity of semiconductors shipped to the United States. For the future, business opportunities exist in tropical hardwoods, petrochemicals, tin, rubber, and infrastructure projects.

Our assessment is that while the potential for internal conflict seems rife, even a short extension of the New Economic Policy, which may be necessary to achieve its economic objectives, won't trigger overt action. And once the NEP's goals have been attained and normalcy returns, Malaysia will rank number three in terms of stability, behind Indonesia and Singapore.

THAILAND'S UNCONVENTIONAL SYSTEM

Another country that merits serious consideration for long-term investment is the Kingdom of Thailand. It presents something of a contrast to Malaysia, in that Thailand appears highly unstable on the surface but actually has a political system that, while unconventional, affords a surprising degree of stability. The government is a constitutional monarchy, but decison-making powers are vested in the prime minister—who need not be elected; a person can become prime minister solely on the basis of his leadership qualities. The army has the final say in who holds the office. This unusual system is due in part to the fact that despite rich rubber and mineral resources, Thailand (formerly Siam) was never colonized by Europeans and has existed as a monarchy since 1350.

However, over the next ten years, the country will experience a drop in stability due to external factors. Because of persistent regional conflicts, especially between Vietnam and Kampuchea (Cambodia), Thailand will continue to divert money from needed civil programs into military activities. The Thai economy is predominantly agricultural. Farming and fishing represent one-quarter of the GNP and about three-fourths of employment. But the living standards in rural areas are quite poor, since the per capita GNP is only $800. Moreover, many of Thailand's agricultural-export customers are improving their own production of rice, cassava, corn, and beans (Thailand's main export crops), so the country needs to diversify its economic base. Thailand is one of the world's principal sources of rubber and tin, and it also has deposits of tungsten, lead, fluorite, and lignite.

Longer term, the outlook is much better. Thailand's oil and gas reserves promise energy independence, and its close relations with China could lead to important trade agreements that would help fund programs to improve domestic living standards. U.S. companies may want to consider establishing operations in Thailand to gain "back-door" entry into China's huge markets.

AFRICA'S IMPRESSIVE RISE

Four of Africa's industrializing countries—Egypt, Nigeria, Zimbabwe, and South Africa—will climb an impressive ten or more places on our stability rankings. By the turn of the century, at least three will present a solid cluster of opportunity at the top of the second tier of countries, sitting above Saudi Arabia, China, Mexico, and Libya. Nigeria is the big question mark among the four. Meanwhile, Libya, which will match their progress during the short term, is due for a spectacular plunge in the late 1990s (as noted earlier).

Of the four, Zimbabwe (formerly Rhodesia) will manage the biggest gains. Slightly smaller than California, Zimbabwe is not only blessed with abundant resources but also boasts the most diversified and self-sufficient economy in all of Africa—achieved in just twenty years of independence.

For most of this century, Rhodesia was a Crown colony and utterly dependent on trade with Britain. It exported tobacco and other agricultural products, as well as mineral ores, and imported essentially all manufactured items. After Rhodesia's unilateral declaration of independence in 1965, Britain and the United Nations tried to exploit the lack of a manufacturing base by imposing a trade embargo. But the move backfired. Instead of forcing Rhodesia's all-white government to submit to demands for more participation by the country's 96 percent black population, the sanctions simply spurred Prime Minister Ian D. Smith's government to emphasize industrialization.

Today, factories employ 15 percent of the work force and generate one-fourth of Zimbabwe's GDP—$7 billion in 1982. Major products include iron and steel, automobiles, textiles, chemicals, leather goods, processed foods, and tobacco products. About 6 percent of the labor force work in mines and produce 8 percent of GNP. The country possesses two-thirds of the world's known deposits of chromite; chromium, gold, platinum, copper, and tin are the other main minerals. Lacking petroleum, the country draws hydroelectric power from the huge Kariba Dam on the Zambezi River and makes up the balance of its needs by burning coal from the rich deposits near Hwange. Still, Zimbabwe's per capita GNP for blacks is less than $700 (versus $13,500 for whites).

Per capita income has been held down in recent years because growth in manufacturing and mining is suffering from shortages of capital, managers, technicians, and skilled workers—largely because of a white exodus after black rule became inevitable under an agreement signed in 1978. Whites owned half of the country's land area and all of the big, efficient plantations; moreover, white Rhodesians or foreigners owned and operated all industrial facilities. There was no way to train blacks to fill the voids as rapidly as the whites left.

After the general election of 1980 brought Marxist-socialist Robert G. Mugabe to power as prime minister, the exodus intensified. Mugabe's strident rhetoric, although frequently tempered with actions designed to soothe the private sector, has cast a pall of uncertainty over foreign investments. The new constitution stipulates that whites be fairly compensated for land that is "resettled" with black farmers, and payments so far have been generous indeed. Yet the mood of uncertainty was intensified when the government recently formed a national minerals marketing company, which many foreign mining interests view as a forerunner of nationalization.

Perhaps Mugabe is just buying time, throwing a bone to the young radicals in his party, the Zimbabwe African National Union (ZANU). He may be hoping that, given time, the radical element will also recognize that pragmatism requires tolerance of foreign capitalists. But whatever the strategy, the move has effectively scrubbed foreign investment—not just in mining but in other industries, too. Those mining companies that aren't selling out are writing down their assets.

Zimbabwe: The Next Five Years—A Crucial Period

For the near term, until the situation shakes out, companies thinking of investing in Zimbabwe will be looking for relatively fast paybacks. That will hamper development in manufacturing and mining. Over the long pull, Zimbabwe will undoubtedly become a socialist state, probably closer to the Yugoslav model than to that of the Soviet Union; Mugabe and the ZANU party have pointedly shunned the Soviets. But in order to attract the foreign money and Western knowhow that the country desperately needs to meet the rapidly rising expectations of its people, some accommodation will be necessary. The government needs to articulate a tough policy for the fair treatment of outside capital. Whether and how that will be accomplished may become clearer after the elections now scheduled for mid-1985.

Of the other problems that cloud the immediate horizon, the most serious are relations with South Africa and the potential for intertribal conflict. Zimbabwe abhors the white-supremacist politics of South Africa. Yet land-locked Zimbabwe must have access to South Africa's railways and seaports to export its goods. South Africa has on several occasions hit Zimbabwe with sanctions to demonstrate just how dependent it is, how easy it would be for South Africa to disrupt the Zimbabwean economy. As a result, Zimbabwe must bite its tongue in criticizing apartheid—a frustrating practicality that fans tempers among ZANU's young turks.

The power base of the minority Ndebele tribe (19 percent of the population) is the Zimbabwe African People's Union, headed by Joseph Nkomo. Initially, Mugabe sought to blunt opposition by bringing Nkomo into his government, but Nkomo was later expelled on charges that he was plotting a coup after large caches of weapons were discovered on ZAPU property. The ZAPU is splintered from within, and Mugabe now seems to be reducing its influence with divide-and-conquer tactics. His ultimate objective is a one-party state, and he is progressing well, in that it's doubtful the ZAPU will be a serious threat in 1985's elections.

Mugabe must still work out a lasting arrangement between the Ndebele and his own Shona tribe (more than 70 percent of the population), but the longer the government continues to avoid extremist policies, and the longer the two tribes continue to avert armed conflict, the better the ultimate outlook for Zimbabwe. If the country's advance continues through 1990, the prognostication for the next decade will be greatly enhanced. And if things keep moving ahead until 1995, Zimbabwe should ring in the new century with a vibrant economy and be well on the road to becoming a regional power.

Nigeria: Not So Much Better as Less Bad

On December 31, 1983, Nigeria's government returned to military hands after slightly more than four years of civilian rule. The change bodes well for the country, at least in the short term, even though the leader of the coup, General Mohammed Buhari, is a political unknown. We doubt Nigeria will try another experiment with democracy before 1995. By then, conditions inside the country may improve sufficiently that a civilian leader stands a chance of remaining in office long enough for the notion of civil government to take hold. Even so, Nigeria's longer-range outlook remains dicey.

The world's most populous black nation (roughly 90 million people, growing by nearly 3.5 percent a year) elected its first government in thirteen years, headed by Alhaji Shehu Shegari, in 1979. While President Shegari was considered scrupulously honest, the same wasn't true of his staff. During Shegari's first term, corruption became rampant. At the same time, the government seemed incapable of dealing with the sudden reversal in the world oil market. OPEC's reduced production and pricing schedules slashed Nigeria's oil revenues by more than half from the peak levels of 1979—foreign exchange earnings plunged from $22 billion to around $10 billion—throwing the country's grandiose development plans into disarray. In the wake of the government's reelection in August 1983, there were widespread charges of fraud and election fixing. Buhari and his senior military followers rushed to take over the government, according to one line of speculation, to prevent a coup by a group of radical young officers.

Nigeria faces a variety of tough decisions, and probably only a strong military head of government stands a chance of dealing with them effectively. Development projects, such as the modern steel complex established in 1982 at Ajaokuta, are notoriously expensive because of official corruption. Although Nigeria is among the world's top ten producers of natural rubber, tin, and hardwoods, the lion's share of export revenues come from oil and petroleum products refined by plants at Port Harcourt, Warri, and Kaduna. The country's agricultural sector, which employs slightly more than half of all workers, has been falling farther behind population growth for three decades. Manufacturing is aimed at import substitution and, despite 30 percent expansion rates in the early 1980s, accounts for only 10 percent of gross domestic product.

Socially, Nigeria is a loose patchwork of some 250 tribes, each with its own language; in fact, more than 300 languages and perhaps 1,000 dialects are spoken. The country is divided into three main parts by the Niger River and the Benue River, which form a giant Y. National unity, already strained, was aggravated further by the bloody civil war of 1967–70, when the Ibo-dominated eastern region attempted to secede and establish independent Biafra. Along the coast, Christianity was transplanted by Portuguese and British colonialists, while Islam took root in the north; in the interior, old animistic religions still prevail. Widespread illiteracy, an unskilled labor force, and excessive dependence on foreign technology and capital compound Nigeria's problems.

Left to stew, these forces and factors could lead to the disintegration of the country. So the resumption of power by the military is likely a blessing in disguise. If a semblance of order is maintained for the remainder of this decade, Nigeria should remain a regional influence and a vocal member of OPEC and the UN. If the military can establish itself as the (now missing) focus of national unity and remain in stable control through the 1990s while delivering on national expectations of universal primary education, better health care, and more jobs, Nigeria could begin to emerge as a viable nation-state in the next century.

However, we base our forecast on the premise that all those "ifs" come to pass. The short-range outlook is immensely better than it was. But the mid-to-late 1990s will likely be the next critical period in Nigerian history. Nigeria's growth will still depend upon the changes listed above.

Egypt's Chronic Growth Dilemma

Egypt, the most populous nation in the Arab world and, after Nigeria, the second-most populous country in Africa, faces several economic problems that will remain intractable so long as its population continues to increase by almost 3 percent annually. More than 96 percent of Egypt's population lives along the narrow Nile River valley—never fertile for more than 10 miles on either side—and the Nile Delta; these areas account for only 4 percent of the total land mass. Most of the rest of the nation lives along the Suez Canal.

Half of Egypt's 47 million people have a hand-to-mouth, subsistence life on farms where antiquated methods limit yields. While cotton and sugar are major export crops, large amounts of food have to be imported; for instance, nearly three-quarters of the wheat that's consumed comes from the United States and other trading partners. Food and other essential imports are paid for mainly with credits earned from exports of oil, Suez Canal fees, tourism, and remittances from the thousands of Egyptians who work in foreign countries. All of these sources of foreign exchange, except for the canal fees, are down substantially since the late 1970s, and the country has been importing about $6 billion more than its $3 billion in exports. As a result, Egypt has amassed the world's tenth largest foreign debt and is heavily dependent on foreign aid.

Despite these troubles, the political system exhibited remarkable stability after the assassination of President Anwar al-Sadat in October 1981. The transfer of power to Hosni Mubarak, Sadat's hand-picked successor, proceeded smoothly and calmly. Mubarak, knowing full well he would remain in office only with the blessing of the military, spent the early years of his presidency establishing a power base within the armed services. He appears to have been successful there, and he also is enormously popular with the public. Finally, he is reestablishing friendly relations with other Arab countries while maintaining the uneasy peace with Israel.

Extremists and fundamentalists still pose a threat to internal stability, as evident from the riots and protests that Sadat put down in early 1981, but Mubarak seems to have gained the upper hand and could, if need be, deal forcefully with such destablizing factions. So Mubarak looks like a good bet to consolidate his authority and thus will likely remain the head of government through at least the early 1990s.

Beyond that time frame, though, the outlook gets more murky. Mubarak has yet to demonstrate the iron will which he'll need to deal effectively with the problems that bedevil his country. Chief among these is the absolute necessity of curbing the birthrate. Otherwise, economic development never will catch up with demand, and an already overburdened welfare-delivery system might even collapse completely. About the best that can be expected of Egypt at the turn of the century is that it will still be a developing country—and one that's on the slow track. And even that hinges on how quickly certain actions are initiated.

Mubarak must turn his immediate attention to attacking the economic problems that plague Egypt. So far, about all his government has done is to list the problems and outline broad objectives. Detailed plans for attaining these goals are still awaited, although Mubarak has continued to support Sadat's *infitah*, a policy of encouraging the private sector and foreign investors to concentrate on manufacturing projects that will erect a foundation for long-range economic growth. Manufacturing must be nurtured because Egypt's oil reserves are quite modest, only about 3 billion barrels. So the current five-year plan calls for shifting the balance of the economy to industry and agriculture, plus slashing the trade deficit by boosting exports and imposing rigid ceilings on imports.

The manufacturing sectors targeted for investment are primarily traditional industries: foodstuffs, textiles, metallurgical products, chemicals, and a growing arms business that promises to be an important source of export revenues. In mining, Egypt has deposits of phosphate, manganese, iron ore, and salt—as well as the Middle East's largest uranium deposit, discovered in 1980. Apart from the uranium mining, all of these industries have been established for many years, but their physical plants have been neglected, due to the balance-of-payments crunch, and badly need revamping or replacement. Similarly, Egypt's roads, ports, and other infrastructure facilities have deteriorated.

Foreign companies that can offer equipment and know-how in these fields may be attracted to Egypt. The country offers various incentives to foreign investors, including preferential tax policies and import duties. At the same time, however, foreign companies will face several hurdles, not the least of which is the glacial pace at which the bureaucracy processes applications. Regulations and controls are cumbersome, and financial assistance will be extremely tight until oil prices increase.

Libya's Castle of Sand

Colonel Muammar al-Qaddafi's one-man rule of Libya is likely more than half over. He has been in power sixteen years, since he led a 1969 military coup that deposed the constitutional monarchy, but his renegade government will probably come tumbling down in another military coup around 1995. That will trigger a period of extreme instability followed, in all likelihood, by Libya's sinking back into obscurity. The country is large—more than twice the size of Texas—but apart from oil (a fairly small reserve of 21 billion barrels that will be dwindling rapidly in the 1990s) it has little to recommend it. More than 92 percent of the land is desert, with few resources other than oil, which generates half the country's GDP and 95 percent or more of foreign exchange credits. Only 40 percent of the country's 3.5 million people are literate.

There is mounting disaffection with the revolutionary regime throughout all levels of Libyan society, and astonishingly little commitment among the apolitical Libyan people to Qaddafi's socialistic ideals. He is not supported so much as tolerated for the materialistic benefits distributed by the government. The standard of living of the average Libyan has improved steadily under Qaddafi. Yet his basic insecurity is reflected in the increasingly frequent purges of tribal leaders, government bureaucrats and employees, university students and faculties, journalists, and military personnel. His decision to nationalize import-export trade and the distribution of key commodities also alienated many businessmen.

The economy is being grossly mismanaged. Libya has been throwing its oil revenues at industrialization, but in a helter-skelter manner. There appears to be little rationale for the diversity of projects, which are generally purchased on a turnkey basis with little technology transfer. With its oil revenues down to about half the 1980 figure of $24 billion, Qaddafi often unilaterally elects to delay servicing the country's debt and paying its industrialization bills if doing so would mean diverting funds from terrorist groups and other international adventures. The banking community is thus understandably leery of further loans.

That opens the real possibility of serious capital shortages in the late 1980s, when Libya will be competing with Saudi Arabia and Europe to sell petrochemical products to a glutted world market. Some development projects could then grind to a halt for want of financing, leaving plants uncompleted. Qaddafi is in a race to modernize industry and agriculture before Libya's oil money peters out. Unless he stops squandering capital, Qaddafi will soon be unable to make good on rising expectations in education, health care, and general prosperity. At that point, his days will be numbered.

Roller-Coaster Rides in Mideast Stability

Two major shifts in stability will keep the pot roiling in the ever-turbulent Mideast. Saudi Arabia, the principal moderating force in the region, is heading for an inevitable confrontation of values, traditional versus modern; the showdown will likely happen before the year 2000 and will surely precipitate a period of grave instability. Conversely, Israel's stability will plummet alarmingly over the next ten years or so, but conditions there should be on the mend by the turn of the century.

Saudi Arabia is a vast desert about the size of the continental United States east of the Mississippi, with no more people than the population of metropolitan New York City. In this vast desert practically nothing grows naturally save for date trees around oases; all of the land under cultivation could be fitted inside the state of Connecticut. But what the kingdom does have in abundance, of course, is oil—

close to 166 billion barrels of the stuff, enough to last (at current production rates) until well past 2050. So the current honchos in the Saud dynasty could, if they wished, sit back and funnel petrodollars to their subjects—and let future leaders of the House of Saud worry about what happens when the oil peters out.

Instead, King Fahd ibn Abdul Aziz al-Saud is pushing aggressively ahead with plans to industrialize the country. And the next Five-Year Plan (1985–90) could mark a turning point in Saudi history. This plan puts more emphasis on alleviating shortages of skilled (and even unskilled) manpower, but that presents a Hobson's choice: The country is desperately short of workers, yet the Saudis are almost paranoid about the contaminating influence of large numbers of foreign workers in their midst. About the only way to expand the labor force from within would be to allow women to work. But that would begin to unravel the fabric of traditional Saudi society, unless the workplace environment can be organized so that women do not come into contact with strange men.

Women working side by side with men from outside their own extended family would be a dire breach of basic Arab values (in their eyes worse than if, say, the United States passed a law requiring all women to disrobe and work in the nude). It would be especially appalling to the fundamentalist Shiite minority in the oil-rich eastern region, just across the Persian Gulf from Iran. King Fahd must therefore tread cautiously toward modernization, else he could provide the Ayatollah Khomeini with an opportunity to foment unrest and dissension.

On the other hand, the House of Saud will also have to contend with rising demand from the nouveau middle class for a political voice. To them, the pace of modernization will probably seem too slow, no matter how fast. Today, Saudi Arabia has no parliament, no political parties, no government at any level except that administered by the House of Saud's princes and princelings.

These rising expectations of the middle class are the fruits of the three previous development plans, which have been remarkably successful. In 1982, with a gross domestic product of more than $165 billion, Saudi Arabia had a per capita income of just under $18,500. The first economic plan (1970–75) focused on infrastructure construction projects: roads, seaports, housing, and utilities. The second plan (1975–80), more ambitious because it was launched after the jump in oil prices, stressed modernizing education and defense, industrialization, and even the creation of two new industrial cities—Jubail on the gulf coast and Yanbu on the Red Sea, both of which are now virtually finished. The third plan (1980–85) continued the investment in industry while seeking to improve agricultural productivity through irrigation, the use of new seeds and fertilizers, and mechanization.

Reconciling the many conflicting pressures to the general satisfaction of everyone will doubtless be impossible. The strain could lead to the overthrow of the House of Saud, or perhaps to a rift in the family. But even if neither of those possibilities come to pass, the stability of Saudi Arabia will almost certainly ebb during the 1990s.

Nevertheless, for companies that can offer the technologies, management training, and automation that the Saudis want, the investment climate will be very favorable. Low-interest loans, tax holidays, and other benefits will be readily provided. The investments accorded the best treatment will be those that help the Saudis lessen their dependence on oil exports. Crude oil and petroleum products now account for 99 percent of all export revenues.

Israel's Rebound

Things have been going from bad to worse within the State of Israel. Divisions have deepened among the country's people and politicians over such issues as economic policy, Lebanon, and West Bank settlements. Without, Israel's usual friends—the United States and Europe—are losing patience with the Likud government's uncompromising policies concerning the Palestine question.

For the near term, these disruptive trends will intensify. To bring the economy under control and arrest the triple-digit inflation rate that has been undermining living standards, severe austerity measures are needed. But it's unlikely that the nation's 4 million citizens would tolerate such a move. External pressures will keep on mounting unless there's a radical change in foreign policy, which also is unlikely.

Yet Israel is only postponing the inevitable time of reckoning. Not many more years can pass before the situation grows critical and these thorny problems will have to be tackled. Depending on which way the country leaps, Israel will either begin to rebound during the 1990s (probable) or it will sow the seeds of its own destruction (possible).

After nearly thirty years of domination by the mildly socialistic Labor party, Israel in 1977 turned to the Likud party under Menachem Begin and Yitzhak Shamir, who has been prime minister since 1983. But that transition pales beside the one due in 1985. Perhaps by the time you read this, the Israelis will have gone back to the polls to choose their next government. This election will mark a pivotal point in the history of Israel, in that many of the "old guard"—the men and women who fought the first Arab-Israeli war in 1948–49, such as Begin—will pass the reins of leadership to a younger generation.

Astute observers will be watching one "leading indicator" of how pragmatic the new government will be: A relatively quick fix to cut costs would be to trim the country's bloated bureaucracy, which employs nearly 30 percent of the work force, or six to seven percentage points more than industry, the next largest employer. Doing so, however, will be politically painful, since many of these positions are awarded as patronage to supporters. Furthermore, the government employees' union is itself a strong political force.

But the crux of Israel's future rests in the resolution of the struggle between those who favor returning to a compact, cohesive nation and those who demand that the territorial gains of recent wars be retained for the sake of national security, even at the expense of internal homogeneity and of continuing enmity from Israel's Arab neighbors. Unless the new government bites the bullet on the Palestinian question and reaches an accommodation on this issue with the Arab world—either granting Palestine independence or at least allowing it to be administered by Jordan—Israel won't be able to devote sufficient resources to its internal troubles; economic conditions will go on deteriorating, and Western support will eventually be decreased to the point where Israel will be unable to maintain its independence.

However, if Israel sacrifices Palestine, the Jewish state's future is all but assured. It has already laid the foundation for a viable economy. Because of its constant vigilance and the need for advanced military technology, Israel has invested heavily in electronics and military hardware. Israeli firms have made important penetrations of world markets for computers, sophisticated medical instruments, and tele-communications. And the Israeli arms industry contributes significant export earnings that help offset the country's lopsided balance of payments: Imports have been running almost double the level of exports ($9-plus billion versus $5 billion). Although some of Israel's high-tech business now faces tough competition, the situation could probably be remedied given time and more R&D funds—both of which would be available if the new government decides it can afford to placate its neighbors and bargain away Palestine.

THE UPBEAT TEMPO IN LATIN AMERICA

Except for Mexico, most Western Hemisphere countries on our stability chart are due for a period of generally rising prosperity and stability over the next twenty years. At worst, gains in the first ten years will cancel losses in the second ten. Argentina, Panama, and Brazil will move up from the bottom half of the list and by 2005 will rank just under Venezuela.

Argentina boasts the most highly developed and diverse economy in Latin America. During the twentieth century, its economy has gradually shifted from large-scale production of livestock and agricultural goods to one dominated by industry and services. But it remains self-sufficient in food. There was even a time, back between the two world wars, when Argentina's level of development ranked right alongside that of a number of European countries. Since the end of World War II, however, economic growth has been hampered by inconsistent and sometimes irresponsible economic policies, and chronic inflation fueled by large deficits, the result of huge public sector spending.

But the Argentine economy hasn't stopped evolving. The country is rich in natural resources, especially oil. Although most of its mineral deposits are too small for world-class development, they support an extremely varied domestic manufacturing base that obviates the need for importing most consumer goods and oil. By the early 1970s, manufacturing and construction accounted for 37 percent of GNP, more than twice the share of any other sector. Since then, services have come on strong and today account for 46 percent of GNP ($130 billion in 1981, or $4,600 per capita), with manufacturing now at 31 percent.

At the start of Argentina's latest experiment with democracy, when Raul Alfonsin took over the presidency at the end of 1983, he faced an inflation rate of better than 400 percent, unemployment of somewhere between 15 and 25 percent, and a foreign debt of $43 billion. The question is, can Alfonsin's government reduce these gloomy statistics enough before public disaffection with the military, due to its defeat in the Falkland Islands (Malvinas), wears off and the threat of yet another coup rears up? There are high hopes that democracy may finally take root in Argentina, but a candid appraisal suggests that the time is not yet ripe.

Alfonsin's challenge is Herculean. He must stimulate economic growth while controlling inflation and avoiding massive labor unrest, then democratize and depoliticize the labor unions without triggering a labor backlash. At the same time, he must reform the military to instill more professionalism and diminish its penchant for political intervention. Only if he pulls off all of the above will Argentina stand a decent chance of seeing one elected government hand over authority to another democratic government. Because there can be no confidence that such a peaceful transition will happen, foreign investors will have to wrestle with this quandry: While Argentina offers attractive business prospects, the periodic upheavals in government tend to touch off radical swings in policy that put foreign investments at risk.

There's an element of Catch-22 here, in that Alfonsin is downplaying involvement in the private sector on the premise that continuity of government will stimulate the investments that industry needs to expand and increase productivity. But without a more concerted move on the economy's troubles, can civilian government last long enough to demonstrate real continuity? The economic strategy formulated by Alfonsin and his minister of economy, Bernardo Grinspun, involves five main elements: 1) dissolving or selling off hundreds of unprofitable state-owned companies acquired under the previous military regime; 2) supplementing price controls with wage limits; 3) reducing the deficit by cutting military expenditures, raising taxes on the wealthy, and improving the collection of taxes; 4) renegotiating foreign debt, and 5) decreasing the growth of money supply.

For the balance of the 1980s Argentina's concentration will remain turned inward. Inflation will probably be curbed, but it will be a slow process—and it will still be quite high by Western standards in 1989. The government will keep adjusting the exchange rate so that the Argentine peso is cheap relative to the dollar, which should maintain the country's favorable trade balance. Agricultural exports will be the chief earners of foreign credit, but manufactured goods will also do reasonably well, especially chemicals and textiles.

Argentina would like to diversify its export mix, particularly in the manufacturing sector, but that effort will be hampered by the lack of foreign funds. The inflow of investments could improve if the government stays in civilian hands, but outside investment would remain sparse through most of the 1990s if the military reasserts a political role. However, no matter which faction rules, conditions inside the country should gradually improve. But a return to military leadership would mean that, despite gains in stability, most U.S. business interests would remain cool to Argentine investments.

Brazil Returns to Democracy, Too

In many ways, Brazil is a king-size Argentina. Brazil's economy also is diverse and balanced, with a well-developed infrastructure. In the interior parts of the country, there's a sense of the pioneer spirit as well—very much like that of America's Old West. Indeed, the Christian work ethic is so strong in Brazil that this country will increasingly give competitive fits to some U.S. companies, and within ten to fifteen years Brazil could become America's chief rival in this hemisphere.

After Brazil gained independence from Portugal in 1822, the country enjoyed unusually long periods of political stability. After independence, the next upheaval was a bloodless revolution in 1889 that overthrew the monarchy. Then things quieted down until the Depression. Beginning in 1930, social and political strife led to the rise and fall of several governments. The political turmoil finally ended in 1964, when the military seized power (and stayed in control for the next twenty-one years).

As in Argentina, Brazil has returned to democracy—even more

recently than its neighbor. Brazil's new 74-year-old president, Tancredo Neves, took office in March 1985. He faces many of the same problems as Argentina's Alfonsin: an intolerable inflation rate (230 percent), massive foreign debt ($90 billion or more, the biggest in the world), state-owned companies that are losing money, and a restive labor force. Many unions are demanding that the country's round of wage hikes, now awarded to everyone every six months to compensate for the vagaries of inflation, should be handed out quarterly, instead. If Neves foolishly gives in, some observers predict that the inflation rate could run up past 300 percent.

The next few years are going to be painful for the largest country in South America (just slightly smaller than the United States). The big unknown is whether the people will endure the necessary austerity measures long enough to correct the country's economic ills.

Apart from dealing with inflation and the inflationary demands of labor, Neves will have to tiptoe around the military to get a grip on the state-owned firms, such as Petrobras. Top management posts in the nationalized companies, which account for nearly 40 percent of Brazil's foreign debt, have traditionally been the private preserve of retired military officers. While the nation was ruled by the military, private businessmen judiciously refused to poach on that turf. Even now, Neves is unlikely to find many volunteers.

Brazil's extraordinary political stability has undoubtedly helped the economy to weather the two boom-and-bust cycles it has passed through: Brazil was the world's leading producer of sugarcane in the eighteenth century, then of rubber in the nineteenth century—and in each case Brazil was overtaken, although both crops are still grown. Today, coffee is the main export crop, and again, Brazil produces more of it than any other country (even though connoisseurs generally sniff at Brazilian beans). Brazil also exports more oranges, beef, and lumber than any other Latin American nation.

For the past few decades, industrial development has been impressive, particularly the development of technology-based industries in the 1970s, when GDP climbed some 8.4 percent annually. By the early eighties, manufacturing, mining, and construction accounted for about one-third of GDP. Brazil is Latin America's champion producer of iron and steel, and it manufactures more automobiles than any other country in Latin America—and more alcohol-powered cars than the rest of the world put together. Most manufacturing is concentrated in the São Paulo area.

When it comes to mineral resources, the parallelism between Brazil and Argentina breaks down. Brazil has tremendous mineral deposits but little oil; in fact, Brazil imports three-quarters of its oil, although that is being trimmed as more people switch to alcohol-fueled cars. Conversely, Brazil is the world's leading exporter of iron ore. It has roughly 25 percent of the entire world's know iron ore reserves, and a recently discovered "iron mountain" in the Carajás Highlands may be the single largest deposit of iron anywhere. Brazil may have as much as half of the world's platinum reserves. The country also is rich in manganese and bauxite—and gold—and it has large amounts of tin, copper, uranium, and coal.

All told, exports of raw materials plus manufactured goods and agricultural items came close to $22 billion in 1983. That tally surpassed the export value for any other South American country, including oil-rich Venezuela. Expanding exports further will be more difficult, though. Brazil is starting to run into protectionist sentiment in the United States and the European community, while some of the markets that Brazil had cultivated—for example, in Argentina, Mexico, Nigeria, and Poland—have collapsed and may not recover for years.

Brazil nonetheless provides a reasonably good environment for prudent foreign investment. Caution is advised because, beyond the common stipulation of 51 percent local ownership and limits on repatriating profits, the government sometimes draws a protective circle around an infant industry, excluding even companies already active in that industry if they have foreign ownership. The most recent examples are the computer and telecommunications industries. Some foreign-owned existing companies making mini- or microcomputers, peripherals, modems, or semiconductor chips were forced to sell out or find a joint-venture partner and accept restrictions on production.

Long term, Brazil will become a formidable competitor for the United States in many regional and world markets (assuming that it manages to extricate itself from its debt problems). Beyond the early 1990s Brazil will likely extend its export drive to include consumer durables and disposables, electronic parts and systems, and military hardware.

Panama Takes Over the Canal

This Central American country has been stuck in the doldrums for over a decade, and improving its lot won't be easy, since Panama is deficient in both energy and natural resources. The transfer of responsibility for the defense and administration of the Panama Canal to the Panamanian government by the year 2000 will impose additional economic burdens, and these will intensify with each year in the 1990s. Because of the canal's strategic importance, however, the United States and probably Japan will provide generous aid and assistance. But that won't solve Panama's basic problem: cultivating a means of raising the wherewithal to pay for past favors and future imports—the country's imports of roughly $1.5 billion are five times its exports.

The 1970s were rough years for Panama. It got hit with a double whammy: soaring oil prices plus falling prices for its traditional agricultural products (mainly bananas and other fruits, sugar, cocoa, and coffee). Because the country has little else to offer on international markets, GDP increased less than 1 percent annually while inflation accelerated at several times that rate, so the real per capita income of most workers declined. That situation was exacerbated by declining employment in the agricultural sector, which still provides about 30 percent of all jobs.

Since the completion of the canal in 1914, Panama's economy has been greatly influenced by this transportation artery. Commerce, finance, and services employ almost half of the labor force. Offshore banking is a major and rapidly growing factor, thanks to strict bank secrecy laws, favorable tax laws, and good communications facilities. Hand in hand with that business, Panama also is thriving as an international insurance center.

Industrial development is hobbled by a grave lack of resources. The only indigenous source of energy is hydropower, and that is barely sufficient for the country's service businesses and few factories. About the only mineral known to exist in commercial quantities is copper, but Panama has tabled exploiting this resource because of the depressed and wildly gyrating price for copper. Instead, Panama is pinning its hopes on attracting foreign assembly and light manufacturing operations to a rejuvenated Free Economic Zone on the outskirts of Colon. The carrot is Panama's participation in the Caribbean Basin Initiative, which affords attractive treatment of exports to the U.S. market. Panama hopes to draw overseas investors eager to tap the American market through the CBI treaty.

The main blemish on Panama's outlook is a recent outbreak of labor unrest. Any serious threat to internal stability would almost surely be quashed by the National Guard, which has been ruling the country in fact or by proxy since 1968—and will continue to be the power behind the new president, Nicholas Ardito-Barletta, as Panama completes the transition to democracy that began with legislative elections in 1980. In any case, labor agitation should subside once the economy begins expanding again.

Even with the enticement of the CBI, it's debatable whether Panama will be able to attract foreign investments as rapidly as it would like. The surge won't occur until the early to mid-1990s, because the new civilian government is too much of an unknown factor, and foreign businessmen will want to see how the wind is blowing before commiting a lot of money. Some foreign observers say that a return to military rule—a distinct possibility if the government proves unable to cope with the tough economic problems—would actually be welcomed by potential investors.

What really would give Panama a shot in the arm, of course, would be the construction of a new canal, big enough to accommodate supertankers and other ships that can't pass through the present canal. But don't look for that until well into the next century.

The Salvadoran Dilemma

El Salvador will rise substantially, short-term, on our chart of political stability. But the improvement will be largely cosmetic and almost certainly transitory, so anyone considering an investment there should be very wary. Any new investments should be designed for extremely rapid payback.

For the immediate future, the situation will improve because the

Salvadoran establishment and President Jose Napoleon Duarte will be under intense international pressure—from the Reagan Administration, from the Kissinger Commission, and from the Organization of American States—to reach some accommodation with the leftist guerrillas who control nearly 25 percent of the country. Duarte and his military sponsors know that, with patience growing thin in the U.S. Congress, they must institute some reforms or face bankruptcy if the U.S. trims its aid.

Still, it's unlikely that whatever measures are adopted will go much beyond tokenism, despite the good intentions of Duarte. El Salvador's troubles are deep, multifaceted, and won't be solved readily. So the government probably will just buy time, hoping that the spotlight of international opinion will shift elsewhere. When that happens, the situation will no doubt regress—and unless the military can assert some control over its radical-right factions and curb the lawless death squads, the country's longer-term prospects could be bleaker than the drop in stability shown in our chart.

The fundamental issue is land reform. El Salvador is the most densely populated Latin American nation, with 4.7 million people occupying an area the size of Massachusetts. That's 570 persons per square mile, most of them eking out a subsistence living from the land. Only about a third of the land is suitable for cultivation, most of that is held by absentee landowners, and meanwhile the population is growing at 2.7 percent annually, one of the highest rates in the Americas.

No workable consensus for alleviating these pressures is in sight, nor is there an institutional framework adequate for the job of achieving a workable compromise among the army, the elite, the guerrillas, the ultra-right wing, and the various labor, peasant, business, and other special-interest groups. Hence, El Salvador seems doomed to a future of internal strife and violence that will thwart attempts to attract outside capital for industrialization. A return to military rule thus seems virtually assured.

The military has been in power almost continuously since 1931, and its response to increasing political unrest has been increasingly strident repression. Political violence escalated sharply after the 1977 election in which General Carlos Humberto Romero Mena became president. He was deposed in 1979 by a group of reform-minded military officers. The military-civilian junta that resulted adopted a partial land reform measure in 1980, ceding most large farms (1,250 acres and up) to cooperatives comprised of the peasants who were working the lands.

However, because the country's huge coffee and sugar plantations were not included—they account for half of El Salvador's foreign exchange earnings—only about 25 percent of the arable land was affected. Subsequent stages of the reform plan, which would have expropriated most of the remaining land held by absentee owners, were blocked after right-winger Alvaro Alfredo Magana was elected president in early 1982.

The economy has been severely damaged by the civil war. Over the past five years, living standards have deteriorated as per capita income has dropped 30 percent, gross domestic product has declined nearly as much, and export earnings fell 35 percent. Small wonder that unemployment is running an estimated 35 to 40 percent. The violence has also exacerbated the tensions between rural and urban areas, since the disparity in public services such as education and health care, already skimpy outside of urban areas, has become even more pronounced.

There seems to be little prospect that a stable, long-range solution to this morass can be agreed upon. Failing that, once pressures from the U.S. and the OAS subside, the Salvadoran economy can only continue to erode. No foreign capital will be available, and what meager public capital has been going to infrastructure and industrial investments will no doubt dry up. If further land reforms can be pushed through, the level of violence may gradually subside and demand for fertilizers could provide a business opportunity in the 1990s. Otherwise, El Salvador presents barren ground for foreign investment for the remainder of this century.

Mexico: Mañana

Declining demand for oil combined with lower oil prices has precipitated an economic crisis in Mexico. In return for loans from the International Monetary Fund to keep the economy afloat, the country has been forced to accept severe austerity measures. The short-term result will be a marginal enhancement of stability, but the IMF's dictates will, in the long run, only help make a bad situation worse.

In Latin America's third-largest country—80 million Mexicans strong—fully 40 percent of the labor force is unemployed, and most workers and peasants suffered a decline in their standard of living over the past decade because of soaring inflation (now down below triple digits, but still in the high double digits). Industrial development has stagnated, and the agriculture sector has been ravaged by drought. President Miguel de la Madrid Hurtado's immediate priorities are to arrest inflation, attract foreign capital to stimulate targeted industries, keep a lid on imports, and boost exports.

While de la Madrid should achieve a modicum of success in the near future, the outlook quickly becomes gloomy again. There is virtually no way to overcome Mexico's underlying structural problems before the turn of the century, if then. The principal reason is the country's birthrate; population growth is marching along at 2.6 percent a year, despite government successes in promoting family planning. That means roughly 1 million new jobs need to be created this year just for the young men and some women who will enter the work force for the first time. Not only won't that happen, but agricultural productivity won't increase enough to feed this year's crop of 2 million newborns. In the past, too much of Mexico's borrowings were devoted to stimulating consumption through price subsidies, and not enough to funding long-term investments in both industry and farm irrigation. Demand for oil, which provides 75 percent of the country's foreign credits, may pick up slightly in the next few years, but that will do little more than help defray the cost of importing more food.

So, unless de la Madrid pulls an economic miracle out of his hat, or the pace of foreign investment picks up drastically, Mexico in the 1990s will noticeably slide downhill. Austerity measures have now been in effect for three years, and resentment among the population is growing and finding expression in local elections, where candidates of the Institutional Revolutionary party, which has held power for the past fifty years, have been soundly defeated. With Mexico's history of political calm during the IRP's tenure, it's unlikely that discontent would turn into widespread violence, but the possibility cannot be dismissed out of hand, at least during the balance of this decade. Once the economy gets back on a growth track, pressure from the peasants and workers should dissipate.

Under Mexico's current five-year plan, the government is divesting most nonbanking interests that it acquired when private banks were nationalized in 1982. De la Madrid has also stated that the government wants to improve the climate for foreign investment by being flexible in interpreting the country's laws as applied to business activities other than mining, petrochemicals, and automotive parts (where foreign holdings are restricted to 40 percent). Special preference will go to import substitution industries and to those that promise export earnings, such as processing raw materials—silver, nickel, zinc, lead, et cetera—before export. A broader petrochemicals industry, including secondary chemical products, is another objective.

In the 1990s Mexico may make substantial inroads in U.S. markets in both petrochemicals and automobiles. The government would like to convert more of Mexico's auto parts industry to doing finished assembly of cars—and expand the country's steelmaking industry in the process. However, even if all this comes to pass, the sheer number and severity of Mexico's endemic problems augur against any improvement in stability. The birthrate issue alone, which is a culturally induced problem and thus is especially impervious to policy initiative from the capital, portends a gradual decline—which could turn precipitous if all the other problems more amenable to corrective actions are not handled effectively.

GERMANY: EUROPE'S NEW BRIDGEHEAD TO THE EAST

The next few years will be a pivotal time for Europe and, indeed, the world. Barring an unexpectedly severe recession in 1986 or '87, we foresee the welcome possibility of a major repair in East-West relations via economic developments in Germany and Yugoslavia. Germany will be well along the road to reunification and a more nonaligned diplomacy by the turn of the century. At the same time, Yugoslavia will prosper from a new sense of national purpose and will be held up as an example of how the precepts of capitalism and communism can be judiciously mixed. The leavening in this otherwise cheery outlook is the distinct chance that Italy's runaway economy will finally end up completely out of control.

The 1980s to date have been rather disgruntling for West Germany, as was evident in 1982 when the Free Democratic party abandoned its long-standing pact with the Social Democratic party and threw its lot behind the right-of-center coalition of the Christian Democratic Union and Christian Social Union. The FDP's surprising move toppled Chancellor Helmut Schmidt and propelled Helmut Kohl into office. Fortunately for Kohl, the world economic situation has since brightened, and his government was returned to office in March 1983.

Germany's problems are far from over, though. Lagging investment in growth industries, especially electronics and biotechnology, has raised serious doubt about Germany's ability to resume its place at the forefront of the world economy. But no matter how successful the country is (or isn't) at tackling that issue, it's hard to imagine any set of circumstances that would really threaten the survival of the current form of government or Germany's position as the most stable democracy in Europe.

What upset the Germans was the unexpected demonstration of their country's vulnerability to world economic trends. Until 1980, the country had weathered the jump in oil prices better than most, thanks mainly to the strength of the deutschmark against the dollar, the currency used to set oil prices. But then the dollar began its long climb in value against the mark and all other major currencies. That aggravated the cost of oil in Germany at the same time that exports were stagnating, unemployment was rising, and overall economic growth was slowing to a standstill. Inflation zoomed to more than 10 percent in 1983, an unthinkable level for West Germany. After oil prices began dropping, the German economy picked up—but no credit to Chancellor Kohl's policies; Germany is simply importing disinflation instead of inflation.

In fact, Germany will have to rectify some fundamental troubles that have been evolving for more than a decade. During the 1970s, Germany's industrial base eroded for want of capital to invest in modern equipment and needed R&D projects. Profits declined because the mark's strength limited exports, while both wage settlements and Social Security taxes outpaced productivity gains. In addition, the federal government's growing interference in business also dampened industry's enthusiasm for new investments.

Most telling are Germany's slippages in such high-tech areas as optics, semiconductors, consumer electronics, and computers. In addition, traditional strongholds such as steel, shipbuilding, and coal are losing ground, and it isn't clear whether Germany can compete in these industries with newly industrializing nations. So the stage is set for some tough industrial policy and private investment decisions over the next few years. So far, Kohl's policies are aimed more at improving the general business climate than direct interference through capital infusions, bailouts, or nationalization.

One might therefore suppose that Kohl's government would regard stimulating innovation by smaller firms and entrepreneurs to be a logical tactic. However, the infrastructure to support U.S.-style entrepreneurship is lacking—even if there are some German businesspeople who are potential innovators, which isn't at all clear. In any event, the issue is moot because there are few venture capitalists, and Germany's ultraconservative bankers are loath to lend money to start-up firms.

For at least the balance of the 1980s Germany is likely to be preoccupied with energy supplies and costs. Economic growth historically has correlated directly with energy consumption—and half of Germany's energy supply is imported oil, while another 10 percent is supplied by imported gas. As the world economy recovers, oil and gas prices should rise somewhat, and Germany could again be faced with imported inflation. The main challenge for the short term will be to prevent labor costs from outstripping gains in productivity so that industry can make the necessary investments to regain a technological edge.

For the longer pull, the enduring problem will continue to be energy. The nation seems to be foreclosing the nuclear option, with nuclear power plants encountering significant resistance from environmentalists. Consequently, industry is mounting a broad effort to develop some of the world's most advanced energy-saving and energy-efficient production equipment, which ought to put the country in good stead by the early 1990s. Closer economic ties with East Germany will also give a boost to West German business. Apart from oil and gas, West Germany is a relatively independent, diversified economy; stronger links with East Germany—and even political reunification is probable by the end of the century—can only improve that situation. At the start of the twenty-first century, then, there is no question but that (West) Germany will be among the strongest powers on the world's economic scene.

THE ITALIAN ENIGMA

As Ian Carson so aptly noted in *The Economist* of May 23, 1981, "With one eye on Italy's political paralysis, terrorism, corruption and scandals, another on the reckless, uncontrolled spending of the state, some foreign economists see Italy perpetually preparing to slide down the road to Bangladesh. But it never does." The Italian economy can indeed be a puzzle. But Forecasting International believes that Italy has finally reached its Waterloo. It may not slide all the way down to Bangladesh, but it will slip dramatically over the next twenty years and end up at the level of Colombia and Iran.

Italy suffers three fundamental problems: unjustifiable public spending practices, galloping inflation, and excessive dependence on imported energy and raw materials. The government recently adopted austerity measures, but there is no convincing evidence that it will really be able to curb reckless spending. Much of the government's handouts, although labeled "investment capital," is actually used to cover losses by state-owned companies in the steel, shipbuilding, and petrochemical industries. That saps the funds which are available for investment, dooming the companies to another term of losses because they don't have the modern equipment they need to be competitive.

Another vicious circle perpetuates inflation. Tax evasion is a national pastime in Italy, compounding the government's deficit woes and forcing it to borrow more than it should have to. When the inflation rate climbs to near South American levels, the Bank of Italy slams on the breaks, squeezing credit and devaluating the lira. But every devaluation makes energy more expensive—Italy imports about 70 percent of its energy needs—and exacerbates the trade deficit. Moreover, it generally sparks another uptick in the *scala mobile*, a wage indexation scheme that covers about three-fourths of the labor force, thus institutionalizing inflation.

Despite years of discussions and rooms full of studies and plans for developing nuclear and other alternative energy sources, Italy continues at the mercy of oil, gas, and coal imports. The recent discovery of offshore oil deposits will do little to alleviate Italy's long-term dependence. And the drop in world oil prices merely postpones Italy's day of reckoning.

In the past, these weaknesses were somehow counterbalanced by a populace that exhibits a fierce entrepreneurial spirit and the ability to pull off eleventh-hour rescues. The hundreds of small- and medium-size businesses in the north are the pillar of the Italian economy. They manage to apply the latest technology to "mature" industries and wrest profit from high-quality textiles, clothing, footwear, leather goods, and jewelry.

However, the entrepreneurs of the north cannot continue indefinitely to compensate for troubles that are dragging at the economy. Italy's honored crisis-management tactics may enable the country to lurch into the 1990s without collapsing, but unless fundamental changes are inaugurated by the early 1990s, when oil prices are apt to rise again, Italy's malaise may soon turn fatal. The government must revise labor laws that constantly drain investment capital from industry; it must install competent managers in its state-owned enterprises or, better still, turn them over to private interests; it must get ahead with a nuclear power program, and it must curb population growth. Without at least most of these admittedly radical reforms, Italy is heading for a series of crises that will bring down government after government in the 1990s and even threaten the continued existence of Italy as a democratic, quasi-capitalist state.

YUGOSLAVIA'S TRIUMPH

Since the death of Marshal Josip Tito in 1981, Yugoslavia has neither collapsed nor been invaded by the Soviet Union, despite dire predictions of one or both. In fact, the country has changed very little—overtly—in the past four years. That no doubt is precisely what Tito intended when he prepared the way for an orderly succession by establishing the concept of a state presidency designed to function without a strong leader.

The subtleties, though, tell a different story. Yugoslavia is at a turning point in history, brought on partly by the recent worldwide recession but mostly by two internal developments: First, the formerly centralized political authority has turned over essentially all economic decisions to regional and local officials. Second, nationalism is on the rise within Yugoslavia's six republics and two autonomous provinces, and the resulting competition is leading to less, not more, efficient utilization of resources. How these two trends are resolved will determine whether the country actually fulfills our optimistic projections.

Few nations can match Yugoslavia for sheer ethnic diversity. It consists of six major "nations" and a plethora of minority groups divided by deep-seated religious and cultural differences, plus a long history of hostile attitudes that often flared into open conflict. Even today, there's great disparity in socioeconomic status among the various groups. Croatia, Slovenia, Vojvodina, and Serbia are relatively industrialized and prosperous. Kosovo, Montenegro, Macedonia, and Bosnia-Herzegovina are mainly poor and agricultural.

The economy is extraordinarily decentralized, postulated on the principle of self-management. Since most decisions are reached at the local or even the enterprise level, workers typically feel involved in the process, so strikes are rare. On the other hand, the economy, as a consequence, is highly fragmented into eight independent spheres, each with its own closed market. The central government, in pursuit of coordinated economic policies, has only one recourse—the blunt weapon of administrative intervention.

During the recent recession, the government was forced to resort to several blunt weapons: It imposed currency controls and rationing, restricted imports and travel outside the country, and devalued the dinar. The upshot has been a decline in living standards plus shortages of materials, capital equipment, and consumer goods. And the evidence suggests that some or all of these measures will remain in place for a few more years, with attendant political risks, in order to preserve central control while the federal government works on structural problems—in particular, broadening the country's export base, reducing the dependence on imported materials and machinery, boosting agricultural output, and attracting more foreign capital.

Western companies will find it relatively easy to operate in Yugoslavia, in that the banking system is modeled more or less after the western European example. Major growth industries over the past decade include oil and gas extraction, electrical machinery, transportation equipment, chemicals, and power generation (although "brownouts" remain a problem). The country has extensive deposits of coal, bauxite, mercury, and zinc.

The austerity program thus far seems to be accepted, recognized widely as necessary. But tensions between the republics are bound to rise over the next few years as they compete for scarce resources. We believe the outcome will be a gradual but significant shift of economic power to the central government, with the republics perceiving that they must compete less with each other and more with outside rivals. All levels of government will be eager to facilitate joint ventures between Yugoslav and foreign companies, hoping to emulate the success stories of joint ventures in such areas as motor vehicles and electrical engineering.

If the central government does, in fact, emerge from this time of testing with a firmer hand, the Yugoslav economy will blossom in the late 1990s, and the country will emerge as a strong, newly industrialized state. Even more important, Yugoslavia will be in a position to act as a cultural and economic bridge between eastern and western Europe. With the two Germanies serving a similar role, tensions between the communist bloc and the West should ameliorate substantially, greatly enhancing the prospects of arms control and lasting peace.

APPENDIX

ABOVE-AVERAGE GAINERS IN AMERICAN TRADE

SITC* No.	Title	Average Annual Change (Percent) 1983–90 Export	Import	1991–2000 Export	Import
3	ENERGY MATERIALS				
33	Petroleum & products				4.1
5	CHEMICALS & PRODUCTS				
51	Organic chemicals & products	4.2	4.9	5.4	4.4
52	Inorganic chemicals & products	4.3	3.6		
54	Medicines & pharmaceuticals	7.6	3.5	6.0	
56	Fertilizer products	4.2	3.5		
58	Plastics, resins, rubbers	4.9	4.1	5.4	
6	PRIMARY MANUFACTURED				
67	PRODUCTS		3.7		
	Iron & steel				
7	MACHINERY				
71	Power generating equipment	7.6	6.3	8.9	5.7
73	Metalworking machinery	6.9	7.8	8.0	7.2
74	General industrial machines	4.5	3.8		
75	Office & computing machines	9.4	8.2	11.9	7.6
76	Telecommunications equipment	6.8	6.7	11.2	6.1
77	Electrical machines, appliances	8.5	6.1	10.0	5.6
78	Road vehicles		5.3		4.3
8	APPAREL, INSTRUMENTS, & MISC.				
87	Prof. & scientific instruments	4.4			
88	Photo & optical, timepieces		5.7		
	OVERALL AVERAGE	3.8	3.4	5.0	3.8

*Standard International Trade Classification

U.S. EXPORTS VERSUS IMPORTS—FORECAST TO THE YEAR 2000

SITC No. / Title	1983 Export	1983 Import	1990 Export	1990 Import	2000 Export	2000 Import
Millions of 1983 Dollars						
0 FOODS						
00 Animals, live	344	534	350	544	315	550
01 Meat & meat preparations	1,191	2,034	1,278	2,211	1,270	2,368
02 Dairy products & eggs	373	403	378	409	337	420
03 Fish & fish preparations	917	3,594	994	3,945	1,007	4,284
04 Cereals, flour, preparations	15,152	316	16,426	338	16,641	354
05 Vegetables & fruits	2,444	2,920	2,686	3,174	2,793	3,399
06 Sugar & preparations, honey	138	1,338	142	1,380	130	1,400
07 Coffee, cocoa, tea, spices	192	3,895	203	4,147	196	4,311
08 Animal feed (ex., unmilled cereal)	2,802	168	3,038	180	3,077	188
09 Misc. food preparations	613	211	682	239	726	270
TOTALS	24,166	15,413	26,177	16,567	26,492	17,544
1 BEVERAGES & TOBACCO						
11 Beverages	166	2,683	176	2,866	170	2,985
12 Tobacco & products	2,647	720	2,681	727	2,390	730
TOTALS	2,813	3,403	2,857	3,593	2,560	3,715
2 MISC. CRUDE MATERIALS						
21 Hides & fur skins	1,010	190	1,036	196	948	200

SITC No. Title	Millions of 1983 Dollars					
	1983 Export	1983 Import	1990 Export	1990 Import	2000 Export	2000 Import
22 Oil seeds, nuts, kernels, etc.	6,337	92	6,799	98	6,758	101
23 Rubber & synthetic rubber	565	909	687	1,136	862	1,483
24 Wood & cork	2,287	2,833	2,585	3,506	2,848	4,517
25 Wood pulp & waste paper	1,741	1,500	1,964	1,722	2,146	1,993
26 Textile fibers (not yarn, fabric)	2,593	312	2,751	334	2,678	349
27 Crude fertilizers & minerals	1,268	517	1,489	620	1,752	765
28 Metal ores & scrap	2,276	2,500	2,743	3,094	2,835	3,986
29 Crude animal & veg. materials	519	736	537	768	490	774
TOTALS	18,596	9,589	20,591	11,474	21,317	14,168
3 ENERGY MATERIALS						
32 Coal, coke, lignite, peat	4,115	97	5,071	114	6,530	135
33 Petroleum & products	4,557	52,325	4,889	58,033	4,860	80,447
34 Gas (natural & synthetic)	827	5,530	745	4,982	532	4,500
TOTALS	9,499	57,952	10,705	63,129	11,922	85,082
4 ANIMAL OILS & FATS						
41 Animal oils & fats	627	10	674	11	673	12
42 Vegetable oils & fats	799	457	857	495	852	512
43 Processed oils & fats	32	18	33	19	31	19
TOTALS	1,458	485	1,564	525	1,556	543

		Millions of 1983 Dollars					
SITC		1983		1990		2000	
No.	Title	Export	Import	Export	Import	Export	Import
5	CHEMICALS & PRODUCTS						
51	Organic chemicals & products	5,326	3,477	7,084	4,857	11,993	7,441
52	Inorganic chemicals & products	3,051	2,567	4,102	3,288	6,214	4,451
53	Dyeing, tanning, coloring products	491	445	542	498	568	556
54	Medicines & pharmaceuticals	2,494	703	4,169	897	7,473	1,207
55	Essential oils, perfumes, etc.	788	460	893	531	983	618
56	Fertilizer products	1,267	997	1,688	1,270	2,101	1,706
57	Explosives & pyrotechnics	87	64	99	74	110	87
58	Plastics, resins, rubbers	3,732	1,098	5,230	1,458	8,855	2,077
59	Chemical materials (misc.)	2,515	968	3,087	1,150	3,944	1,398
	TOTALS	19,751	10,779	26,894	14,023	42,241	19,541
6	PRIMARY MANUFACTURED PRODUCTS						
61	Leather, dressed skins	411	582	397	642	324	702
62	Tires & tubes	304	1,400	323	1,504	314	1,575
63	Cork & wood products	492	1,358	566	1,713	645	2,268
64	Paper, paperboard, & products	2,553	4,215	2,818	4,720	2,953	5,274
65	Textile yarns & fabrics	2,368	3,225	2,828	3,948	3,488	5,008
66	Nonmetal minerals	1,770	5,330	2,133	6,241	2,205	7,432
67	Iron & steel	1,478	6,791	1,733	8,746	2,045	11,932

		Millions of 1983 Dollars					
SITC		**1983**		**1990**		**2000**	
No.	**Title**	**Export**	**Import**	**Export**	**Import**	**Export**	**Import**
68	Nonferrous metals	2,033	7,422	2,485	8,816	2,640	10,717
69	Metal products (misc.)	3,443	4,504	4,021	5,379	4,684	6,590
	TOTALS	14,852	34,827	17,304	41,709	19,298	51,498
7	MACHINERY						
71	Power generating equipment	8,718	5,274	14,558	8,078	33,993	14,118
72	Specialized industrial machines	9,081	4,848	11,766	5,878	17,184	7,357
73	Metalworking machinery	1,121	1,480	1,792	2,501	3,858	5,028
74	General industrial machines	7,980	4,837	10,823	6,259	17,215	8,597
75	Office & computing machines	11,669	6,759	21,857	11,712	67,480	24,415
76	Telecommunications equipment	3,804	11,278	6,021	17,723	17,389	32,129
77	Electrical machines, appliances	11,936	12,499	21,101	18,943	54,681	32,612
78	Road vehicles	14,611	36,421	17,363	52,178	21,722	79,747
79	Other transportation equipment	13,659	2,731	15,615	3,058	15,800	3,417
	TOTALS	82,579	86,127	120,896	126,330	249,322	207,420
8	APPAREL, INSTRUMENTS, & MISC.						
81	Lighting & plumbing fixtures	272	272	295	320	303	422
82	Furniture	593	1,866	675	2,326	768	3,336
83	Luggage & handbags	51	1,004	45	1,055	39	1,188
84	Clothes & furs	818	9,583	927	11,619	1,032	16,803

SITC No.	Title	Millions of 1983 Dollars					
		1983 Export	Import	1990 Export	Import	2000 Export	Import
85	Footwear	102		112		118	
			4,010		4,628		5,947
87	Prof. & scientific	5,856		7,905		12,383	
	instruments		1,911		2,387		3,432
88	Photo & optical,	2,217		2,873		4,155	
	timepieces		3,401		5,023		5,155
89	Misc. manufactured	5,338		6,127		7,000	
	articles		9,659		11,310		14,846
	TOTALS	15,247		18,959		25,798	
			31,706		38,668		51,129
9	COMMODITIES &	7,009		9,118		14,910	
	TRANSACTIONS		7,742		9,770		12,948
	NEC.						
	GRANT TOTALS	195,970		255,065		415,416	
			258,023		325,788		463,588

INDEX

ABOUT THE AUTHORS

Marvin Cetron, president and founder of Forecasting International, Ltd., in Arlington, Virginia, has been accurately predicting the future, through economic and statistical analysis, for the last fifteen years. His clients have included the U.S. Congress, the Atomic Energy Commission, and the departments of Commerce, Defense, Energy, HEW, Labor, and State; UNESCO; the governments of Australia, Brazil, Canada, Finland, Israel, Japan, Kenya, Poland, South Africa, Sweden, the United Kingdom, and Yugoslavia; AT&T, Citibank, Control Data, Du Pont, GM, Hartford, Honeywell, IBM, 3M, Union Carbide, Westinghouse, and Xerox; the European Economic Community; and NATO. An expert in scientific forecasting, Dr. Cetron has been on the faculties of American University, M.I.T., Georgia Tech, and George Washington University. He has lectured extensively throughout the world, and his work has been published in nine languages. The latest of Dr. Cetron's twelve books include *Encounters with the Future, Jobs of the Future,* and *Schools of the Future.*

Alicia Pagano is a management consultant and is also an adjunct professor at the City University of New York and at Marymount Manhattan College. Dr. Pagano was formerly a senior executive with the United States Committee for UNICEF.

Otis Port has been Technical Editor at *Business Week* since 1977, and before that was Engineering Editor at *Modern Plastics* magazine. His work has won several honors, including awards from the National Association of Science Writers and the Aviation and Space Writers Association.

Date Due			
APR 8			
APR 1 8			
MAY 2 1			
NOV 2 0			
DEC 1 0			
Sum. '69			
APR 7 1981			
MAR 0 2 1990			
FEB 2 2 1996			

Library
Marymount College
221 E. 71 St.
New York 21, N. Y.

1. Reference books, such as encyclopaedias and dictionaries, are to be used only in the library.
2. Reserved books may be borrowed for one period, or at the close of classes, and should be returned before the first class the following morning.
3. All other books may be retained for two weeks.
4. Two cents a day is charged for each book kept overtime. Additional fines are charged for reserved books.
5. Injury to books beyond reasonable wear and all losses shall be paid for.
6. No books may be taken from the library without being charged.